T0290534

MELANESIAN LAND TENURE IN A CONTEMPORARY AND PHILOSOPHICAL CONTEXT

David Lea

University Press of America, Inc.
Lanham • New York • London

Copyright © 1997 by
University Press of America, ® Inc.
4720 Boston Way
Lanham, Maryland 20706

3 Henrietta Street
London, WC2E 8LU England

All rights reserved
Printed in the United States of America
British Cataloging in Publication Information Available

Library of Congress Cataloging-in-Publication Data

Lea, David
Melanesian land tenure in a contemporary and philosophical context /
David Lea.
p.   cm.
Includes bibliographical references and index.
1. Land tenure--Melanesia. 2. Commons--Melanesia. I. Title.
HD1120.Z63L43   1996   333.3'0995--dc20   96-28822 CIP

ISBN 0-7618-0456-0 (cloth: alk. ppr.)

⊖™The paper used in this publication meets the minimum
requirements of American National Standard for information
Sciences—Permanence of Paper for Printed Library Materials,
ANSI Z39.48—1984

Contents

Introduction

Since the Enlightenment, most social philosophy which has dwelt on the subject of ownership has been primarily concerned with private rather than corporate or communal. This has been the case with the modern masters, e.g., Locke, Kant and Hegel, as well as the most contemporary of works devoted to this topic. In the numerous number of recent books, there is a tendency to assume that ownership has a univocal meaning which is synonymous with private property. Accordingly the focus is upon the moral and practical considerations which are alleged to support this institution. This issue is often approached from a variety of moral and social perspectives encompassing the spectrum from the extreme deontological/libertarian to the consequentialist/welfarist. But despite the variety of arguments treated, there is the frequently encountered common residual presumption that private ownership represents the natural condition of man in his social context. As the tendency of philosophers, since the Stoics, has been to been to associate man's natural state with moral principle, there has been this corresponding inclination to believe implicitly that there is a moral point to private ownership with universal application, the central disagreement only remaining the articulation of the presumed moral perspective, or the distinguishing of the appropriate principles operative in the process of private appropriation.

A survey of some of the more prominent of recent works on this topic indicates that this is the case. Alan Ryan's two influential books on the subject of ownership: Property and Political Theory and Property both investigated arguments which justify private ownership, the former canvassing the general gamut from Locke to Marx, the latter considered the connection between private ownership and freedom in works from Plato to Robert Nozick.[1] James Grunebaum in Private Ownership similarly provided a comprehensive account of the justificatory theories of private ownership categorizing the possible arguments into a triad of natural perfectionists, first appropriationists, and conventionalists.[2] More recently Alan Carter, in The Philosophical Foundations of Property Rights, considered attempts to derive private property rights (in Honore's modern liberal concept of ownership) from the nature or predicament of humanity prior to (logically or chronologically) obligations to civil society.[3] Finally I will mention of Jeremy Waldron's book, The Right to Private Property, whose substantive work considers the moral derivation of private property rights from two rights based perspectives, that of general rights and that of special rights, which he claims offer different distributive implications.[4]

Unlike most philosophical works on ownership, this book offers a comparative study of ownership. In this respect we compare and contrast customary communal ownership as found in Melanesia with the Western paradigm of private ownership. The intent is to gain a perspective on the Western institution of private ownership through a contrast with a form of land tenure endemic to a very different sort of culture, a subsistence agrarian society with simple technological means of production. In this undertaking we study the axiological background which grounds customary communal property and compare this with the theories of value which supposedly ground the Western institution of private property as articulated by certain prominent Western liberal philosophers, specifically, Locke, Kant, Hegel and Robert Nozick. It is expected that this approach will offer fresh insight into moral and social structures of both societies: the Melanesian and the Western.

At the same time, our approach is historical in that we trace the evolution of European ideas concerning ownership as they developed from the prominent notion of collective human ownership in the writings of the early Church fathers towards the embrace of individual ownership during the Reformation and in the writings of the leaders of the Enlightenment. In indicating the historical evolution of our ideas concerning ownership, we seek to exhibit the development of the ideas and moral justifications for individual ownership as both influenced by, and influencing, changing conditions in Europe. Ultimately the aim is to achieve an appropriate focus on ownership, which, as far as possible, is not coloured or blurred by an endemic framework of contemporary Western culture. By concentration on the historical genealogy of modern Western institutions, and evaluation through comparison with the very different social paradigm found in Melanesia, it is hoped that we will be liberated from cultural subjectivity so as to attain some objectivity with respect to the effects of this Western institution on social and environmental conditions.

In many ways this work should be read as a critique of private ownership, and, perforce, the philosophy of liberalism which emphasizes individual liberties, notably those associated with private property. In the context of recent philosophical thought, this book falls within the recent developing controversy between the so called liberal philosophers and the communitarians. Communitarian criticism has emerged as a much needed questioning of the liberal perspective. The specific positions assumed by the communitarians can be seen as derivative from the general criticism that liberals are insensitive to the virtues and importance of our membership in a community and culture and in so doing have exaggerated our capacity for individual choice because they have misconstrued the relationship between the self and its social roles and relationships. Accordingly, this controversy has been assessed from a variety of perspectives: individualism versus collectivism; the priority of the theory of rights versus the theory of the good; the priority of universal values versus the priority of culturally specific principles.

Though this work as far as possible attempts to avoid the overly technical and dry discussion which characterizes much of contemporary political philosophy, I will briefly mention some of the more prominent communitarian authors and their works. This is primarily intended for the reader who may wish to research some of the finer points of the debate in more detail. A brief canvassing of the literature indicates the general outlines of the communitarian criticism. Michael Sandel, for example, rejects Rawlsian liberalism on the grounds that he and other liberals advocate the "thin" view of the self in which the self relates to its end as mere "system of desires".[5] These desires, he says, can perhaps be rationally ordered according to their relative intensity but they do not essentially determine the self's identity.[6] This, claims Sandel, undermines the very notion of moral agency for this must be a self without "character, without moral depth", incapable of self knowledge in a morally serious sense. Essentially, concrete people for Sandel are always bound together by ties of community and tradition which are deeper than and potentially more valuable than they are morally understood.[7] Similarly Charles Taylor rejects the atomistic disengaged subject of seventeenth century rationalism which he presumes to be the inheritance of contemporary liberal thinkers. In contrast, Taylor asserts that human identity and selfhood are defined by a commitment and identification with a tradition.[8] Likewise, Alstair McIntyre attempts to formulate a moral theory centred on the notions of virtue and the rationality of tradition.[9] Thus, he sees our current moral crisis as the product of a failure in consensus due to the fragmentation of our tradition. Finally, Michael Walzer in Spheres of Justice: A defense of Pluralism and Equality, has argued that criteria of Justice cannot be specified independently of an account of the society where they are supposed to work, despite the familiar liberal talk of universal natural rights or primary social goods.[10]

The above is not meant to offer an exhaustive canvassing or compression of the communitarian literature but rather to provide a representative sample of some of the more prominent works. There are two possible broad interpretations of the communitarian criticisms. The first, liberal theory, simpliciter, is misconceived because it fails to account for the communal and societal background in which the self functions. The second possibility is that liberal theory simply represents the values of a community which overemphasizes individualism at the expense of communalism which leads to unhappy consequences. My own view is a conflation of these two notions. In this work liberalism will be regarded not simply as a misguided theory but rather as an expression of the ideological and social tendencies of Western civilization, however, it is nevertheless a theory which distorts social realities when applied to other cultures and to some extent distorts realities when blandly accepted as an accurate and consistent self description of Western culture.

However, if social values and moral principles are a function of our social context, as communitarians state, how is it possible to escape subjective relativism? Here much depends upon the claims of the hermeneutical approach advocated by some communitarians, principally Charles Taylor. In any hermeneutical study it is recognized that cultural activities and social concepts are rooted in a socio-historical setting. One aspect of this approach involves the articulation of this historical development through the language of societal and cultural self perception. This avoids formulation by universal laws and concentrates on the specific case in its historical and cultural context and so insists on the inseparability of fact from value, detail from context and observation from history. In a sense this is a study in the evolution of our own language of self description and here we are in agreement with communitarians like Charles Taylor who point out that not only our feelings but also the actual social structure of our relations with one another are defined by language, which as he points out, is not to say that such relations are not shaped by power and property but that power and property themselves are shaped by language, and for our purposes this includes the very meaning of property itself.[11] However, the other important aspect of our hermeneutical approach to this subject involves an understanding through what Charles Taylor has called the "language of perspicuous contrasts".[12] An historical perspective no

Introduction

doubt helps to free us from tyranny of the current ideology by allowing us to recognize the cultural specificity of a normative ideal. However, a more complete understanding must go beyond description according to its own terms and one further way of doing this is to compare and contrast diverse cultural phenomena. Taylor argues that this can be achieved in a language in which we formulate the forms of life embodied in two cultures as alternative possibilities in relation to some human constants at work in both. According to this so called "language of perspicuous contrasts", one understands the practices of another culture in relation to one's own culture and this means that one cannot understand the other culture until one has understood one's own better as well. The idea is that the workings of a specific social arrangement become more apparent through comparison with the workings of those of the other culture. This means equally that the shortcomings of the other culture will also become more apparent where there is discrepancy between the claims of self described workings of the system and the results of the comparative study. Taylor himself says that employment of the language of contrast may well show us that the language of self understanding of the other culture is distorted or inadequate in some respects or it might show that our language of self understanding is inadequate. This he says could well lead to an alteration in self understanding and hence in our form of life which has happened in the past. Here, no doubt Taylor is thinking of the Reformation and the rise of Western protestantism, one of the central foci of this work. Taylor believes, among other things that studying cultures in terms of contrasts avoids the erroneous belief in the universality of North Atlantic behavioural types and "functions" which so vitiates much of contemporary comparative politics.[13]

This described hermeneutical study serves to outline the essential structure of this book. In this work we will look for our "perspicuous contrasts" in a comparison between the Melanesian communal property with that of Western private ownership. In this undertaking it is hoped that we will discover certain aspects of the Western concept which have gone unnoticed and even unearth certain contradictions or illusions associated with the reality of Western practices and beliefs about the latter. Also as we mentioned previously, our undertaking is in part historical as we study the historical transformation of European thought on ownership and its presumed moral basis. These various alterations in thought were often subtle and mutually contributory and it is the purpose of this book to delineate certain of these central themes. In this manner our end is to achieve a hermeneutical project of completer understanding through both avenues.

This demonstration which aims at a more catholic appreciation will proceed by emphasis as well as argument. We initially underline that private ownership was not always seen as natural to man's social condition and accordingly these rights could not be regarded as having any special moral validity. At the heart of this book lies the argument that moral attitudes towards private ownership were often strongly antithetical before human thought was transformed by the intellectual revolutions of the European Renaissance and the Reformation. These movements reformulated man's attitudes towards himself and his standing in relation to the cosmological and spiritual orders with the consequent that these emerging ideas were then incorporated in the prominent works of the fathers of the liberal tradition through the resulting articulation of humanism and "rights of man". This essentially is the design of this work in terms of scholarship and analysis. However, this book also contains an important sub-theme, one which questions the environmental soundness of the institution of private property and suggests that earlier more communal forms of ownership as found in Melanesia should be reconsidered in the interests of environmental protection.

Having adumbrated these central themes, we will make explicit the structure of this work in order of chapters. The first chapter considers communal ownership within the holistic society as it existed and continues to exist in Papua New Guinea. P.N.G. with its endemic societies presents non-cash economies inset in a stone age culture expressing social modalities which offer a sharp contrast to Western cultural paradigms. In the course of this exposition we compare the axiology which governs Melanesian communities with that of the modern liberal Western community which enshrines private forms of ownership. Going beyond the mere highlighting of philosophic and institutional contrasts we consider how P.N.G. has sought to reconcile customary forms of ownership with the liberal forms inherited from colonial rule and pose questions as to the viability of this syncretic solution in relation to protection of the environment and sustainable development.

The following three chapters further explore, from varying perspectives, the reality of cultural communal ownership in P.N.G. In the first chapter we focused on the community, its cultural values and its preference for certain forms of social/political arrangement rather than others. In the second chapter we look a little more closely into the individual Melanesian character and in so doing illustrate the social conflicts and even disorder which results when relations with the communal land base are undermined. We demonstrate in part how economic development and the subsequent alteration in his or her natural habitat undermines the constraints which determine the individual within the communal context subsequently bringing about social disintegration. The main points underlined, will be illustrated through reference to developments which led to the so called "Bougainville crisis" - an insurrection which began on the island province of Bougainville in 1989 and which is continuing to this day.

In the third chapter we offer a comparative perspective as we present and evaluate the existing Fijian system of land tenure. Fiji is sometimes seen as a virtual sister state of P.N.G., a Pacific Island state with similar Melanesian traditions though with a much stronger Polynesian influence. For our purposes Fiji offers a comparative though somewhat different model of land tenure from that of P.N.G. In contrasting and comparing the two systems we hope to arrive at accurate evaluations of the economic, political and social realities as they are influenced by the existing land tenure systems.

In the fourth chapter I consider aboriginal title to land in greater philosophical detail and evaluate the sense in which customary title to land can be said to exist in pre-civil society. Ultimately, I argue that using Lockean natural rights arguments based on acquisition through labour, one can successfully defend customary title to village sites, gardens and related areas of aquaculture and silviculture, but less successfully areas of the uncultivated "wilds".

The following five chapters offer a general comparison of communal and private ownership concentrating on issues relating to the evolution of European thought, the association of private ownership and personal liberty, distributive justice and finally environmental protection. In the fifth chapter we return to the topic of modern Western notions of ownership and consider matters of historicity as they apply to the evolution of these notions. It has sometimes been said that individual ownership is the essential paradigm of ownership. In this chapter we consider whether this has always been held to be the case, even in Western culture. We begin with the attitude of early church embodied in the patristic writings. Our researches indicate that these thinkers either tended to disregard the moral significance of property in general or saw ownership as founded in a grant from God which gave rights of propriety to mankind in general and not to single individuals. In this respect, primacy is attributed to communal rather than private property.

Subsequently we consider the shift in conceptualization effected by the Renaissance and the Reformation. Here I argue that the humanism of the Renaissance and Reformation re-orientated man's perception of his relation to "material reality" and reformulated this relation in terms of domination which demanded a private rather than communal relationship. Ultimately what began as a religious reorientation within Christianity became reflected in the secular philosophy of the Enlightenment which founded social arrangements on individual liberties and private rights.

In the sixth chapter I focus specifically on the presentation of private property in the political philosophy of John Locke through a comparison with political culture and forms of ownership found in Melanesia. The prominence of John Locke in Western political thought and specifically in the Anglo/American inheritance cannot be denied and therefore clarity on this issue is of undeniable importance. Recent Lockean scholarship, especially in the work of James Tully, has questioned the traditional interpretation which saw Lockean civil society as structured to protect individual rights and privileges gained in the state of nature. In place of this interpretation, Tully argues for a Locke who embraced the Thomistic vision of a human community of ownership, which in civil society, claims Tully, becomes translated into the primacy of communal rather than individual rights. However, I argue in favour of the traditional interpretation through a contrasting of the concerns of Locke's Political age with those endemic to Melanesian communal society. By this means I argue that communal forms of ownership were inconsonant with the struggles and concerns of Locke's political era which sought to reconcile the sovereignty of the monarch with growing middle class individualism. Given this background, it is demonstratable that Locke sought to articulate a political system founded on individual rights thereby rejecting both the models based on Kingly Divine Right and the communal model as found in the Melanesian social paradigm.

In the seventh chapter, we consider the principal thought of the German Enlightenment as embodied in the political writings of Kant and Hegel. In this chapter I point out that though Locke's influential political writings are preoccupied with the legitimization of civil authority through individual rights, the connection between concerns of individual autonomy and private property rights remains somewhat inchoate. The major contributions to the development of linkages between individual autonomy and private ownership are more obvious in the works of Kant and Hegel. However, the German tradition offers us two differing notions of individual freedom and autonomy each of which is roughly traceable either to the philosophy of Kant or that of Hegel. In general, modern liberal philosophy actually defines property and modes of distribution differently depending on which of these two distinct notions of autonomy is embraced. Finally, I argue that despite the fact that the strongest proponents of private ownership, the libertarians, trace their intellectual antecedents to Kant, Hegel, in fact, offers a stronger argument for the moral linkages between private property and their particular concerns. Specifically, I indicate that though the modern libertarian tends to rely on the Kantian notion of autonomy, the articulation of this notion is in fact Hegelian with unavoidable communitarian implications.

In the eighth chapter, I look at the important issue of "desert" and the moral justification of the modes of acquisition in the modern market economy. The issue of desert is enlightening because, in fact, it reveals the central problematic in the belief that ownership is primarily private and individual. To this point we have offered a fairly extensive discussion of the liberal attitude which regards the institution of private ownership as necessary to maintain the personal liberty or autonomy of the individual. It must be recognized, however, that this is simply an argument for the institution of private property per se, there yet remains the issue of acquisition, its procedures, methods and moral justification. In conducting this inquiry, I concentrate on the contribution of Rawls in a Theory of Justice. Enlarging on Sandel's analysis in Liberalism and the Limits of Justice, I argue that a proper understanding of the issues with respect to personal entitlement underlines the communitarian rather than the individualistic nature of ownership.

In the final chapter I consider the environmental implications which follow from the embrace of either the Hegelian notion of private ownership, or the Neo-Kantian Libertarian understanding. Previously I demonstrated that these two notions offer differing interpretations of private ownership and emphasize different aspects of this institution. Though each interpretation gives emphasis to different aspects of modern ownership, I point out that whichever interpretation of private ownership is embraced, the environment will not be sufficiently protected from deleterious consequences. In the concluding sections I argue that a worsening environmental crisis may require that we abandon the moral view which requires that property remain a matter of exclusive, entrenched, private control. Environmental protection may well require that we mitigate our concern for individual autonomy and reinstate more communal approaches to ownership as exemplified in certain intrinsic values found in the pre-colonial societies of P.N.G.

---

[1]   Alan Ryan, *Property and Political Theory* (Oxford Blackwell, 1984); and *Property* (London: Open University Press, 1987).
[2]   James Grunebaum, *Private Ownership* (London: Routledge, Kegan Paul, 1987).
[3]   Alan Carter in *The Philosophical Foundations of Property* Rights (London: Harvester Wheatsheaf, 1989)
[4]   Jeremy Waldron's, *The Right to Private Property*, (Oxford: Clarendon Press, 1989).
[5]   Michael Sandel, *Liberalism and the Limits of Justice* (Cambridge: Cambridge University Press, 1982).
[6]   *Ibid.*,14.
[7]   *Ibid.*, 180.
[8]   Charles Taylor, *Philosophy and the Human Sciences: Philosophical Papers 2* (Cambridge: Cambridge University Press, 1985); *Sources of Self: The Making of Modern Identity* (Cambridge: Harvard University Press, 1989).
[9]   Alstair McIntyre, *After Virtue* (Notre Dame· Notre Dame Press, 1981); *Whose Justice? Which Rationality?* (Notre Dame: Notre Dame Press, 1988).
[10]   Michael Walzer,: *Spheres of Justice A defense of Pluralism and Equality* (New York. Basic Books, 1983).
[11]   Charles Taylor, *Human Agency and Language: Philosophical Papers 1* (Cambridge: Cambridge University Press, 1985), 218-227.
[12]   Taylor, *Philosophical Papers 2*, 125-129.
[13]   *Ibid.*, 39.

Chapter 1

A General Comparison Of Melanesian And Western Cultures and Their Systems Of Land Tenure

Melanesian culture in Papua New Guinea has been preserved through time and isolated from the forces and trends of civilization as it developed in Europe, Asia and Africa. Until most recently Papua New Guinea was wholly a stone age culture following the relations and forms of life suited to that particular subsistence form of living. This is a world without money or cash, profoundly agrarian, cognitively and spatially limited by one's small linguistic group. In its social character, the Melanesian society is usually egalitarian, and non-nomadic. This can be linked to a subsistence agrarian economy utilizing a simple technology which does not require complexity or rigidly structured hierarchy in its social relations. In this context, feudalism and capitalism are entirely foreign to the social arrangements of the subsistence economy. In this circumstance, economic relations are not structured to further a more intense utilization of the resources such as we find even within the feudal system. However, at the same time this non-nomadic group requires stable relations and defined modalities of control with respect to natural resources and above all, the land base. It may well be the case that this form of ownership represents a more fundamental form of tenure than that embraced by the individualistic Western culture. With this in mind it is worthwhile to consider the essential character of property and the values which animate and bind these communities in which it is found. In doing so I believe we will also come to appreciate better the axiology which Western societies embrace and its relations to the form of private ownership often

From *Journal of Agriculture and Environmental Ethics*, volume 6, number 1 (1993).

enshrined in our jural frameworks. In the spirit of enquiry based upon a study of "perspicuous contrasts", this acquaintance with the Melanesian social structure will hopefully allow us to gain a critical perspective both with respect to the Melanesian and the Western systems.

As I have said, this study is a study in contrasts, in which understanding is to be gained through comparison of certain salient aspects of the two cultures, the Melanesian and the Western. In accordance with this aim, I will proceed to compare generally certain Western attitudes towards "individual freedom", self interested behaviour", "individual and communal interests", "private ownership" with attitudes and values expressed in the traditional Melanesian approach. In order to demonstrate the latter, I will briefly touch upon the phenomena of "wantokism" and indicate how the Melanesian values, associated with this concept, find their locus in the system of "customary communal ownership". Subsequently, I will describe how the emergence of a cash economy and the attachment to Western gadgetry and products have undermined values which have previously maintained Melanesian social cohesion and effected injury to the environment. While admitting that little can be done to eradicate the desire for cash and the products it can buy, I suggest that Melanesian communities and the environment itself would receive more protection if future development in Papua New Guinea embraced a system which incorporated certain of the traditional Melanesian values through the preservation of the communal form of land tenure. Ultimately, I suggest a way in which customary communal land tenure can be integrated into the established Anglo-Australian legal system

In the course of this chapter, I point out that the traditional holistic societies of Papua New Guinea have been affected by the individualistic Western societies and so have suffered incredible transformation and ensuing damage to their environment It is the argument of this chapter that inimical social change and environmental damage can, at least, be limited or slowed by formal attempts to maintain the holistic nature of Melanesian communities. It has been well argued that the desire of individuals for increasing shares of superfluous gadgets and the products of advanced technological/economic activity undermines present communities and environment, at the expense of future generations.[1] Papua New Guinea offers a striking illustration of this thesis. In particular, community disruption is most perspicuously evident in the "cargo cult" phenomena, as we shall see. However, before discussing this topic, one first needs to gain some understanding of fundamental Melanesian social arrangement through acquaintance with the phenomenon of "wantokism"

Wantokism

The character of Melanesian interpersonal relations is best understood through the phenomenon of "wantokism" "Wantokism" refers to the mutual duties and responsibilities which exist between those individuals who share the same language. Wantok is a Melanesian pidgin English term which refers to all those who share this language, who are called "wantoks". (But as in all lexical matters, this term has a shifting usage and is often applied to individuals who come from the same country or neighbourhood.)[2] Responsibilities for those within the wantok system can be extremely demanding. Wantoks are always under heavy responsibility to help other wantoks in terms of providing food, shelter and cash. Essentially its strictures prescribe mutual sharing of the advantages and benefits which a particular wantok may acquire. To deny one's wantok is a grave matter which generates social repercussions which threaten one's place or standing within the community This brings us to the cosmic view which supports and buttresses the wantok system of social responsibility.

According to Melanesian cosmology, the individual always finds himself situated in a web of relationships. These relationships consist not only of relationships within the community, but also connections with ancestors, with other communities and with the entire environment. One must maintain the proper attitude towards all these elements including one's ancestors Individuals are not free to execute their plans according to chosen life styles, their activities are circumscribed by these linkages to ancestors, communal traditions and the other sentient and insentient creatures which make up the environment. Because one must carefully observe these relationships, individuals find themselves subject to very strong restraints.

The principal source of constraint is, of course, the community. Community existence is central to the Melanesian, to the point that life itself is not conceivable outside one's community A community is thought to consist not simply of a particular aggregate of individuals, but individuals in a number of specified relationships.[3] The Melanesian understands the community in terms of these relationships and, according to this understanding, these connections are seen to carry more importance than the individuals who are so related. As The community is thought to be made up these relationships, the community and thus, life itself, may be disrupted or threatened if these relationships are ruptured. Clearly, the community can sustain the loss of certain individuals but if the appropriate relationships are not maintained the community itself may be destroyed and with it all the individual members. Thus, Melanesian cosmology expresses itself in an implicit Melanesian axiology, one which finds its basis in the idea of community and whose ethical implications will be seen to impose severe restrictions on the ideas of autonomous and self-interested behaviour.

Wantokism, itself, has its roots in the traditional pre-eminence of community values over individual preferences. Mantovani, a cleric with extensive experience in the Highlands of Papua New Guinea, points out that in the traditional clans of the Highlands, individuals frequently put aside their most personal preferences (for example, marriage preferences) in favour of decisions which would be more advantageous to the group and the community.[4]   Furthermore, Mantovani indicates that since the community is the primary value, the ethical rules will respond to this primary value. In other words, what is considered bad behaviour in terms of the individual's actions is that which hurts the community. What does not hurt the community is not bad despite what the Western courts may say about individual guilt. Mantovani mentions the case of some villagers in Chimbu Province who were not much concerned about some petty crimes which some younger members were committing in another village except that those crimes might affect the safe travel of their own villagers who had to pass by that village. The community, thus, responds to what the individual does as it is seen to bring harm upon the community.

It is not difficult to appreciate that these Melanesian attitudes contrast strongly with the Western cultural attitudes which have been concomitant with our market economy and technological advance. Western thinking for over a hundred years has been dominated by liberal philosophy which holds that the function of the community and civil society is to afford the maximum expression of individual freedom and autonomy. This formula has been often repeated by liberals and libertarians from John Stuart Mill to Robert Nozick.[5] What is meant is that individuals should be, as far as possible, free of social pressure and coercion from both government and the community, so that they can construct their lives according to their ideas and plans, and of course these sentiments are traceable to the seventeenth century enlightenment in which, for example, Kant promoted the ideal political community as a "Kingdom of Ends", a free association of self-legislating autonomous individuals. In liberal ideology autonomy is the intrinsically valuable property of the individual who creates his life through a rational plan and whose behaviour is seen to conform to his own self legislation. Accordingly, society has no intrinsic value but only instrumental value - that of ensuring that individual autonomy can proceed without interference.   In traditional Melanesian society, however, the established order of the cosmos and the ultimate value of the community impose themselves upon the individual and there is little room for individual planning which does not take account of the ends of the community.

In the Western ideology the individual and his personal rights are not only promoted from the so called deontological perspective which enshrines the personal capacity for individual autonomy (through individual rights) but also from a complementary utilitarian evaluation. In earlier modernity Herbert Mandeville and Adam Smith taught that the promotion of one's self interest and occupation with one's personal affairs was ultimately contributory to the public benefit without the necessity for conscious promotion or regulation to ensure the collective interests. The laissez faire economists who followed this thinking understood self-interested individualistic behaviour as conceiving the greatest social benefit guided as it were by an invisible hand. In the famous words of Adam Smith.

> It is not from the benevolence of the butcher, the brewer, or the baker, that we expect our dinner but from their regard to their own interest. We address ourselves, not to their humanity but to their self-love, and never talk according to them of our own necessities but of their advantages Nobody but a beggar chooses to depend chiefly upon the benevolence of his fellow-citizens [6]

Again this thinking minimizes the role of the community and communal action. The rational pursuit of individual interests and ends will maximize the general interest and correspondingly there is no particular value in the community or society which needs to be enhanced. The role of the community or even the state is simply to facilitate, not regulate, the free intercourse and interaction between rational individuals and to this end the proper function of the state is to ensure individual liberty, and especially those liberties which pertain to the market exchanges, ensuring that they are free of force, fraud or coercion.

However, all this emphasis upon individualism may well have engendered a certain blindness both in understanding our own social affairs as well of those of other cultures; all of which is precisely the point of the communitarian critique. It is interesting that in conformity with the general critique of communitarian philosophers, certain anthropologists have remarked upon the impossibility of understanding indigenous Melanesian culture through the Western "individualistic" paradigm, which pervades Western analysis. For example, the anthropologist, Daniel De Coppet, has asserted that our modern approach to society is exceptional in that it disregards society as an ultimate value, to the benefit of a quite opposite and non-social value, the individual. He argues that as the liberal ideology values nothing beyond the individual, the continuous move towards its expanding freedom discredits society as a value and makes understanding society even more difficult.[7] De Coppet contrasts Individualistic societies, like those of the Western world with holistic societies - societies in which the ultimate value is society itself. Daniel de Coppet locates the initial expansion of individualism in Medieval ideology During this period, he alleges, there was a growing difficulty to assign a place to society in the context of (in and beside) God, Christ and King. With the inability to effect an appropriate definition of society, there began a very slow and gradual drift of ultimate value from society to the indivisible individual, he claims. It may be said that in so far as Western culture has tended to conceive society from an individualistic bias, it has failed to comprehend the function of society and the individual's place in it, both with respect to its own society, and that of others.[8]

I would argue that medieval Christianity undermined the identity of given communities through its single minded focus on the one universal God head thereby undermining the local gods and local spiritual realities. The animism and the various forms of ancestral worship, we associate with traditional Melanesian life, for example, has and have a local topology, which like the land base itself, maintains the identity of communities and clans over time and given space. Various forms of animism and a topology of local spirits also characterized the life of pagan pre-Christian Europe. Christianity required that Europeans abandon their local gods and those spiritual realities specifically associated with their communities and exclusively focus upon the one universal *Summum Bonum* embodied in the three persons of the Trinity. Responsibilities to those spirits and gods who traditionally maintained the well being of the community was thereby lost which only served to vitiate and undermine identity of community Naturally with this diminution of the communal, the importance of the universal God (in the persons of the Father and Son) grew, as did the importance of the King often seen as God's representative in the realm of temporal affairs. With these developments obligations to God and King left little room for those obligations, which in earlier age found their source in a profound sense of society or community. In a subsequent chapters we will see how the Reformation and Renaissance Humanism promoted an increased awareness of the value and importance of the individual and how Locke especially, seized upon this individualistic ideology in opposition to the circulating notions of Kingly sovereignty, and derived the legitimacy of civil society from beliefs in the preeminence of individual rights and private property. However these are issues which we will explore more fully later.

Looking at the present state of affairs, and the current environmental crisis, it is apparent that what is also evident is that this elevation of the individual has been paralleled by the devaluation and depredation of our natural environment. In a word, environmental damage can be seen in the movement of value from society to the individual.

Traditional Communal Ownership Melanesian identification with the community is intimately and inextricably connected with the parallel identification with the communal land holding. A.P. Power asserts that the lynch pin of the Melanesian group which ensured the continuity of its community life and history was the land holding.[9] The communal land holding provided the locus for the community's cultural activities: political, military and social Because of this, Power believes Melanesians cannot fully disassociate themselves from their land.[10] In drawing from his experiences in the East Sepik Province, Power concludes that the Melanesian concept of a sale of land is really something like the Western concept of a lease. After Melanesians sell their land they maintain a proprietary interest in the land by some form of interest in the subsequent use of the land by the new owner.[11]

Given this cultural setting, it is worthwhile to pursue the subject of ownership rights. Power asserts that as land through generations was held by force of arms through social groupings, the fundamental ownership of land is by groups of some sort or other. The important constant, he remarks, was that the group owned, and individuals used the land. "Individual land usage rights did not remove the reality that the group was the basis for ownership and the basis for the defense of these rights."[12] Similarly Heider in his study of the Dani of Irian Jaya also observes that individual holdings correspond to usage rights rather than the Western idea of ownership [13] Crocombe in his study of land tenure in the P.N.G. states "...the major land rights were held by ongoing groups within which individual usufruct and control was a consequence of group membership through birth, adoption or refuge,

land was not subject to inheritance in the European sense of the term."[14]
Essentially, one can say that alienation or conveyance of land plus
transmission of property through inheritance by will, in the modern
understanding of these practices, was unknown in the traditional
communal form of land tenure.

I would briefly contrast this conception of ownership with the
Western form of ownership (both real and personal).   Within the
Western experience, the paradigm of the ownership right has been the
private property right.   Since the beginning of the seventeenth century
enlightenment Western thinkers like John Locke began to attach
fundamental moral importance to private individual ownership, finding
this right morally binding even in the unstructured circumstance
defined as the so called "state of nature".[15] Beginning from that period
Western theorists began to see the moral legitimacy of the organized
community, civil society and the state as derivative, *inter alia*, from a
commitment to protect such rights.   Consistent with this analysis, the
Western liberal attitude tends to regard community rights as ancillary
to, if not derivative from, individual rights

The individual's right of ownership in Western society has included
the power to control resources and the means of production, something
which is unknown in Melanesia where the principal means of
production is the land base, which is under communal rather than
individual control.   Furthermore, within the Western institution,
restrictions on unilateral prerogatives of personal control are seen as
contrary to very notion of ownership. In his detailed study of the
modern liberal notion of ownership, A.M. Honore concludes that this
notion will always include, *inter alia*, " the right to capital, the power to
alienate a holding or to consume waste, modify or destroy it."[16] He
asserts categorically that the right to capital is a necessary component in
any legal system which claims to possess a modern concept of
ownership. Western treatment of this right has been normative as well
as descriptive.   The strongest articulated moral defense of these cluster
of rights is to be found in Robert Nozick's *Anarchy, State, and Utopia*,
in which he expands the application of this Western arrangement to
universal significance in asserting that the right of the individual to
control and transfer holdings, without any external interference,
constitutes the natural moral endowment of every human individual.[17]
Here, no doubt we see evidence of the tendency of liberals which the
communitarians emphatically decry, that of universalizing Western
social and institutional paradigms.

Furthermore, those who have espoused this view of the primacy of individual ownership and the right to capital have seen it as an essential concomitant of the free market economy. This embrace of individual property rights has been put forth both in deontological natural rights and utilitarian language. Locke and Nozick are frequently associated with the former view. With respect to the latter, people like Smith and more recently the votaries of the Austrian School of economics, have seen the individual's ability to transfer holdings, including capital investments and means of production, as essential to an optimum generation and distribution of utilities.[18]

From Subsistence to a Cash Economy

One of the initial startling responses to the arrival of the white man's cargo was the appearance of the so called "cargo cults". Worsley summarized these events in the following terms. First, there was seen to be the adoption of new rituals - based on the behaviour of the whites - aimed at the control and acquisition of these modern goods and gadgets. Indigenous people came to regard the behaviour of the whites as ritual behaviour with a magical connection to the arrival of the desired cargo. Hence the Melanesians imitated the behaviour of the whites, dressing in western clothing, scribbling notations on bits of paper and passing them around. Second, there was a desertion of traditional ways and labouring activities in expectation of the arrival of the desired cargo. Ultimately, the desired cargo never arrived and the cultists reasoned that they had yet to master the rituals properly.[19]

The cargo cults demonstrate a pattern of dealing with a modern industrialized world, key elements of which, remain evident in current Papua New Guinea. In part, Papua New Guinea, in emerging as a modern nation has attempted to embrace the outward forms and procedures of Western culture yet these rules and procedures are not deeply rooted in the values or traditions of the people. Thus, the conflicts between those who apply, yet only partially understand the meaning of those rules, and those who reject them outright. These problems are reflected in a growing law and order problem linked with an alien and often inappropriate legal system.

The emergence of the cargo cults was a more familiar phenomenon before attempts were made to integrate the forms of life of the indigenous people with those of the colonizers. In subsequent developments the colonizers introduced the modern cash economy. Fundamental and irreversible changes have been effected in the

Melanesian way of life with the transformation of Papua New Guinea from a subsistence to a cash economy With the demand for cash one observes a push to alienate land from communal holdings to forms of tenure other than communal. When this occurs, control of the means of production no longer resides with the community Subsistence farming of commons would not have such an effect, since these lands, after one or two generations of family use, would revert back to commons. Cash cropping, however, which uses land on a permanent basis has had the effect of permanent transfer from communal control Power, who has observed this phenomenon in the East Sepik alleges that this has led to winners and losers and the breakdown of the communal nature of social organization.[20] Those who are not sufficiently enterprising have been alienated from the social organization and the results are now encountered in terms of urban drift, crime and urban unemployment.

To this stage our description of Melanesian society has been one which associates collectivist values with communal land tenure. However, social organization according to collectivist or communitarian values does not imply development according to a socialist model, as many westerners often assume Western individualism and Western forms of socialism are equally seen as anathemas to the communitarian ideal embodied in the traditional notion of local communal rights. R.W. James, a Guyanese who teaches land law at the University of Papua New Guinea, has explained that the traditional communal form of land tenure enshrines the values of participatory democracy[21] Thus, while the individualistic liberal position with its emphasis on individual decision making and control does not accommodate traditional modes of collective control, it is also the case that the socialist orientation, which promotes centralized governmental management rather than local management, is equally antithetical to the traditional collective mode of local control through participatory democratic structures. This, according to James, does definite work in explaining resistance, both within Melanesia and parts of Africa, to the imposition of forms of land tenure based either on the individualistic liberal model or the socialistic central management model.   In practical terms, maintaining the primacy of the customary land holding within the agricultural sector, means management on the local community level through the democratic participation of the recognized members of the community.

Communal tenure, despite the emphasis on the collectivity, actually endows the individual with considerable scope for individual control of those events which affect him personally.   As is often the case in Melanesia, changes in arrangements and developments cannot proceed without near unanimous consensus [22] This may well amount to one of the most egalitarian systems known. If we contrast this with the reality of the Western system of private ownership, in which individuals do not acquire these collective rights because of their membership in a community, it becomes apparent that individuals often have less control over events which profoundly affect their lives and their community. If we look at the phenomenon of corporate ownership, in which private companies own and acquire vast resources, we find that decisions can be implemented which profoundly affect the community without the legal necessity to consult with community members One need only the reflect upon the phenomenon of the "company town" to remind oneself of this reality. In part our emphasis on the inviolability of private ownership promotes this result as many liberals and especially libertarians insist upon a private right of capital - the right to waste, destroy, transfer or alienate the resource without public interference.

By way of contrast, what is interesting is that certain Western philosophers have emphasized the close connection between these aspects of property rights and individual liberty. According to the most prominent view, to have a right is simply to have a liberty which others ought to recognize. As Alan Ryan explains this attitude "liberty is maximized, if indeed unscathed, if one employs only what is theirs. The only way liberty is invaded is by incursions on what is not ours. We have here the classical defense of the simple system of "natural liberty" beloved of Adam Smith."[23] On this view my liberties are essentially proprietary rights with which others should not interfere unless their exercise is causing harm to others and among my liberties are the rights associated with private property Thus, the argument which demands personal control for what is privately mine is argued to be synonymous with the right of private ownership. Aside from the obvious circularity of this argument, Ryan points out that the modern concept of ownership includes more than a requirement that we be left alone. It includes rights of capital, rights to alienate, waste or destroy the holding and also the rights of transmissibility, the right to make a bequest. To accomplish these rights one needs the active engagement or an active participation of other individuals. For example, others must actively do something if the wishes expressed in my will are to be carried out, or even if I am going to transfer my freehold estate into your hands. Obviously, it does not follow from the modern concept of ownership that in general people are thereby less constrained by institutional and social arrangements However, a more cogent argument is advanced by a libertarian like F.A Hayek, who argues that liberty is maximized through private ownership because it expands my options.[24]   When contrasted with feudal and customary communal ownership this may certainly appear to be the case In the feudal system the individual is subject to a hierarchical system in which personal options are severely limited. In the customary communal system in which the tendency is for group ownership, decisions often proceed by consensus, and thus unless the individual can convince the group of the value of a certain arrangement, his or her preferred line of action cannot be implemented. In this sense, therefore, the modern institution of ownership seems to expand private options because it removes traditional restrictions on unilateral decision making with respect to holdings.

However, at the same time in which individual liberty appears to be enhanced, there is also the introduction of elements of uncertainty, and possibilities of domination, control, and exploitation which were not present in the Melanesian or even feudal systems.   The former phenomena have been skillfully documented by Foucault in associated studies of modern liberal institutions and the emergence of the disciplinary sciences.[25]   In the following pages we touch briefly upon this issue in distinguishing Western from Melanesian forms of ownership.

The modern understanding of the private property right (as a universal natural right) is an exclusive rather than an inclusive right. This is to say that the right guaranteed is not that of universal access to resources or benefits (an inclusive right to be included in the distribution of social goods) but simply the right to use and to deal with one's holdings without interference from other individuals or the groups; this can be called an exclusive right - it is a right to exclusive control and thereby the right to exclude others.[26]   By implication, this universal natural right to property is not a benefit or a claim right, that is a fundamental claim to certain resources and services which one can claim as of right.[27]   For example, in Western society the father can disinherit the son whereas in Melanesia individuals usually don't inherit, but acquire rights on recruitment to a descent line. This means the Melanesian enjoys inclusive rights simply through membership in a group, i.e., certain claims to benefits and social goods based on membership in the clan.

Unlike claim rights, the rights to exchange and transfer holdings include a cluster of rights which Wesley Hohfeld would call power rights and liberty rights. A power right endows the capacity to alter legal arrangements, in substance, empowering one to effect or create new rules through the conferral of new responsibilities, duties and powers, all backed by legal sanctions. A good example, is the act of making a will which on one's death creates new legal rights, responsibilities and duties which did not previously exist. On the other hand a liberty right guarantees that one can undertake a given course of action without interference, but it does not guarantee that one will meet with success in this endeavor. For example, the right to engage in the activities of the free market, protects one from interference in the exercise of this right but in no way ensures the outcome of these endeavors or success in these activities. Rights to transfer and exchange holdings protect one against interference in these undertakings and also stipulate that successful performance will alter legal arrangements, but otherwise do not ensure against performative failure.

Thus, the rights we associate with the Western institution of ownership guarantee nothing in the way of personal benefit, but do secure a protected sphere of autonomy. In order to implement changes in the legal structure of holdings, one does not require a wide group consensus, one simply needs the agreement of several interested parties; and though the agreement may only be effected by several interested parties, the arrangement now is binding upon and valid for the rest of the society. But at the same time there are no rules or principles of social order which stipulate that these exchanges must occur; and one operates with necessary uncertainty within this matrix of indeterminate interaction. One observes that this very precariousness of circumstance exposes one to new liabilities and possibilities of domination.

This becomes apparent in considering the basis on which claims are established. In the individualistic free market ideology of the West, one understands that to gain what you may want and even need, your fundamental recourse is to the untrammeled liberty of exchange. But if you are without special skills or material resources in this free market context, the propertyless worker must exchange and sell the only resource left, i.e., personal labour, as Marx pointed out. Thus, the employee/employer relation is in a sense a concomitant of a right of property which only guarantees the liberty of exchange, transfer and undisturbed control. In this way the emergence of what at first appears to be a new right and a valued expansion of personal freedom engenders new possibilities of domination and power as uncertain circumstances force individuals to submit themselves to modes of dependence and domination in order to avail themselves of society's social goods. In fact, in the final chapter we will amplify this point and demonstrate how this has occurred in concrete social circumstances.

Because Western ownership is characterized by the liberties associated with privately willed transfer, whether before or after birth, rather than fixed customary or traditional principles of distribution applicable from the moment of birth, the character of the legal and social order in Western society is constantly shifting and modifying through the exercise of these personal rights Because these rights are exercised not merely as ends in themselves but to secure certain benefits and prerogatives, one must ask oneself who does benefit ultimately in the instantiation of this system. The answer axiomatically is those who possess the resources and or skills to institute favourable arrangements. Whereas in previous systems the social order was characterized by universal law or cosmic order and obedience to order or law, in the Western system we observe the emergence of private "exclusive" rights and the domination of others through the exercise of those rights. In pre-colonial Melanesia, individuals found themselves subject to rules which reflect the cosmic order and the necessity to maintain certain prescribed relationships. On the other hand their place within that order guaranteed them an appropriate access to societies resources as proprietary claims are pressed on the basis of clan membership, and maintained through performance of community service and adherence to prescribed relationships In the Western system one is freed of many communal demands in this respect, but also denied the security of inclusive claim rights derivative from group membership.

The capitalistic system with its particular forms of property appears to create a situation of uncertainty and even insecurity when compared with communal systems of Melanesia. What therefore have been the social advantages of embracing such a system? In part, what one points to is the dynamic nature of such an economic system. Hayek has argued that the great virtue of capitalism is derived from the fact that success is indeed an unpredictable gamble; this reality calls forth energies no other system can match and thereby it secures greater prosperity for everyone, or so it is claimed.[28] In the following section we will discuss some of the disutilities associated with maintaining this particular point of view.

Environmental Advantages of Communal Land Tenure

Social analysts have pointed out that the free market system with its characteristic modes of property has engendered the domination of other human individuals with strong connections to the domination of nature. The domination of nature has been perhaps an illusion as the incalculable effects of environmental damage accumulate from the exercise of intense industrialization and resource development and begin to threaten the future of the human race But though the idea of domination vis-a-vis nature is perhaps an illusion, the relation between our activities in this respect and environmental loss is definitely not an illusion. Papua New Guinea has certainly suffered identifiable environmental damage with the introduction of the cash economy and disruption to customary land tenure and subsistence modes of production. In a chapter of this length there is certainly insufficient space to provide an exhaustive survey of the environmental and social damage effected by the transfer and alienation of land from communal holdings. With respect to the environment one witnesses the emergence of extensive plantations for producing rubber, oil palm, sugar, cocoa, tea, coffee etc. Thus, the cyclical use of land for subsistence farming is replaced by the cash cropping of plantation crops which utilizes the land on a permanent basis. The usual environmental strain on the land and depletion of this resource have begun to occur Furthermore, this desire for cash has also led to the foreign backed and controlled developments in the areas of gold and copper mining. These events have resulted in the release of toxins and other detritus into the alluvial systems, as has occurred especially on the Jaba River system in Bougainville and on the Fly river system on the main land. (Ultimately the damage to the Jaba river system has been seen as one of the significant factors which contributed to the closing of the Bougainville Copper Mine and the current Bougainville crisis) Add to all this the emergence of the logging industry, and one encounters the host of familiar environmental problems which are beginning to plague all third world countries and the world in general

One observes that environmental damage has apparently gone hand in hand with the inroads on the communal land system and the traditional forms of production. It is the suggestion of this book that the injury to the environment and the communal way of life can be combatted by maintaining the communal form of land tenure which has been associated with traditional Melanesian values and modes of production. However, there are many, among them the World Bank and the government in recent budget reports, who assert that the most efficient development is through changes in the customary system of communal land holdings.[29] The World bank has proclaimed in the past that the "...problem of reconciling traditional land customs and western practices persists and has delayed productive use of some areas of land."[30] Nevertheless, it is the view of this author that the projected efficiency should be sacrificed if an alternative communal ownership is better suited to minimize social and environmental problems. Here I would echo the words of Andre Gorz, the French ecologist and philosopher, "...ecology ...reveals.. an appropriate response ...must be sought not in growth but in the limitation or reduction of material production. It demonstrates that it can be more effective and "productive" to conserve natural resources than to exploit them, to sustain natural cycles rather than to interfere with them."[31]

This point, therefore, touches upon the central ecological benefit of communal ownership To be specific the institution of communal holdings encourages traditional agricultural methods and resource usage which harmonize with natural cycles, while permanent alienation of land into individual holdings for cash cropping denies these cycles. Subsistence farming of commons allows communal lands a period in which to replenish and revitalize, since these lands, after one or two generations of family use, would revert back to commons.   Cash cropping, however, which uses land on a permanent basis has had the effect of permanent transfer from communal control and thereby the land suffers depletion through constant use.

However, an additional important reason for continuing communal ownership is the fact that this form of land tenure is congruent with local environmental control and economic bioregionalism. Environmentalists praise local community control of productive activities because it allows for the close monitoring of data in order to determine if the use of resources is occurring at a sustainable level. It has been pointed out that often a large amount of data is necessary to determine if a particular resource is sustainable.[32] It is undeniable that the local clan will be in the best position to observe the effects, for example, of a palm oil plantation on their traditional land, and subsequently implement policies to mitigate possible deleterious consequences.[33] Thus, traditional Melanesian communal land tenure accords with the ideals of bioregionalism, which advocates decentralized economic activity through the local management of resources.

Social and Economic Reasons for Communal Ownership

In addition to these ecological reasons, there are certainly socio-cultural reasons for maintaining the present form of entitlement. Melanesia has always invested ownership of the means of production - land - in the community. This has been the traditional Melanesian approach, one which is associated with traditional Melanesian values and the primacy of the community. This orientation contrasts sharply with the form of Western development which has proceeded with absolute individual ownership and the right to capital at its centre. The nexus between Melanesian values and this institution indicates that social and cultural stability may inevitably depend upon the preservation of this well established system. The Starnberg Institute, for example, suggests that the undermining of the communal land system, through the institution of the Bougainville Copper Mine and its subsequent activities, effected significant social disruption by undermining the traditional value system eventually triggering the current Bougainville crisis [34] However, a fuller discussion of this issue will be offered in the next chapter.

At the same time, the communal form of land tenure remains an important source of economic and social security as well as political stability for the 85% of the population which lives in the rural sector. The presence of this system ensures that demographic displacement and nutritional deprivation will be unlikely within the future development scheme so long as individuals still have recourse to traditional rights within the communal system. To this point Papua New Guinea has yet to witness those familiar scenes of third world horror which occur when unmanageable numbers of displaced landless peasants find themselves in conditions of urban squalor or rural famine Given this positive role as an economic safety net and the deep social and cultural attachment to this system of land holding, it would seem that any scheme for modernization and development which does not take into account this basic institutional factor will carry too great a social cost.

However, aside from the issues of social viability and cultural continuity, there are what might be described as purely economic reasons for maintaining the system. Indeed a recent study by the Starnberg Institute emphasizes that this form of land tenure has been integral to the generation of a productive surplus within the subsistence sector.[35] This is due to the fact that small-scale agriculture is both economically efficient and often superior to plantation production when measured in terms of cost per yield.[36] Furthermore, this surplus, they argue, has reduced the need for additional government investment in agriculture and provided ".. considerable support to the mobilization of domestic resources for public capital formation".[37] In this respect, therefore, the communal form of land holding which has maintained self-subsistence communities and high labour productivity has

promoted rather than hindered development and the efficient utilization
of resources within Papua New Guinea

Traditional Communal land Tenure and Anglo-Australian Law

In these final pages I argue that customary forms of communal
ownership should be given legal status within the current Anglo-
Australian common law system   I don't promote this move as an
ultimate panacea for the current environmental crisis, however, I think
this is necessary to pre-empt those pressures which seek to dissolve
communal holdings into individual holdings Though customary
ownership is definitely at variance with the Anglo-Australian common
law system, which is the legal inheritance from the Australians, there
are ways in which the traditional system can be realized within the
modern legal framework. Modernization doubtless requires that Papua
New Guinea harmonize its traditional values and distinct cultural
approach with the legal infrastructure of the modern world economy.
The English common law system is the evolved legal reality of modern
market relations, a legal reality with which Papua New Guinea must
come to terms. But the necessity for accommodation is not an
insurmountable barrier to the continuation of communal ownership.
Certainly customary land tenure can be adapted to the modern legal
modalities according to the following procedures Initially, one must
ensure that the clan is endowed with a legal status which it may
presently lack. Without legal status a clan will be unable to enter into
enforceable legal arrangements which may be necessary to control the
future development of the communal land holding. One way of
accomplishing this, suggested by Power, would be to register the clan as
an incorporated company.[38] There may, however, be other avenues to
achieve legal status which I would leave for the exploration of other
legal theorists. In any case, it is essential that the legal status of a clan
be closely tied to the communal land holding so that the clan will be
regarded at any point in time as a discrete group of people owning a
discrete amount of land.

A further absolutely essential requirement is that this legal model
for future development should preclude any permanent alienation of
land from the community. This means that individuals may be granted
land to use and develop themselves, while compensating the clan in
general for the loss of usufructuary rights However, individuals do not

have the right to transfer permanently or alienate the land to third parties. Any form of transfer of land should be regarded as a form of leasing, even if the clan consents to some form of major development on its communal entitlement.   The advantages of following these suggestions would be both ecological and social   Such moves would retard and control the transfer of traditional commons to individually owned land. A clan could, for example, decide that the general interest of the clan requires an area of permanently protected clan commons. This will have the advantage of maintaining certain areas of land for casual use as in subsistence farming and hunting. This will help to minimize the environmental damage occasioned by permanent cash cropping, while allowing security for those members of the community who have been alienated from the struggle for cash and the means necessary to generate it. With respect to the latter, there will always be some clan commons which the individual can, on occasion, utilize for subsistence farming or hunting - or if not, some form satisfactory compensation for the loss of such rights.

Furthermore, if the clan does transfer land by lease for large scale development, it will continue to have legal interest in the land developed as all land reverts back to the clan   In this way the clan will be able to ensure that the land is not impaired for the enjoyment of future generations. As the clan is held to consist of both past, present and future members, the current membership would be legally bound to manage the clan's resource of land so that it is neither impaired nor destroyed.

However, the reader may well entertain doubts as to whether traditional values, supported by legal communal land ownership, will be sufficient, given the Melanesian history of cargo cultism and the continuing lure of cash and Western gadgetry   Even the communal management may succumb to the desire for immediate cash and squander natural resources. (Mistakes, for example, have been made in certain areas of the East Sepik where customary land owners have agreed to logging which has devastated their natural habitat.) However, it is not the aim to promote communal ownership as the infallible panacea for the environmental problems of Melanesia This paper maintains that communal ownership is preferable to the Western form of individual ownership for two essential reasons 1) because this form of ownership supports the traditional holistic community with its traditional values which have taught respect for the land and the environment; 2) because communal tenure preserves local control as opposed to extrinsic control of land holdings As 97% of holdings are still held in customary communal tenure, the encroachment on these holdings has not yet become significant But we have already outlined the threat to this form of tenure and stressed the need for stronger legal protection. In essence, the outlined thinking is in sympathy with that of other non-Western environmental groups like the Chipko movement of India which conflates political ends and environmental protection in its strategy "...to wrest control of nature away from the state and the industrial sector and place it in the hands of rural communities who live within that environment but are increasingly denied access to it because, "These communities have far more basic needs, their demands on the environment are far less intense, and they can draw upon a reservoir of cooperative social institutions and local ecological knowledge in managing the "commons" ..on a sustainable basis".[39]

It is my conclusion that providing legal protection for customary communal ownership in this suggested manner, is the most viable course for maintaining sustainable development, development that meets the needs and expectations[40] of the present without undermining the ability of the future generations to fulfill their needs

---

[1]   Phillip Catton, "Marxist Critical Theory, Contradictions and Ecological Succession," Dialogue 28 (1989) 637-653, Andre Gorz, *Ecology as Politics*, (Boston South End Press, 1980), Andre Gorz, *Path to Paradise: On the Liberation from Work* (London Pluto Press, 1985), Ivan Illich, *Celebration of Awareness: A Call for Institutional Revolution* (London Calderand Boyars, 1971), Ivan Illich, *Imprisoned in the Global Classroom* (London Writers and Readers Publishing Cooperative, 1976)

[2]   F Mihalic, *The Jacaranda Dictionary and Grammar of Melanesian Pidgin* (Port Moresby Jacaranda Press, 1971), 202

[3]   Ennio Mantovani, "Traditional Values and Ethics," in *Ethics of Development: The Pacific in the Twentieth Century,* eds S Stratigos and P. Hughes (Port Moresby U P.N G Press, 1987)

[4]   Ibid.

[5]   See for example J.S Mill, *Liberty* (Harmondsworth Penguin Books, 1974), (Original work published 1859), R Nozick, *Anarchy, State, and Utopia* (New York Basic Books, 1974)

[6]   Adam Smith, *Selections From the Wealth of Nations,* ed G.J. Stigler, (Arlington: A.H A. Publishing, 1957 [1776])

[7]   Daniel de Coppet, "The society as the ultimate Value and the Socio-cosmic Configuration," *Ethnos* 55 (1990). 140-151

[8]   Ibid

[9]   A.P. Power, "Resources development in the East Sepik Province," in *Ethics of Development: Choices in Development Planning,* eds C. Thirwall and P. Hughes (Port Moresby: U.P.N G Press, 1988).

[10]   Similarly, Rodman speaking of the Melanesians of Longana Vanuatu states that, "Being a Longanan is inseparable from Longana as a place" in "Margret Rodman, *Masters of Tradition: Consequences of Customary Land Tenure in Longana Vanuatu"* (Vancouver University of B C. Press, 1987), 158.

[11]   A.P. Power, "Resources development in the East Sepik Province".

[12]   Ibid., 272.

[13]   Karl Heider, *Grand Valley Dani, Peaceful Warriors* (New York: Holt, Rinehart & Winston, 1979).

[14]   Ron Crocombe, *Land Tenure in the Pacific* (Suva: University of the South Pacific, 1987), 339.

[15]   John Locke, *Two Treatises of Government,* ed P Hazlett (Cambridge: Cambridge University Press, 1967 [1690]).

[16]   A.M. Honore, "Ownership", in *Oxford Essays in Jurisprudence,* ed A.G. Guest (London. Oxford University Press, 1961), 112-128

[17]   Nozick, *Anarchy, State, and Utopia*

[18]   See for example, Adam Smith, *Selections From the Wealth of Nations.*

[19]   P.M Worsley, "Cargo Cults," in *Anthropology, Contemporary perspectives,* eds. D. Hunter and P Whitten (Boston· Little, Brown and Co., 1975).

[20]   A.P. Power, "The future of clans in Papua New Guinea in the 21st Century," in *Ethics of Development: Choices in Development Planning,* eds C. Thirwall and P. Hughes (Port Moresby· U.P N.G Press, 1988).

[21]   R.W. James, *Land Law and Policy in Papua New Guinea, Monograph 85* (Port Moresby: Papua New Guinea Law Reform Commission, 1985).

[22]   See for example, Douglas Oliver, *A Solomon Island Society, Kinship and Leadership among the Siusi of Bougainville* (Cambridge Mass: Harvard University Press, 1955), 350-370.

[23]   Alan Ryan, *Property* (Stony Stratford Open University Press, 1987), 83

[24]   F.A. Hayek, *Law, Legislation and Liberty,* vol II (London· Routledge and Kegan Paul, 1967), 85ff.

[25]   Foucault demonstrates this through the emergence of modern institutional frameworks realized in prison systems, corrective institutions, health clinics and even school systems Foucault underlines that as our individual civil rights have been promoted and expanded since the enlightenment, new and more immediate micro systems of power have emerged which provide a new and even more effective network of control One identifiable micro-system of power is the modern institution of private property. What many modern writers and especially libertarians have seized upon as fundamental to ownership is the right to transfer, exchange or convey holdings freely, and they see this as an important expansion of individual freedom. But

there are new elements of domination and control which realize themselves in this very expansion of individual freedom One need only reflect on the aspects of control which can be incorporated in the modern will or its codicils For example, "Life estate to my wife and then after her demise, to my eldest son so long as he stops drinking and remains married, the remainder to my youngest son so long as he has issue etc " Clearly some very detailed forms of domination and control can be maintained even after the grave, a possibility which would not have been realizable in previous systems of tenure, which did not recognize inheritance in this modern European form Furthermore in accordance with the Foucaultian insight this form of domination does not merely seek to prohibit it aims to bring about a specific effect or result Whereas previous forms of tenure, either customary communal or feudal, constrained the individual through a tradition of informal and formal social structures, control remained prohibitive, general and far less specific. However, with the institution of modern property rights domination can become more specific and focused, with widely dispersed loci of control The exercise of these rights can bring about the implementation of more efficient and effective control with the object of constraining the behaviour of specific individuals and groups and tailored to specific local conditions but with agendas which may be indifferent to local interests In this manner, modern property rights represent a general power structure whose topology can permeate local affairs, and so act with other modern institutions to supplement the vertical power of the state, whose coercive action proceeds from remote centres with far less specificity.Michel Foucault, *Discipline and Punish: the Birth of the Prison*, trans A Sheridan (New York Vintage Books, 1979)

[26]   For a fuller discussion of this point, one recommends the treatment of "common property" in J Tully, *A Discourse on Property. John Locke and his Adversaries* (Cambridge Cambridge University Press, 1980)

[27]   Wesley Hohfeld, *Fundamental Legal Conceptions* (New Haven Yale University Press, 1964), 38

[28]   F.A. Hayek, *Law, Legislation and Liberty*, vol II

[29]   International Bank for Reconstruction and Development, *Papua New Guinea: Its Economic Situation and Prospects for Development* (Washington The World Bank, 1978), See also Power, *The Future of the Clans in the 21st Century*

[30]   International Bank for Reconstruction and Development, *Papua New Guinea*, 46.

[31]   Andre Gorz, *Path to Paradise: On the Liberation from Work* (London: Pluto Press, 1985), 16.

[32]   D.B. Botkin, *Discordant Harmonies: A New Ecology for the Twenty-First Century* (New York. Oxford University Press, 1990)

[33]   Cf. G.R Harris, "A Practical and Theoretical Assessment of Sustainable Development - A Case Study," *International Journal of Environmental Studies* 39 (1992) 313-323

[34] The Starnberg Institute, "Economic-Ecological Development in Papua New Guinea," *Catalyst* 21 (1991) 13-112

[35] Ibid

[36] Also cf. Ghillean Prance, "Fruits of the Rain-forest," *New Scientist* 13 (1990)· 35-45.

[37] Starnberg Institute, "Economic-Ecological Development," 111.

[38] Ibid.

[39] Ramachandra Guha, "Radical American Environmentalism and Wilderness Preservation A Third World Critique", in *Social Ethics: Morality and Social Policy*, eds T Mappes and J Zembaty (New York McGraw Hill, 1992), 519.

[40]

Chapter 2

The Bougainville Crisis And The Hermeneutics Of Distributive Justice

In the last chapter we became acquainted with the communal form of Melanesian property and the communal value system which binds these communities together. At the same time we contrasted this Melanesian social phenomenon with that of the West. In doing so we adumbrated the modern liberal ideology with its emphasis on individualism and its enshrinement of private property rights. We went on to discuss the environmental advantages of the Melanesian customary land tenure and recommended that it be maintained and in some way integrated with the modern common law legal system. In the enquiry conducted in the last chapter we focused on the community, its cultural values and its preference for certain forms of social/political arrangement rather than others. In this chapter we want to look a little more closely into the individual Melanesian character and in so doing illustrate the social conflicts and even disorder which results when relations with the communal land base are undermined. We demonstrate in part how economic development and the subsequent alteration in his or her natural habitat undermines the constraints which determine the individual within the communal context subsequently bringing about social disintegration. The main points underlined, will be illustrated through reference to developments which led to the so called "Bougainville crisis" - an insurrection which began on the island province of Bougainville in 1989 and which is continuing to this day.

More specifically, in this chapter I want to evaluate two models of explanation which social scientists have utilized to understand the "Melanesian personality" and behaviour. Both of these models are intended to offer informative contrasts to the Western patterns familiar

From *Alternatives: Social Transformation and Humane Governance,* volume 19, number 1 (Winter 1994), Copyright © 1995 by *Alternatives.* Reprinted with permission of Lynne Rienner Publishers, Inc.

to the researchers and their readers. The first is the allocentric/idiocentric distinction which has recently become popular with psychologists engaged in cross cultural studies. The second model of explanation emphasizes the ritualized nature of Melanesian behaviour as contrasted with the less ritualized or even non ritualized behaviour of the Westerner. This second explanatory paradigm is most often employed in the writings of anthropologists. In various ways I find both these models to be unsatisfactory as explanatory keys. I shall be discussing the allocentric/idiocentric distinction immediately and therefore I will postpone the statement of my objections. With respect to the anthropologist's emphasis on understanding through the framework of ritualized action, I will articulate my objections later in the chapter with specific reference to the Bougainville crisis. Essentially I argue that the employment of this model to explain certain actions which led to the North Solomon's rebellion is overly simplistic and misses the more important conflict between different conceptions of distributive justice which actually precipitated the disorder and the rejection of the mine.

The Allocentric/Idiocentric Distinction

The allocentric/idiocentric distinction formulated by Triandis et al., refers to a cultural difference in the personality dimension which equates "..to the distinction between cooperation and individualism at the cultural or group level."[1] This distinction has been used to explain perceived evaluative bias in psychological testing when employed in the Melanesian context. For example, Frewer and Bleus in a study of Eysenck Personality testing attempt to explain differences registered in the Personality Inventory. The authors claim that allocentric societies confound the results of tests (like the E.P.I.) devised in idiocentric societies in that "...what is perceived as socially desirable will be different in an allocentric culture. The response bias will be towards the perception of the self as an in group member; the positive self image will reflect positive in group identity rather than portrayal of the self-as-an-individual".[2] The conclusion reached is not that this fact invalidates Eysenck Personality testing but that "...cultural -specific instruments that take into account the allocentrism of the culture should be developed".[3] What I question is the implicit idea that the concepts of allocentrism and idiocentrism can do any meaningful work in suggesting the development of cultural-specific instruments which serve to reinterpret results as one moves from one culture to another.

Individualistic societies, like those of the Western world have been contrasted with holistic societies - societies in which the ultimate value is society itself. Indeed, Daniel de Coppet, an anthropologist, finds our modern approach to society exceptional in that it disregards society as an ultimate value, to the benefit of a quite opposite and non-social value, the individual.[4] The point taken is that in so far as Western culture has tended to conceive society and community from an individualistic bias it has failed to comprehend the function of society (and the individual's place within it) both with respect to its own society and that of others. This has been, more or less, the thesis of the continental post-modern movement in contemporary philosophy. To be precise, the demand that explanation be decentralized and deconstructed so that the individual subject or self as effective agent does not appear in the discourse. The post modernist manifesto proclaims that we have fundamentally misconstrued the human individual and his place in society by maintaining this theory or fiction of "the sovereign rational subject - atomistic and autonomous, disengaged and disembodied, potentially and ideally self transparent".[5]

I have no intention of offering an extensive illustration of post modern thought, but attention to the definitions offered by Frewer and Bleus underline the appositeness of the a post modern critique.

We are told that in one culture the self is perceived as an "in group member" in the other culture there is a "portrayal of self-as-an-individual". What is to be concluded? In one culture the individual is a construction derived from his relative standing within the group with an implicit assumption that this standing is a function of his relation to the group's welfare. In the other case, the individual perceives his value not in relation to his or her group membership but on his or her individual standing to be calculated as some function of his or her individual welfare (by what ever criteria that is measured.) The problem is that whether you are a team player or an individualist one's perception of oneself will be ineluctably based on one's standing within the group. Lacan, in his criticism of humanist based psychoanalysis, argued that the perception of self is always a reflection of the others perception of myself; there is no self which is transparent to itself independently of interpersonal interaction.[6] The individual human being can only conceptualize itself through another. This necessarily occurs within language, and it is within the terms of language that the self is constructed. Certainly those who promote the idiocentric model cannot blandly assert the notion of the "self as an individual" without addressing the issues raised by Lacan's research.

Ultimately, the reality in all types of societies is that the individual is a construction of the forms of life, systems of language and general cultural milieu in which the subject operates. The myth of Western thought has been that the subject is prior to and indeed constitutes these systems which condition his action. I would add that the idiocentric individual is part of this fiction, specifically the fiction which holds that the individual authors his destiny independently of group evaluation.

Furthermore, the Western concept of the individual necessarily conveys associated notions of individual interests as contrasted with group interests - otherwise little sense can be made of the allocentric/idiocentric distinction. But this also raises problems. To say that the Westerner acts for his individual interests in contrast to the Melanesian, who acts for the group's interest, still leaves one ignorant with respect to the content one ascribes to the notion of "individual interests". Indeed as we have said, there are no "individual interests" per se which are not defined within a cultural milieu and determined by criteria which are cultural specific and which are highly dependent on definitions articulated by the "group". Madison avenue advertisers have known this all along. For various reasons the sort of behaviour which tends to be valued in the Western context is autonomous agency. One very important way in which this is expressed is through bargaining and contracting between the autonomous agents, which finds its special expression in the modes of distribution particular to the Western model of private property. In the West as in any other culture, the group defines what is acceptable individual behaviour and acceptable forms of "individualism" and, of course, is just as intolerant of individual pathologies which threaten group stability as in any other culture.

We conclude, therefore, that the distinction between the portrayal of self as "in group member" and "self-as-an-individual" is not an entirely viable distinction because the self is a construction of group interaction whose context is always cultural specific. Individuals who are preoccupied with enhancing self value assign self value which is based on the norms, axiology and systems of evaluation endemic to their society, just as individuals who strive to enhance in-group standing depend upon the identical source for their judgements.

But it may be argued that I have misconstrued the reference of the idiocentric/allocentric distinction. The cultural variation in the emphasis put on collective good over individual welfare is not a matter of private motivation, one might argue, it is objectively manifest in the informal norms, societal rules, morals and general philosophical orientation of the culture. Within Melanesia it is evident that the norms and general morality promote the collective good rather than individual welfare, whereas in the West the converse is true. If this is indeed the thesis, I think it is carelessly overstated. H.L.A. Hart has pointed out that despite variance in cultures and their attendant moralities and legal systems, they all exhibit the universal tendency to focus upon the goal of survival. The aim of survival, he says, is an empirical yet contingent truth about individuals and human communities and it colours the structures of language, thought and rules of conduct which any social organization must contain if it is to be viable.[7] All existing successful communities reflect this goal, the unsuccessful are simply not around to exhibit the obverse.

My own feeling is that within the Western culture, the promotion of individual welfare over the collective good is more apparent than real. It is true that we tend to encourage competition over cooperation (to some extent) and personal saving over sharing, however, this emphasis merely obscures the underlying utilitarian tendencies. Those who stress the West's commitment to individualism forget that this has been rationalized on the grounds that competition and rational self-interest most effectively realize the greater social good. Individualistic self-interest has been tolerated in the West because it is the avenue to greater collective good, if this were otherwise, it would be rejected. Theory from the classical economists to modern libertarian free market apologetics has stressed the general advantages of enlightened self interest.[8]

However, to colour all societies with general survivalist tendencies may operate to obscure and blur the important variations within the general strategy. For this reason I would like to qualify what has just been said. Certain elements in Western societies promote a myth of idealized individual autonomy, but this does not deny that the myth itself promotes individualism as a important Western value. However, what the allocentric/idiocentric distinction conveys is an overly literal reading which gives rise to hasty generalizing and misleading half truths. Studies do support the idea that in Melanesia behavioural norms do constrain the individual to act in favour of the group in contrast to Western norms which, in certain respects, tend to ease these pressures to allow the individual to determine his own life according to his personal preferences and personal interests.[9] Nevertheless, this point, if true, is yet insufficient to license the conclusion that in Melanesia the individual invariably acts for the group interest and in the West he/she tends to act from personal interest (the allocentric/idiocentric position) or that cultural differences are simply reducible to other regarding and self regarding societies.   Generally, I think that a more appropriate interpretation sees individual Melanesians tending to value the group or clan to which he belongs somewhat more than the Westerner because, in part, he sees the clan as the means to a fulfilled life and personal satisfaction.   In contrast, the Westerner somewhat erroneously sees his own success and personal happiness as an individual achievement and not something he has gained through appropriate participation in group activities.   In other words, what the allocentric description obscures is the very real instrumentalist attitude towards the group which is common in the Melanesian context.   It is not simply the case that all the components of group value project the group as an end in itself.   The Melanesian more so than the Westerner sees the group not only as a value in itself but also a means to his own personal satisfaction and fulfillment.   What this indicates is that group relations can be highly unstable in the Melanesian community when the individual feels that the group is unjustly failing him or denying him his share in the appropriate social goods.   I believe this principle is demonstratably useful in making sense of the social upheaval and violent disorder which occurred during the Bougainville crisis and I will touch upon this later in the chapter.

When we look at the salient aspects of the Bougainville crisis, it will be apparent that this crisis with its attendant rebellious behaviour is neither predicable nor understandable through the employment of the allocentric model. The allocentric model of Melanesian behaviour would hardly suggest or predict the decidedly self interested behaviour which contributed to the social dissatisfaction and disintegration. Far from offering predicative possibilities, this paradigm would not even offer post facto insight into the unfolding of events. In fact, reliance on the validity of this description of behaviour would persuade one that the course of self interested behaviour, which occurred with respect to the disbursement of compensation monies, could not have happened. But this is exactly what happened and we will look into these events in more detail in a few pages.

This leads me to make two points which ought to supplement the simple model of allocentric behaviour. The first is that the Melanesian tends to rely on the group to a greater degree than the Westerner, and consequently when feelings of deprivation occur, he is more likely to blame the group and express this dissatisfaction violently. The second point, is that the allocentric model is entirely unreliable, when there is uncertainty as to the rules governing the distribution of social goods as when there occurs a definite conflict in cultural values. In this case, self regarding and self interested behaviour are quite likely to occur. Both these tendencies were manifest during the Bougainville crisis.

The Melanesian "Cultural Field"

The more general problem with the allocentric model is that it does not adequately explore the cultural background and context in which the Melanesian acts and behaves. In an effort to achieve the unambiguous clarity which occurs in the natural sciences it seeks to reduce cultural complexity to a single dimensional property which ultimately offers misleading half truths. Beginning with Dilthey through to Habermas[10] and recent communitarians like Charles Taylor[11] and Alstair McIntyre[12] there has developed a strong tradition of hermeneutical analysis which offers an understanding which departs from the epistemic models of simple empiricism. In these critiques we are admonished not to confuse the study of human subjects with natural science which is grounded in verification principles and procedures associated with the epistemology of empiricism. The differences in this approach entail first of all that one cannot assume the universal nature of the subject which exists independently of any cultural context; secondly, as the subject cannot be completely understood independently of his cultural context, understanding will require a complete familiarity with a cultural tradition.

Hermeneutics teaches that the failure of normal categories of empiricism in the study of human "nature" is a function of a human identity which is always a matter of self definition. To understand a human subject we must understand his own categories of self definition. This means, inter alia, understanding how the subject views him/herself in relation to the natural environment, available resources and what we may loosely define as "property". This ensemble which concatenates in the cultural context is sometimes referred to as a "cultural field".[13] I argue that the human subject is only understandable within a cultural field or context, and this will be exhibited in self definition which reflects the meanings which attach to this field. By implication, the psychologist, sociologist, and criminologist etc., must go beyond the unidimensional significance of the allocentric/idiocentric distinction to a more detailed study of the culture itself in its multifaceted complexity.

Having said this we must proceed to say something about the specific character of the "cultural field" in which the Melanesian finds himself. With reference to some of the literature on this subject and our remarks in the last chapter, I will briefly summarize the principal points before passing on to a consideration of the Bougainville crisis. I feel this is necessary in order to consider in more detail the motivation which underlies individual behaviour and the social "field" in which this behaviour occurs. I believe the Bougainville crisis indicates how disruptions to this cultural field through rapid development lead to the abandonment of traditional forms of life and specifically traditional constraints which ultimately fostered the creation of a guerrilla insurgency.

Given this program we categorize the "cultural field" according to the following general points:

1) The Melanesian ideology recognizes society as the ultimate value through which individual satisfaction is achieved. With this recognition one observes the importance of relationships over actors.[14]

2) However, the community does not constitute the entirety of concern, the greater whole to which all social action is geared is society and universe combined.[15] The whole consists of humans, ancestors, deities, plants, animals or things drawn from temporary conjunctions of different socio-cosmic combinations. In this context the Melanesian sees cyclical and not linear development in the universe and cosmological relations - things do not improve incrementally, rather phenomena are regenerated, renewed or restored in a cyclical movement. This is the motif suggested by the expressions found in the studies of anthropologists: "regeneration of total society",[16] "renewal through time",[17] "life giving death",[18] "ronde des echanges", "circulation", "ritual system".[19]

3) Melanesian identification with the community is intimately and inextricably connected with the parallel identification with the communal land holding.[20]

4) The fundamental ownership of land is by groups, the group owns and the individual uses the land.[21] It is important to distinguish customary usufructuary rights from the modern exclusive forms of private ownership enjoyed in Western culture. James Tully, using MacPherson's terminology in his commentaries on Locke, refers to the latter form as an "exclusive right", because this right gives the proprietor the prerogative to exclude others from that to which the right refers (the "res"), in addition to the other moral and legal powers over the "res" - rights of abuse and alienation. In contrast, the rights assigned within a communally held commons situation are

termed inclusive rights, because they invest a right not to be excluded from the use of that to which the right refers.[22]

5) Finally, one of the principal forces working to overturn this traditional system of land tenure in Melanesia is the cash economy initiated with the institution of money.[23] The demand for cash, unlike subsistence farming, requires the use of land, not on a cyclical basis, but on a more or less permanent basis for cash cropping.[24]

Aside from undermining the particular relationships which ensure specific forms of cyclical movement within the socio-cosmic ordering, one observes that the transformation of communal lands into forms of individual tenure, if unchecked, denies the individual inclusive rights which characterize the individual's standing with respect to communal property. Again this particular right refers to the right not to be denied access to communal lands with its obverse - the duty to make available land and other resources for other members of the community. When these inclusive rights are undermined there is real danger that certain individuals will be marginalized and the holistic community ruptured and divided into identifiable classes of apparent winners and losers.

The Bougainville Crisis and Ritual Behaviour

The Bougainville crisis illustrates in microcosm the profound changes that occur when customary relations between clan member and the environment are ruptured through the rapid introduction both of the cash economy and Western development. In the seventies and eighties, one of the largest copper mines in the world operated on Bougainville Island. In the unfolding of events it was the rejection of this huge development and its attendant works which precipitated the closure of the mine and the attempts by Bougainvilleans to secede from the P.N.G. union.

I will now summarize from some excellent research provided by Filer and others found in Ron May's work on this subject.[25] There was first of all the environmental damage. On a small Island the degradation of the surroundings becomes more readily apparent. Prominent was the pollution of the Jaba River. As a significant proportion of the population were affected by waste disposed within the four mining leases stretching from Rorovana to the mouth of the Jaba River, there was potential for a high proportion of disgruntled and dissatisfied customary landowners. The further problem was the social disruption effected by the institution of the mining leases on customary communal land and this second consequence is by no means unconnected to the first. In this case of the use and abuse of communal lands by the Bougainville Copper Limited, there was little permanent alienation of customary land into forms of individual private tenure. But following established federal legislation, the mining company sought to compensate the traditional owners for the use and abuse of traditional lands on which the mine was constructed through leasehold arrangements. In implementing the leases the company subdivided the leased areas into blocks which were said to belong to particular family groups. Each block was then drawn on a map and registered under the name of an individual title holder, usually a male who had convinced the company of his leadership of the clan. These determinations then founded the calculation which fixed the proportion of royalties, occupation fees and compensation payments the family group received as rent from the lease of their land. It was then presumed that the individual titleholder would use these monies for the benefit and general welfare of the landowners belonging to his family.

In the unfolding of events, however, many landowners charged that titleholders never distributed the compensation money.[26] Thus, we have the undeniable recipe for social disaster set in the context of the Melanesian social unit. As we have intimated the cohesion of the Melanesian community depends upon identification with the customary communal land. The necessary corollary states that degradation of the communal land base will undermine and ultimately destroy the community, unless some powerful cohesive element is substituted to replace this ruptured relationship. B.C.L. had began the process of destroying the communal land base by excavating the huge open pit copper mine and polluting the Jaba River with its waste. The compensation monies were intended to compensate the owners for this loss and ultimately sustain present and future community through the creation of trust monies, the intended pecuniary substitution for the losses to the land base. Ultimately these plans went awry, the general landholders did not receive or received insufficient benefits while the trust monies simply fell into the hands of a more sophisticated group of businessmen and speculators.[27] Consequently, revolt began as groups claiming to represent the landowners quarrelled and embarked on internecine war, first among themselves and subsequently with the mine and the P.N.G. government.

One, of course, could argue that the expectations of the P.N.G. government and B.C.L. would have been realized if it were not for the greed of a minority of local "leaders". However, it has been suggested that the failure to distribute the compensation monies or use them for meaningful benefits for the people could be attributed to the lack of ritual governing the disbursement of cash amounts.[28]   Inheritance is usually matrilinear whereas cash crops have been thought to belong to the male line. Thus, it is claimed that the leaders, rather than operate in conditions of confusion in which the dissemination of benefits would ultimately lead to controversy, decided instead simply to keep the money for themselves. Perhaps this is a convenient rationale for the cupidity of certain individuals whom one may prefer not to condemn. On the other hand, it may well indicate the disruption which will be effected by the introduction of cash, and indeed large amounts of it, into a subsistence agrarian economy where the principle means of production is the communal land base. In order that the infusion of cash act as a general benefit rather than a further source of contention, it is necessary that there exist rituals governing distribution as the business of exchange exhibits a highly ritualized character in traditional Melanesian societies.

Inevitably It is not a light matter to abandon rituals relating individuals through customary devolution of property and power - which are understood through primary relations to the land - and substitute Western fiduciary relations associated with trust monies in which the trustee (titleholder) bears the sole responsibility to act unselfishly in the interests of his beneficiaries. Even the idea of general benefit or interest though clear to Western utilitarians may have been somewhat of an opaque idea to the Melanesian. (Within the Melanesian society, exchange is primarily a way of building relations within the community or restoring ruptured ones.) Furthermore, the idea of investing these monies in the future of the community to create schools, health care systems and other Western conceived public goods would be an equally foreign undertaking. Indeed, it may never have occurred to the family leader that creation of these public goods were meant to substitute for the losses to communal land base, though something of this nature was no doubt intended by the sponsors (B.C.L. and the P.N.G. government) of these arrangements. Though they took no steps to ensure this was done.

However, though this interpretation of events is highly interesting and even intriguing, I think that there is a real danger that it oversimplifies and endorses misleading implications. Explanation of indigenous behaviour and performance through the paradigm of ritual clearly falls within a recognized tradition of anthropological scholarship. The focus of much of this research has been directed to "action" which seeks to control natural phenomenon through certain rites closely associated with the practice of magic. In this instance one finds a history of interpretation which goes back to Sir James Fraser which sees magical rituals as proto-technology, or primitive efforts to control natural phenomenon which are thought to prefigure the more rational, reliable and more advanced techniques of modern science. Thus, Implicit in these explanations is the ethnocentric view that Western man has escaped the tyranny of ritualized behaviour and magic, and embraced a more rational enquiring (scientific) attitude towards natural phenomena. Though recently certain thinkers have questioned this interpretation of magical rites as proto-science,[29] there remains this tendency of anthropologists to view the behaviour of indigenous people as essentially ritual behaviour or behaviour which is uninformed by rational deliberation. However true this may be with respect to natural phenomenon, it may well be an unwarranted extrapolation to maintain in the same way that Melanesians are excessively captured by ritual in their social behaviour to the extent that social break down is imminent where rituals are absent or lacking. And of course, this explanation fosters a misleading attitude of ethnocentric superiority, for we can only understand how ritual may constrain rational response if we know of other people who do not suffer from these constraints, namely ourselves.

Besides hidden ethnocentric attitudes embodied in this sort of explanation, there are other more serious problems. It is no doubt true that rites and ritual behaviour are highly prominent in magical or quasi-religious ceremonies among indigenous peoples, but this fact may well lead one to overvalue the importance of ritual in everyday life. Filer's thesis is that the Bougainvillean could not properly deal with the circumstance of money because in this changed situation, there were no rituals to guide action.   This explanation suggests a paralysis in Melanesian behaviour caused by lack of ritual for changed circumstances which, in turn, precipitated a rebellion as parts of a disgruntled population reacted violently to the sudden wealth of a small number of its members. What Filer's analysis misses or obscures is the dynamics of a cultural conflict which provoked enmity and resentment as different groups felt that the rules governing the distribution of social goods were being misapplied.

It may of course be true that Filer's employment of the term "ritual" was really intended in a more general and broad sense so as to cover what are normally understood as rules and procedures governing the distribution of social goods. If this is the case, I think it should have been more clearly stated, because emphasis on the absence of rites misses the dynamic and more fundamental cultural conflict which precipitated the social uprising. But furthermore, emphasis on the absence of ritual raises other fundamental questions which cannot be answered by this point. For example, if the more widespread dissemination of compensation monies was restricted because of lack of ritual, why should the other unlucky Bougainvilleans have felt resentful if they also knew that there existed no ritual which could guarantee them a share in the compensation monies?

This brings us to the discussion of social goods, an area in which the rules and procedures are complex and culture bound. Individuals, one can say, define themselves in terms of a tradition and a culture which in turn offer narratives which explain and define the good life. Our self conception grows from the latter definitions. In any tradition, the definition of the good life will include reference to various natural and social goods which constitute the elements which concatenate and alloy in various accepted forms of the good life. As Michael Walzer has explained, the character and nature of the various social goods are described and interpreted differently from one culture to another, and impacted in the very notions of these different social goods are distinct rules and procedures governing their distribution. Our various notions of distributive justice are derived from our unique understanding of these rules governing disbursement.[30] It is Walzer's view that these different interpretations do not offer a single universal concept of justice as different social goods are to be distributed according to different reasons and different procedures.[31] Thus, distinct social goods imply distinct principles of distributive justice, whose immanence creates what he calls a distinct "sphere of justice". As social goods vary from culture to culture, it is mere vanity to pretend to universal trans-cultural principles of distributive justice implicit in Western "spheres"; everything depends on context and a consideration of the social good embedded in the ethnic and cultural circumstance.

This I think does some work in explaining why Westerners are so non-plussed by the failure of the designated titleholder to redistribute the compensation monies to their communities, and begins to explain why there was resentment over the undistributed monies. Essentially Westerners are familiar with money as a social good, its "sphere" of operation, and the principles and normal procedures which govern its distribution. From this perspective of cultural familiarity, it is obvious what should occur, i.e., how the money should be distributed and also more primary in this case, that justice requires that it be redistributed. In the Western world, claims Walzer, the distribution of money operates within a sphere (a "sphere of justice"), which is distinct from other spheres, e.g., from that of office holding or that of religious grace.[32] Money, Walzer says, is distributed by the rules of exchange which means that usually one can only legitimately claim and receive money if one has exchanged something to obtain it. In this context the titleholder may well not have fully understood that the money had been generated by implicit exchange between the mining company and the community and that his role was merely to facilitate disbursement of this wealth to the community who had really made the transaction through surrender of their rights with respect to the communal land base. In this respect, the titleholder may have eagerly accepted the idea that the presence of money in his hands amounted to something like elevation to public office, or the recognition of some privileged status, i.e., that he was receiving an individual benefit or social good in recognition of his personal merit and not simply that he was acting as a mere third party trustee in a transaction between the two principals, the beneficiary (the community) and the mining company.

On the other hand, lack of acquaintance with the implicit rules associated with the distribution of money on the part of the titleholder would not lead other bougainvilleans to excuse the unequal pattern of distribution. The fact that the distribution of benefits ultimately was restricted to the titleholder and certain landowner groups violated what might be called the "deep structure" associated with the Melanesian systems of social entitlement, i.e., a Melanesian grammar of social entitlement which limits and proscribes certain unacceptable patterns of distribution. Throughout Melanesia the pattern of distribution is controlled by a primary notion of communal "property" such that individual rights tend to be inclusive rather than exclusive rights. This expresses itself in the innate feeling among all members that they have a right to a share in the community's social goods, whether it is land or some other fundamental resource. The titleholder may have been unable to locate appropriate rules and procedures for distribution with respect to money, however, his actions or lack thereof still left him in violation of this "deep structure". It is no doubt this sense of violation which can be seen to have generated the social discontent and resentment which erupted as armed conflict between rival landholding groups. Ultimately we can criticize the titleholders for a failure to be more creative in their thinking and for failing to fashion some response which would have been more consonant with the "deep structure" of Melanesian social relations.

Moving beyond the actions of the titleholders, there is a problem connected with the fact that B.C.L. sought principally to compensate landowners and did not distribute benefits widely throughout the Island community. Why they would operate in this manner is no mystery to the Western mind but in the Melanesian cultural context it was felt to be unacceptable, in part for the reasons we have just mentioned. According to Western thinking, which is drawn from a culture of bargaining agents, there is a belief that those outside the contractual arrangement cannot makes demands for the benefits of the arrangement. Though, Walzer indicates eleven distinct spheres of justice within our society, I am sure most people would agree that for most aspects of our Western lives, distribution proceeds by the rule of exchange which operates within the sphere of money. Westerners as it were, grow up within a tradition in which this is so well understood that it hardly ever occurs to us that things could be otherwise. As Charles Taylor has pointed out, we are essentially a culture of bargainers and this has led to an ideology which sees all political arrangements as the results of bargaining between agents and all social interaction as the interaction of bargaining agents.[33]

By contrast to the Western context, within Melanesian society there is a greater emphasis on group consensus, and furthermore, on the notion that all group members have certain inclusive rights to a share of society's social goods.[34] Thus, regardless of the existence or non existence of certain rites or rituals, Melanesians don't readily accept the idea that social goods are distributed principally by contractual arrangements between individual agents, because, as members of the community, they believe that all individual members possess prior inclusive rights to a share of these goods. As we have underlined, distribution contrary to the notions embodied in these implicit rights, precipitate feelings of injustice; and disorder and unrest can be readily effected. These distinct attitudes with respect to the distribution of social good were, I believe, the source of the cultural conflict between the owners and managers of the mine and the indigenous population.

By illustration, I should mention a Bougainvillean student of mine, who attempted to explain the causes for revolt, by referring to the fact that most of the roads leading from the mine to the airport and the harbor were paved and well maintained, whereas the road to his village was unpaved and decrepid. He regarded this as evidence of the unfairness of the arrangement. My initial response to this statement was that his complaint was ridiculous, if not irrational. Did he not see that the mining company had no reason to pave roads to a remote village when there was no obvious necessity or advantage to the company? Again, however, my thinking was being coloured by a pervasive Western framework - social interaction and most social goods proceed by exchange - and therefore as a remote village had nothing to offer the company by way of valuable access why should the company consider bestowing the social good of a paved highway. What I failed to appreciate perhaps is the element of consensus is stronger in the Melanesian culture than our own and often operates in instances when we would assume that there must be an exchange relationship. Additionally there is the previously mentioned tendency to assess social arrangements as they affect the community as a whole, and with this the strong feeling that benefits should in some sense accrue to all members and the community in its entirety. In short, distribution should proceed on a more equitable basis. In contrast, the Westerner tends to compartmentalize and atomize the community and in so doing selects those groups and individuals who are seen to offer benefits and advantages consequently identifying only these people as the ones who should receive various benefits and social goods by way of exchange. The Western thinking, therefore, excludes certain groups and individuals from consideration in the distributive process. This is contrary to Melanesian understanding of distributive justice which follows the notion that distribution should proceed with reference to the inclusive rights of all the individual community members, rather than remain matters of individual or fractionalized group arrangement.

Over all, the Island witnessed the enrichment of certain individuals and the rewarding of certain groups in a manner which was contrary to a culturally innate sense of justice. Thus, we begin to see the malcontent, resentment and envy which unfolded within the Island community as grounded in a profound cultural sense of injustice. Having said this, there is an obvious objection to this central argument, which argues that I have added the hidden premise that the entire Island possessed a sense of communal identity which is not entirely probable. This indeed has been a hotly contended issue, however, I tend to side with people like Griffin who do believe that Bougainvilleans look upon themselves as a unique and distinct people apart from all other Papua New Guineans.[35] With other Papua New Guineans the sense of community does not extend much beyond their extended family or localized linguistic group, as until quite recently, communication with other groups was linguistically limited and contact often restricted to war like incursions. However, with the Bougainvilleans it is certainly arguable that these limitations had been overcome through a much earlier contact with Western civilization and the earlier work of the Catholic missionaries. With this early contact with both Westerners and through them other Melanesians, they began to see themselves as different from other Island groups and mainland P.N.G. aided in part by their extremely dark skin colour. Earlier on therefore, Bougainvilleans understood themselves to be a distinct Island community which was different racially and historically from the rest of P.N.G. One could safely say that within no other province in P.N.G. do the people recognize a similar cohesive identity throughout the territory, and accordingly, with respect to Bougainville, one can speak of a sense of community which extends beyond localized groups and envelopes the entire Island.

Conclusion

Our conclusion is that the individual Melanesian more than the Westerner defines himself in terms of the community and the communal land base. With respect to personal access to society's social goods, it is the case that he/she does not does not believe that the principal modalities of distribution should be dominated by the procedures of individual or personal exchange. There is an understanding that distribution should benefit the community as a whole which implies the distribution of benefits or social goods should be sufficiently widespread and thereby not a distribution which is determined and restricted by arrangements between the principal individual bargaining agents. As we mentioned before, most Melanesians feel themselves to be members of a community which endows them with certain "inclusive rights", i.e, rights which require that they have a share in society's social goods. In contrast, the Westerner regards as his inalienable rights, liberties or rights to transfer and exchange what he personally possesses and to do so without interference. Obversely, he feels that arrangements must ideally proceed by individual arrangements, without regard to some overall social good. In Bougainville, the industrial world attempted to introduce the latter ideology and value system in its development of the Island, not from some intentional view to cultural domination, but simply because they understood development, economic distribution and themselves (as embodiments of development) through this framework. In Bougainville the result was confusion followed by a sense of injustice as many observed the distribution of benefits proceed contrary to their innate understanding of justice. These feelings led many Bougainvilleans ultimately to reject violently the mine as the source of pollution, social chaos and unjust societal arrangements.

Generally one could say that within Melanesia development which occurs within traditional holistic communities in one way or another undermines the communal land base and its environment and effects the destruction of the Melanesian community. Bougainville illustrates the difficulties and pitfalls of substituting cash for land and the Western social relationships based on business and consumption for the traditional relations of the agrarian community. Bougainvilleans had the opportunity to observe the rapid westernization of their community and the rapid ascent of a new class of entrepreneurs and businessmen. Ultimately the Bougainville social unit could not sustain the ruptured social relations which occurred with the empowering and enriching of this new class. Elsewhere in Melanesia events associated with development and the generation of new inequalities have yet to provoke a similar crisis, but this is probably because, *inter alia*, they lack the rapidity or magnitude of the development which occurred in Bougainville. For example, Rodman in speaking about the introduction of capitalism and plantation cropping in Longana Vanuatu, finds that the course of differentiation is proceeding very slowly which allows the illusion to persist that the inequality between ordinary people and the wealthy landowners is fundamentally no different from the inequalities between ordinary men and those of rank in the past.[36]

In terms of the allocentric/idiocentric distinction, what is important is not so much that the individuals in Melanesian society tend to act for the benefit of the group rather than individual self interest, clearly the Bougainville crisis, in many of its facets, suggests contrary evidence. But this does not mean that the majority of Melanesians on Bougainville did not invest a central value in the community group from which value they derived strong expectations of individual benefit and reward. The lesson drawn is that the sense of group cohesion and stability is fragile and is susceptible to dissolution and disintegration when sufficient numbers of individuals feel that aspects of the community are denying them access to what ought to be communal benefits. In Bougainville we observed the emergence of a new form of life, that of leadership by guerilla insurgents, understandable only if we appreciate the collision of cultures and value systems - that represented by the mine and Western development and that represented by the traditional communal society. Those who rejected the mine and sought to restore and maintain the latter, could only do so violently. In the traditional Bougainvillean society leadership was achieved principally through consensus;[37] in contemporary Bougainville it became imposed by violence and force of arms, a new form of life which was neither the preferred Western personality model nor traditionally Melanesian.

Furthermore the idea that there is pervasive ritualization of Melanesian behaviour and that social and individual disorders can be explained by disruption to or lack of governing rituals is oversimplistic and intellectually unsatisfied. Ultimately it   fails to explain to Westerners what appears to be inherent irrationality in the Melanesian personality and its subsequent violent and rebellious response to introduced development.

The conclusion I promote, therefore, is that what occurred in Bougainville exhibits not merely the failure of ritual in the face of changing circumstances, but rather a profound conflict between two fundamentally different conceptions of social justice. To appreciate this conflict one needs to point to the Melanesian unfamiliarity with the Western social goods embedded in the cash economy.   Applying Walzer's insight, I argue that particular social goods entail distinct modes and procedures of distribution, and these Western social goods carried their own appropriate rules of distribution which were misunderstood by many Bougainvilleans. These social goods, especially money and capital, are distributed through a free market system based on individual freedom of   exchange and contract.   Justice for the Westerner is achieved if the rules and understandings of the market are respected, for example, if it is free of force, fraud and coercion. For the Melanesian, however, a market of freely determined contractual arrangements is a far less dominant mechanism in the distribution of property and social goods.   In contrast, membership in a particular community with specific attachments to a defined land base are more important determinants of rights to holdings, as these facts determine the inclusive rights to claims on society's social goods. Furthermore, as we have said, there is a deep structure to all modes of distribution which understands that all aspects of the community should derive benefit from society's social goods, and this certainly promoted the feeling that the entire Island should benefit from the wealth of the mine.

On the specific issue of money, Filer points out that there was uncertainty as to appropriate definition of money as a social good within the context of customary Bougainville culture, which in turn lead to confusion as to appropriate mode of distribution. In this situation of confusion, certain opportunistic individuals prospered.   However, despite the acknowledged confusion there remained a deep seated resentment and feeling that developments were proceeding unjustly. Again this was due to a conviction that distribution was proceeding without reference to the needs of the greater Island community which remained directly proximate and related to land base from which the wealth was being generated. Ultimately, great numbers of Bougainvilleans felt that the greater proportion of the wealth unfairly benefited a small number of indigenous businessmen and titleholders, together with expatriate foreigners and the citizens of mainland P.N.G. who had no organic links to the community or the land.

---

[1]   L.Frewer, A.V. Bleus, "Personality assessment in a collectivist culture," *South Pacific Journal of Psychology* 4 (1991): 1;   C. Triandis, R. Bontempo, H. Betencourt, M. Bond, K. Leung, A. Brenes, J. Georgas, H. Hui, G. Marin, B. Setidadi, J. Sinha, J. Verma, J. Spangenberg, H. Touzard, G. Montmollin, "The Measurement of Etic aspects of Individualism and Collectivism across Cultures," *Australian Journal of Psychology* 38 (1986): 257-267; C. Triandis, R. Bontempo, M. Villareal, N. Lucca, "Individualism and collectivism: Cross Cultural Perspectives on self-ingroup Relationships," *Journal of Personality and Social Psychology* 54 (1986): 323-338.

[2]   Frewer & Bleus, "Personality assessment in a Collectivist Culture," 1.

[3]   Ibid., 4.

[4]   Daniel de Coppet, "The society as the ultimate Value and the Socio-cosmic Configuration," *Ethnos* 55 (1990): 140-151.

[5]   Thomas McCarthy, "Introduction," in Jurgen Habermas, *The Philosophical Discourse of Modernity,* trans. F.G. Lawrence, (Cambridge: MIT Press, 1991), IX.

[6]   J. Lacan, *Feminine Sexuality,* trans. M.& J Rose, (London: Macmillan Press, 1987).

[7]   See H.L.A. Hart, *The Concept of Law* (Oxford: Clarendon Press, 1964).

[8]   See for example, Adam Smith, Selections From the Wealth of Nations, ed. G.J. Stigler, (Arlington: A.H.A. Publishing, 1957 [1776]); or F.A. Hayek, *Law, Legislation and Liberty,* Vol. II, (London: Routledge and Kegan Paul, 1967).

[9]   Ennio Mantovani, "Traditional values and ethics," Ethics of Development: The Pacific in the Twentieth Century in eds. S. Stratigos and P. Hughes, (Port Moresby: U.P.N.G. Press, 1987).

[10]   See Habermas, *The Philosophical Discourse of Modernity.*

[11]   Charles Taylor, *Philosophy and the Human Sciences· Philosophical Papers 2* (Cambridge: Cambridge University Press, 1985); and *Sources of Self The Making of Modern Identity* (Cambridge Mass.: Harvard University Press, 1989).

[12]   Alstair McIntyre, After Virtue, (Notre Dame: Notre Dame Press, 1981); and *Whose Justice? Which Rationality?* (Notre Dame: Notre Dame Press, 1988).

[13]   Taylor, *Philosophy and the Human Sciences: Philosophical Papers 2.*

[14]   Mantovani, "Traditional values and Ethics".

[15]   Ibid.; de Coppet, "The society as the ultimate Value and the Socio-Cosmic Configuration".

[16]   A. Gell, *Metamorphosis of the Cassowaries Amide Society, Language and Ritual* (London: Athlone Press, 1975).

[17]   Annette Weiner, *Women of Value, Men of Renown New Perspectives on Trobriand Exchange* (Austin and London: University of Texas Press, 1976).

[18]   Daniel de Coppet, "The life giving Death," in *Mortality and Immortality· The Anthropology and Archaeology of Death* (London: Academic Press, 1981).

[19]   Andre Iteanu, *La Ronde des echanges: De les circulation aux valeurs chez Orokaiva* (Cambridge: Cambridge University Press, 1983).

[20]   A.P. Power, "Resources development in the East Sepik Province," in *Ethics of Development· Choices in Development Planning,* C. Thirwall and P. Hughes, (Port Moresby: U.P.N.G. Press, 1988).

[21]   Ibid.; Annette Weiner, *Women of Value, Men of Renown;* Ron Crocombe, *Land Tenure in the Pacific* (Suva: University of the South Pacific, 1987).

[22]   J. Tully, *A Discourse on Property: John Locke and his Adversaries* (Cambridge: Cambridge University Press, 1980).

[23]   A.P. Power, "Resources development in the East Sepik Province,"; A.P. Power, "The future of clans in Papua New Guinea in the 21st Century," in *Ethics of Development: Choices in Development Planning,* eds., C. Thirwall and P. Hughes, (Port Moresby: UPNG Press, 1988).

[24]   A.P. Power, "The future of clans in Papua New Guinea in the 21st Century".

[25]   C. Filer, "The Bougainville rebellion, the mining industry and the Process of Social Disintegration," in The Bougainville Crisis eds., R.J. May & M. Sprigs, (Bathurst: Crawford House Press, 1990).

[26]   Ibid; H. Okole, "The politics of the Panguna Landowners's Association".

[27]   See Ibid.

[28]   C. Filer, "The Bougainville rebellion, the Mining Industry and the Process of Social Disintegration".

[29]   P. Winch, "Understanding a Primitive Society," *American Philosophical Quarterly* 1 (1964): 307-324; Taylor, *Philosophy and Human Sciences Philosophical Papers 2*

[30]   Michael Walzer, *Spheres of Justice: A defense of Pluralism and Equality,* (New York: Basic Books, 1983).

[31]   Ibid., 6.

[32]   Ibid.

[33]   Taylor, *Philosophy and the Human Sciences: Philosophical Papers 2*, 40-49.

[34]   R.W. James, *Land Law and Policy in Papua New Guinea, Monograph 85* (Port Moresby: Papua New Guinea Law Reform Commission, 1985).

[35]   J. Griffin, "Bougainville is a special Case," in *The Bougainville Crisis,* eds. R.J. May & M. Sprigs, (Bthurst: Crawford House Press, 1990).

[36]   Margaret Rodman, *Masters of Tradition. Consequences of Customary Land Tenure in Longana Vanuatu* (Vancouver: University of B.C. Press, 1987).

[37]   See for example, Douglas Oliver, A Solomon Island Society, Kinship and Leadership among the Siusi of Bougainville (Cambridge: Harvard University Press, 1955), 350-370.

Chapter 3

Legal Realities O f Papua New Guinean And Fijian Communal Tenure

In the first chapter we strongly recommended that P.N.G. maintain elements of customary communal land tenure in the post colonial development period. We suggested that this could be accomplished through incorporation of clans and their formal registration as owners of the communal land base. To this date the incorporation has not been widespread, however, landowner companies and associations have been significant players in those areas which have experienced foreign backed development of customary lands. Perhaps because the incorporation of clan membership has legislative approval the courts tend to recognize the interests and rights of landowner groups whether incorporated or not. Many of these groups have been quite aggressive in asserting their claims and demands often utilizing the judiciary and legal counsel to effect their interests. As we have mentioned these associations and companies have galvanized in those areas where foreign interests are contemplating or have established large scale projects involving the extraction of either renewable reserves (principally forestry) or non-renewable resources (principally, copper, gold, silver and petroleum).

Prof. R. G. Ward of the Australia National University has recently demonstrated that there is a variance between custom, practice and legal principle in the land tenure systems throughout the South Pacific.[1] While admitting the accuracy of this observation, in this chapter I wish to compare generally bureaucratic and legal practice as they apply to land in Fiji and P.N.G, and further compare the effects of these realities on the practicalities of development, legal implementation, effective management of social change and social impact, and in the case of Fiji, the broader issues of social justice.

With this general project in mind I will seek to bring these diverse points together through focus upon the communitarian principle of empowering communities or cultural groups rather than concentrating on the rights of individuals. In effect this is the theoretical framework within which we will conduct our enquiry. Recently writers such as Will Kymlicka, Joseph Raz, Avishai Margalit, and Vernon Van Dyke, among others, have argued for the devolution of state powers to members of cultural groups so that they might maintain the integrity of their cultures, customs, norms and languages which compose their way of life.[2] Communitarian and so called culturist critiques of liberal theory have questioned the liberal tendency to articulate principles of justice premised on the "bi-polarity" of the individual on the one hand and the state on the other. Will Kymlicka has argued that cultural communities, particularly "indigenous peoples", ought to be accorded special protections of the law so that their culture is not undermined in so far as an attenuated cultural structure damages the individuals who live within it.[3] Also in line with this thinking, Niraja Gopal Jayal of the Centre of Political Studies, Jawaharlal Nehru University, for example, has recently proposed that the notion of citizenship be redefined in a manner which will incorporate differences so that cultural communities can gain collective rights like trade unions and corporations.[4] The idea conveyed by those we might call culturists or communitarians[5] is that justice must go beyond the idea of equal rights for all citizens and provide special rights for communities and cultural groupings in order that these cultural communities will endure in the face of overwhelming threats to their traditions. In the course of this paper I would like to look closely at the notion of the presumed connection between according special rights to community groupings and preserving the indigenous culture and the social cohesion of the original community. I intend to test the application of this principle by assessing the social consequences of *mataqali* land rights in Fiji, and the social consequences of those accorded to the traditional landowner groups in Papua New Guinea.

Our method of evaluation, which we have utilized throughout is that of comparison. Certainly land tenure in Fiji does offer a relevant model for comparisons. Fiji is sometimes seen as a virtual sister state of P.N.G., a Pacific Island state with similar Melanesian traditions though with a much stronger Polynesian influence. The current system of land tenure in Fiji represents a colonial and post colonial effort to preserve perceived elements of customary communal land tenure through the participation of the government bureaucracy in the form of the Native

land Trust Board, rather than through the legal incorporation of land
holding groups.

History and Colonial Origins of the Contemporary Fijian System of Tenure

In Fiji the land tenure system which continues to this day was
instituted by the British in the late nineteen hundreds and alleged to
correspond to the traditional Fijian system which was said to reflect a
form of communal ownership which was inalienable. In 1874 all lands
not already European owned or likely to be occupied by Fijians were
placed under control of the *mataqali*, a Fijian kinship group, which by
legislative decree was established as the rightful "landowner" in a
virtually new land tenure system which, with minor modifications, exists
to this day.[6] This move can be better understood through reference to
social conditions in Fiji at the time of cession.

Before the British assumed control of Fiji as a colonial unit, the
European planter community was rapidly buying up Fijian land with the
purpose of creating sufficient acreage for their plantations. At the same
time, it was intended that the purchase of extensive holdings would have
the effect of separating the native Fijians from their customary lands so
as to create a pool of unemployed available labour.[7] European
acquisition of customary land was facilitated through sales conducted
through the agency of the Fijian chiefs. It is usually understood that in
order to protect Fijians and their lands Chief Cakobau in the eighteen
seventies ceded the entire country to England "...believing (according to
B.H. Farrell) like his colleagues that the lands of Fiji were vested in the
ruling chiefs".[8]

Subsequently, Sir Arthur Gordon, the first Governor General of Fiji
(later Lord Stanmore), also became alarmed at the encroachments which
Europeans had made on Fijian land; and at the same time became
enamored with the Fijian people and their customs and determined to
preserve both - though it has also been suggested that Gordon was
inclined to preserve the customary system of chiefly rule in order to
maintain his own position through the agency of existing ruling elites,
rather than risk imposing an alternative rule with insufficient resources.
In any event, he believed that one policy which might promote these
ends would involve the registering of all land according to communal
tenure as belonging to the *mataqali*, and rendering it inalienable. It was
hoped that this policy would have the effect of voiding future sales by

the chiefs and ensuring that the Fijians did not become a mere dispossessed enslaved labour force. At the same time the chiefs also became persuaded of the wisdom of these views as in 1877 the Council of Chiefs held that the true ownership of the land rested with the *mataqali* and the Fijian land was inalienable. *De Facto*, as matters now stand, 83% of land remains in Fijian control (as *mataqali* units), while 1.7% is owned by Indians who make up roughly 50% of the population, while the remainder is either freehold or Crown land.[9]

Many writers have stressed the discrepancies between the pre-contact land tenure practices and what became the orthodox codified model of "traditional" Fijian land tenure. J. Gerard Ward has recently succinctly categorized these discrepancies into three: mobility of the people, alienability or transferability of land, and the levels within the hierarchy in which land was held. With respect to mobility, Ward emphasizes the frequent moves from one settlement to another, the splitting of the *mataqali* or *yavusa* and subsequent relocation of the parts, and the coming together of groups which had no prior kinship links. Thus, instead of fixing time honoured connections which existed from time immemorial, the formal registration of ownership boundaries may simply have ossified a more fluid system, rather than preserving customary practices. This point had been made by France and Walter in earlier works. Walter attempts to capture the aspects of this colonial policy in the term "traditionalisation" by which he means a process "...where an omnipotent alien administration has seen fit to codify a traditional social system - or what is reckoned to be a traditional social system - thereby ossifying it into exactly the tightly functional, static system the preconception deemed it to be."[10]

On the matter of alienation, Ward underlines that the appropriate chief could transfer and sell land to others, and so pre-cession events clearly contradict the assertion in the record of the Council of Chiefs meeting of December 1877 which states that Fijian land "cannot be absolutely alienated". With respect to the last point Ward, following Thompson, emphasizes that land fell into three categories of ownership to which different types of rights might be held by different groups or individuals.[11] For example, the *veikau* or forest, within a group's area of influence "...was considered to be the domain of the broadest social or settlement unit, the *yavusa*".[12] On the other hand, areas which were cultivated or gardened belonged to the individual or extended family which had cleared and planted them, whereas house sites within the village belonged even more strongly to the occupying family or individual.

To varying degrees, several of these criticisms of contemporary formalized Fijian land tenure are also applicable to formalized land tenure in P.N.G. With respect to Ward's first point, one can claim that similar events were not unknown in P.N.G., and so the P.N.G. practice involving the formalizing of customary title through incorporation also runs the same risk of distorting the pre-contact practices. On the other hand, the absence of the chiefly system in P.N.G. would clearly indicate that customary land could not be invested in individuals so as to empower them to transfer land unilaterally as happened in Fiji. For example, B.H. Farrell noted that the Polynesian influence on Fijian institutions renders it unclear whether land was communally owned or looked upon as the property of the chief as in a feudal system.[13] He states that unlike other Melanesian societies which exhibit "unilateral exogamous clans", a relevant characteristic of which is that of complete equality among all members, and subordination of the individual to the clan as a whole, the behavior of chiefs and nobility in Fiji appear to be essentially Polynesian. With respect to the third point which recognizes varying degrees of communal, family (extended family) and individual rights within the system, it cannot be denied that in many respects this was also the case in P.N.G., however, I do not believe these observations are sufficient to deny the overall communal character of customary ownership.

We should now turn to Fiji and expand the evaluation. In weighing these criticisms it is important to point out that in general any modern legal or bureaucratic attempt to formalize customary ownership can never adequately capture the full character of any customary form of tenure because of the essential informal nature of these arrangements. Any registering of land according to European legal bureaucratic principles in itself creates a foreign non-indigenous institution which imposes itself into customary interpersonal relations and creates novel affiliations and corresponding modalities by connecting certain members of the clan and the bureaucratic officials or legal representatives. Events elsewhere point to this difficulty of preserving communal ownership through formal institutionalization. For example, in Tanzania, legislation was passed which was intended to reemphasize communal ownership of the means of production, land and resources. However, one commentator observes that this did not satisfactorily return communal control to the village level but did bring bureaucracy to the village level, and "...Although the villagers have a measure of control over land and resources, the penetration of state machinery to the village level is obvious."[14] Thus, to expect formally registered forms of tenure to capture fully all the elements of customary ownership is an impossible demand, in the sense that the act of legal registration itself introduces elements which must alter the internal structure of the customary arrangement.   In any event, what was apparent in Fiji, and what is apparent now in P.N.G., is that land tenure must be formalized so as to meet novel and changing socio-political realities.[15]   Though it may be illusory to believe that customary arrangements will be preserved intact through formal registration, in making these changes, it is important to include, as far as possible, many of the original characteristics of customary tenure so as to maintain the cultural identity and integrity of the indigenous social units.   I would agree that in the case of Fiji, the system of ownership which was formally recognized was significantly at variance with the pre-colonial system, but at the same time I think we will see that important elements of customary ownership do remain recognizable within the contemporary system.

Keeping in mind this general observation we should look more closely at Ward's specific criticisms and their application to traditional Fijian land tenure.   With respect to Ward's first point as to the fluidity of the original system and the solidifying effect of the imposed system, it is obvious that this aspect could never be preserved as recorded registration of land does just that, fix, index, codify and thereby determine shifting or fluctuating ownership claims.   On the other hand his second point as to the transferability of land is certainly a significant departure from customary practice, but can be politically justified when seen as a modification in the traditional system designed to ensure that the Fijians continued to hold their lands and certain traditions which it accomplishes by precluding the possibility of customary land conveyance.   Finally, the third point which Ward raises, "the level within the social hierarchy at which land was owned", alleges that the imposed system seriously simplified traditional land tenure which recognized elements of community, clan, family and individual ownership.   However, it might be said on behalf of the contemporary system, that these complexities could not be easily captured in a system of formal registration.   The fact that the colonial administration emphasized the communal aspects becomes understandable as an avenue to preserve the integrity of the customary land base.   Vesting title in the community again precludes sales, grants or conveyances by avoiding the vesting of land title in individuals especially the chiefs who could consider themselves the owners of the land on which the rest of the community lived and depended.

Furthermore, Ward himself has asserted elsewhere that in general the customary land tenure system of the South Pacific cultures "...rarely gives absolute and alienable rights to users" in that the dominant element appears to be individual usage rights to that which is owned by groups of one form or another - the community, clan, extended family or family.[16] Ward's description of Fijian land tenure, despite qualifications accords closely with his general depiction of land tenure systems of the South Pacific in that for the most part it allows for individual usufructuary rights which strongly implies the greater interest or title rests with the community, clan or individual family.[17] These are the important elements which distinguish customary communal ownership from modern individual private ownership as recognized in Western societies. In any event, it is undeniable that these essential elements of communal ownership existed in precolonial tenure and therefore an emphasis on these elements, to the exclusion of certain exceptions, would not have created a situation which was foreign to the Fijian experience. From what has been stated and written, it is obvious that one cannot easily say, as we can in the European system, who holds the ultimate title to land: the community, the clan family, the individual, the chief etc. However, the characterization which has been provided points, I believe, to the dominance of some form of group ownership and this view has been confirmed to me by the leading indigenous Fijian authority on Fijian socio-political history.[18]

Assessing Fijian Land Tenure Today

At this stage further discussion is needed to bring us up to date. When in 1874 the *mataqali* was declared the rightful owner of Fijian lands, the colonial government instituted the Native Lands Commission to register and record *mataqali* boundaries. In the 1940s the colonial administration set up the Native Land Trust Board to administer policy, especially the leasing of inalienable *mataqali* land. The latter powerful bureaucratic institution endures to this day.

It is also significant that in the late nineteen hundreds Sir Arthur Gordon imported indentured Indian labourers to work the sugar cane plantations; a policy which had already been implemented in the British Island colonies of Trinidad and Mauritius. This was intended to satisfy the European plantation owner's need for labour and protect the Fijians through the introduction of a non-Fijian labour resource. Both the introduction of the Indians who now number around 50% of the population of the Island and the institution of the Native land Trust

Board to administer leases are crucial to an understanding of present economic, social and political affairs.

Today much of the island economy is still heavily dependent on the production of sugar, which is the major export. It is now, however, the Indians who manage most of the sugar plantations and who supply their labour. On the whole the Native Fijians have been disinclined to take on these businesses and where they have, they have failed to be competitive with the Indians, with the exception of some island groups.[19] In any circumstances the production and harvesting of sugar cane is not an easy business. At the same time the system of land tenure which was instituted by Sir Arthur Gordon has obviated the need for Fijians to take on this work as they can exist on rents from those who do.

The renting of land, however, is not an unregulated laissez faire matter between the lessor and lessee. In order to set up their businesses the Indians must rent *mataqali* land, however, the Indian cannot rent directly from the *mataqali*, but rather must rent through the Native Land Trust Board. One of the functions of the Board is to assess the unimproved value of the land and calculate an appropriate rent which is based on a formula which should not exceed 6% of the unimproved value of the land.[20] The *mataqali* does not get all the rent money paid by the renter as the N.L.T.B. absorbs up to 25% of the rent in administrative costs. However, despite the bureaucratic costs involved, the system of land tenure set up by Sir Arthur Gordon has provided the native Fijians with a significant source of income through the economic utilization of their land without either risking loss of ownership of the land through credit transactions or otherwise, or having to provide the expertise or intensive labour necessary to render the enterprise productive.

The question is have these parties benefited from this system of ownership and property rights. Generally one might argue that based on the yardstick of mere economic benefit, the answer would appear to be yes.   Among the independent islands in the South Pacific, notwithstanding Australia and New Zealand, Fiji leads in per capita income with $1930 (U.S), compared with, for example, Tonga's $1280 (U.S.) and P.N.G's $800 (U.S.).[21] This, however, is not to say that everyone is existing in a state of contented coexistence. The 30 year leases currently held by the Indian farmers expire from 1996 onwards, and there is genuine uncertainty as to whether they will be renewed or whether indigenous Fijians will pressure to resume control of their lands. It is obvious that this is a source of anxiety for the Indians whose access to land depends upon both the will of the indigenous Fijians and the policies of the Native Land Trust Board. On the other hand Fijian nationalists led by Sakeasi Butadroka have demanded the abolition of the N.L.T.B. as well as return of all control to the grass roots village level.[22] This group emphatically declares the N.L.T.B. to be a vestige of colonial paternalism which is separating Fijians from achieving higher standards of living through higher rent revenue and greater autonomy in their own affairs. In expanding on his views Butadroka claims that P.N.G. and Vanuatu are better off because of greater grass roots control of land.

Indeed these remarks indicate to us a significant avenue of assessment through comparison of the socio-economic consequences of each system. Furthermore, I think one will see that this comparison offers an informative means of contrast which puts into relief the difficulties and disorders which have been avoided in Fiji through its formally registered system of land tenure while unfortunately highlighting the problems which have been visited upon P.N.G.

Comparative Evaluation of Land Tenure in Fiji and P.N.G.

Unlike Fiji, customary land, for the most part, in P.N.G. remains unformalized and unregistered; A system of formal registration was attempted in 1952 when the Native land Commission was established to enquire into ownership of each tract of unalienated land and record the rights of the traditional owners, but the program was pursued for ten years with little practical result.[23] (In July 1995, the Chan Government considered, as part of the I.M.F. structural readjustment package, the possibility of registering customary land, but caved into demands from a combined protest of university students and army personnel, and dropped the proposal.) Also unlike Fiji, the colonial government in the 1960s pursued a policy of substituting individual registered titles (freeholds) for traditional communal forms of land holding and the replacement of customary law by English real property law.[24] However the legislation intended to implement the plan efficiently was ultimately defeated by the P.N.G. members of the House of Assembly in 1971.[25] Significantly, in 1974 the Land Groups Incorporation Act was passed and provided for the legal recognition of traditional groups and their incorporation for purposes of acquiring, holding, disposing and managing land.[26]

It is certainly arguable that because customary land holdings in P.N.G. have not been formally fixed and determined through registration as was done in Fiji during the last century, there is great potential for conflict between competing claimants. However, so long as clan lands remain in a relatively undeveloped condition, the registration of these lands is not a particularly tangible advantage or disadvantage to the clan, but these matters usually undergo a dramatic change when some particular major development project is contemplated and there is the prospect of acquiring significant development money.

No doubt because of the legally unformalized nature of customary ownership in P.N.G., the legal status of any agreements between the customary owners and outside interests actually fall outside the protections of the law. P.N.G. legislation provides that all dealings with respect to customary land between customary owners and non-citizens are void and unenforceable.[27] In order to avoid this result the customary owners can either lease their land to the government who then acts as agent for the landowners and negotiates rents and compensation payments; or the customary owners can incorporate, and deal more directly with the foreign developers. In recent years the latter route has become increasingly more popular as local landholding groups seek a more direct negotiating role. With respect dealings in timber, the Federal Government through the agency of the National Forest Authority buys the timber rights from landholders in a forest management Agreement. The Authority then sells the rights to a developer through a timber permit, and the landowners get a royalty with the premium which is negotiated with the developer.[28] In any event, in the cases of both mining and timber harvesting, landowners are frequently forming associations and negotiating their position through hired lawyers.

The history of recent events indicates that within P.N.G., land owners have only been motivated to form associations when foreign interests have expressed an intent to develop their land. Unfortunately the result has been a recurring problem of frequent, protracted and sometimes violent disputes over land ownership which most often galvanize when there are proposals for a large development project like a mine or an oil pipe line. Where the development and use of land tends to be extensive, the developers, the government and especially the judiciary are often faced with a monumental problem of unravelling, researching and adjudicating often numerous conflicting and competing land claims. Every large scale project must, therefore, address and resolve this problem before any further financial investment can be made. If the colonial or post colonial government had surveyed and registered all clan lands throughout P.N.G., in their original relatively undeveloped condition, as was done in Fiji, the necessity to address and settle the issue in a heated, politically pressurized climate would have been avoided, not to mention the bitter disappointments and social unrest which have often followed the decision making process. It is undeniable that much work is being generated for the large law firms in Port Moresby and Lae who are presently engaged representing the different landowner groups, but it is questionable whether the increasing economic and social cost of ever escalating and expensive litigation is really supportable in the context of a developing economy.

What is at issue in this instance is not the institution of clan incorporation and subsequent registration of land through the corporation but rather the untimely approach which has been tolerated. If development is to proceed effectively and efficiently by means of clan incorporation, then government, provincial or federal, ought to ensure clan and communal lands are registered well in advance of the appearance of foreign investors and developers, otherwise the developers, government and especially the judiciary leave themselves open to an almost uncontrollable situation - a situation in which they will have to fight off specious, tenuous if not fraudulent claims, and at the same time exercise the wisdom of Solomon to decide between groups who affirm competing but equally plausible rights.

Also if we consider the situation subsequent to the contractual agreement, conditions in P.N.G. indicate that it would be an advantage to have a permanent bureaucracy like the Native land Trust Board whose mandate is to regulate relations between the lessor and lessee. The existence of an experienced and competent third party to regulate and adjudicate differences between lessor and lessee would go far to stabilize relations especially in those instances where the landowners may feel that they have been given an unfair deal. The existence of a bureaucracy like the N.L.T.B. would offer to the P.N.G. land owners an alternate procedure of complaint rather than the frequent recourse to either costly litigation in order to settle points of agreement or in some cases violence or forcible interruption to the activities of the developer.

Beyond the issues of clarity and the regulation of relations, additional and serious problems have occurred in the stages subsequent to effective performance, that is, after the clan or group has duly received the agreed upon monetary consideration. Again relying on custom to guide the distribution of these monies has often proved to be a serious miscalculation, sometimes with some unforeseen additional disastrous consequences. The most striking example of this form of misadventure occurred during events which led up to the so called Bougainville crisis. As compensation for the use of customary lands for the purposes of this huge mine, Bougainville Copper Limited paid money for each of the clans to a designated principal title holder with the expectation that these monies would be distributed to the families and individual clansmen according to indigenous customs.[29]   In most cases, however, the individual titleholders kept all the money themselves, and ultimately the Bougainville crisis began as clansmen quarrelled and first fought over money and leadership ultimately precipitating a secessionist movement which forcibly closed the Panguna mine and called for the creation of an independent Bougainville.

As we saw in the last chapter, Colin Filer, formerly of the Anthropology Department of the University of Papua New Guinea, has suggested that this failure to distribute the compensation monies or use them for meaningful benefits for the people could be attributed to the lack of ritual governing the disbursement of cash amounts.[30] Filer notes that inheritance in the North Solomons is usually matrilineal whereas cash crops have been thought to belong to the male line. Thus, he claims that the leaders, rather than operate in conditions of confusion in which the dissemination of benefits would ultimately lead to controversy, decided instead simply to keep the money for themselves. Whether or not this analysis presents a convenient way to let the titleholders off the hook, it does underline the glaring mistakes which can occur when one trusts that cash will be equitably distributed according to custom, especially when the cash economy has been a colonial introduction.

More specifically these remarks point to the difficulties of the incorporation model of development as it applies in context of P.N.G. social realities. In the Bougainville case there existed a landowner's association and separate from this a trust fund (The Road Mine Tailings Lease Trust Fund) which was administered by the twelve aforementioned titleholders who represented the landowning clans and communities. The trustees were to invest the money received from the mine "...for future generations while spending the income for the benefit of the wider community". As it turned out the trustees violated their fiduciary duties and kept the money for themselves.[31] In his analysis of this situation Colin Filer strongly suggests that the variance between customary procedures for disbursement of social goods and the expectations of the Western developers, who understand the procedures, rights and duties with respect to fiduciary arrangements, ultimately led to an unhappy series of events which precipitated a full rebellion. By holding on to the money the trustees created a small elite of enriched titleholders and associated businessmen, thereby freezing social power and material wealth in their personal holdings rather than allowing it to devolve naturally according to indigenous social customs - though, of course, cash payments could not devolve naturally by customary procedures because there were no customary procedures which governed this newly introduced "social good". This state of affairs understandably created dangerous jealousies exacerbated by a conflict between generations as the younger rising members of the community began to demand a greater share in the wealth and participation in the control of the disbursements.

The fundamental problem is, of course, that a landowner company or association has to function as trustee of other people's money; and the risk is that those who are not sufficiently acquainted with the cash economy may fail to appreciate adequately their responsibilities through insufficient acquaintance with the cash system and the various mechanisms and procedures whereby it is held, distributed, acquired, and invested. At the very least the principals in the corporation have to be sufficiently aware that the corporate structure provides for a distribution of company shares to individuals and families and by law the revenues have to be paid out proportionately through dividend payments. If the trustee/directors do not sufficiently appreciate and comprehend their role as in the Bougainville case, disastrous results will ensue as individual clansmen/clanswomen, the intended beneficiaries, begin to feel that they have been dispossessed and defrauded.

Overall what also becomes evident is that the introduction of cash and large amounts of it into the context of the Melanesian community has a destablizing effect because of it's very non-customary character.[12] When one understands the nature of a social good, as Michael Walzer has pointed out, one comprehends the appropriate modes of acquisition and appropriate avenues of distribution and disbursement. As cash in Melanesia is a non-customary social good, these modes and procedures are often not understood or only partially grasped. Those who by fortuitous circumstances or even accident find themselves in possession of monetary wealth as in the case of our Bougainville titleholders, may still have only a clouded understanding of the attaching uses, powers, modes of distribution, rights and responsibilities. They may simply lock their money away as happened in Bougainville and thereby sustain their own social status so creating a new social class who unaccountably command social power, prestige and access to cargo simply because of their closer relation with the monetary forms of wealth. These events, of course, are at variance with, and disturb customary modes and procedures whereby social power, prestige and material wealth devolve through the Melanesian community and pass from one generation to the next.

On a more practical note I would conclude from these general remarks that it is important to minimize the social impact of cash and certainly an obvious course is to reduce the amount which is made available through foreign development projects. In the first chapter, following the suggestion of A.P. Power, we recommended that future development in P.N.G. proceed through incorporation of the clans. I still maintain the advisability of this move for reasons of self reliance, clan autonomy, self development and self respect etc., however, with certain reservations. Advisedly this would be the optimum course of procedure in cases where the clan initiates its own modest scale projects or developments, and maintains its own management and control of the enterprise, for example in cases of agriculture, aquaculture, sylviculture and animal husbandry. These would be projects which accord with the principles of bioregionalism and sustainability, rather than development through unsustainable resource extraction through the agency of multinational companies. Community, clan autonomy and self reliance is enhanced through the former type of development, whereas the latter will most often have deleterious effects, especially when the concern is the well being and continuity of the indigenous community.

My following remarks, therefore are intended to refer to relations between land groups and multinational interests in the context of development involving large scale resource extraction requiring the infusion of large amounts of foreign capital, and foreign expertise and management. In these instances, I believe, the government bureaucracy needs to assume a more regulatory role comparable to that of the Native land Trust Board in Fiji. In addition, to ensuring that land is already adequately surveyed and assigned to appropriate clans before the possibility of future development is widely known, the government needs to set by formula, according to uniform and strict rules, the amount which should be payable to the clan in terms of rent and compensation for the abuse and waste of clan land. The money paid by the foreign interest to the land owners certainly should be sufficient but certainly not overly generous to avoid a corrupting affect. Through all stages of negotiation through to actual payment and distribution of monies, the government bureaucracy should deal directly with the foreign interest as the agent for the clan. This is also important from another perspective, since at present, Landowners deal with the foreign companies through the lawyers for the landowners group, and often the interests of the lawyers may be at variance with those of the government, the land owners and the foreign company. For example, it may be in the financial interests of the lawyers to continue litigation rather than settle negotiations out of court.

Though landowner payments from mining interests are uniformly substantial, it has been alleged that this has often not been the case with respect to payments from foreign timber harvesting interests. This problem is attracting global interest as the Island of New Guinea contains one the World's last vast remaining rain forests. It has been alleged that international logging interests have frequently paid P.N.G. clansmen relatively little for the billions of kina worth of timber which have been harvested on their lands.[33] Unlike mineral wealth, which supposedly belongs to all the people of P.N.G., and therefore cannot be developed without the participation of government, timber rights belong to the owners of the land, and so logging interests, once they have obtained their licenses can deal directly with the traditional owners without the same government supervision. This has given an unfair advantage to the logging interests who are often dealing with remote villagers and clansmen who are often hungry to experience even the simplest and least expensive benefits of civilization. In Fiji the existence of the N.L.T.B. legally precludes the logging interests dealing directly with customary owners and in P.N.G. a similar bureaucracy might do the same and so monitor relations between the clansmen and the business interests.[34] Within P.N.G. the need for some form of permanent "watchdog" over these interests is becoming vital as evidenced by the recent urgent appeal made by Premier Bernard Vogae of Papua New Guinea's West New Britain demanding that the National Government review all existing timber agreements in light of the environmental problems currently experienced in the province.[35]

Finally what is crucial in any of these situations is the disbursement of money to the landowners through the government bureaucracy. It is essential that some P.N.G. counterpart of the Fijian N.L.T.B. assume control of the disbursements, deduct administrative cost, and than distribute the money to the clan members on a pro-rata basis. Here it is important that the money be given directly to the individuals and not given indirectly through the landowner groups; this will ensure that all individuals derive equal and comparative benefit from the project. Taking over the disbursement of moneys in this manner ought to avoid situations which have happened in Bougainville and elsewhere in which individual clan members have received disproportionate or no development monies because other individuals in the landowner's association have for one reason or another failed to make appropriate distributions. This is not to say that unincorporated or incorporated bodies representing the landowners should not exist or undertake investments for the clan, but what I believe should happen is that the individual members of the clan first receive their money directly through the government bureaucracy and then as members of the clan and eligible shareholders in the clan corporation, they can decide to proceed with the option of investing their entitlement money in clan projects through the purchase of shares.

As I pointed out, in Fiji the flagrant form of misappropriation which happened in Bougainville could not have occurred because the Native Land Trust Board carefully distributes proportionately to individuals and families, though the proportion paid to the chiefs is greater than that distributed to the commoner, but again this is in accordance with Fijian custom. In Fiji 30% of the rent goes to the three principal chiefs of the owning group - 5 percent to the *traga i taukei*, 10 percent to the *turaga ni qali* and 15 percent to the *turaga ni mataqali*.[36] In any event it would be impossible as occurred in Bougainville, that the majority or even any member of the clan could be denied a share in the revenue money paid to the clan.

Ultimately with respect to P.N.G., I maintain the position that small scale projects which are within the competence of the clan and require modest amounts of initial capital should proceed by the method of incorporation described in the first chapter. However, in those cases in which we are talking about projects of larger scale which require significant amounts of foreign capital and foreign expertise, then I would propose that money which is paid to the clan for the rental, or use and abuse of clan lands, should be negotiated for by the government according to some set of uniform principles and formulae and paid to individuals directly through the government bureaucracy.

This may limit the autonomy of the clan or the landowner community, but the benefits more than balance this deficiency. Firstly, this will preclude impossibly high compensation demands, the product of either unreasonable expectations or encouragement of lawyers, and also the alternative situation in which unsophisticated indigenous people have agreed to inequitable arrangements. Secondly, though this move may appear to limit the control of the community in reality it does not. The community will still have the option of refusing any package which is offered to them. Thirdly, this arrangement will allow the clan to decide soberly whether the costs of development are worth some reasonably determined monetary compensation and at the same time it does remove the possibility that they will be induced to accept serious depredations to their environment because they have by blinded by the allure of instant wealth.

For the above reasons I believe that the overall benefit to the clans would be greater if these events were managed by a "responsible" government bureaucracy. In any case, the landowner companies which are now assuming a negotiating role are not entrepreneurial enterprises in the true sense of the word, but rather represent brokers or middle men interposed between the foreign interest and the customary landowners. Given this reality, the interests of those managing the landowner company may not coincide with the best interests of the traditional customary owners. For example, it has been demonstrated that landowner companies which apeared in Manus Province in the late nineteen eighties actually frustrated the Province's efforts to manage the timber harvest on a sustainable basis. Against the Province's wishes they interposed themselves into negotiating roles with foreign logging interests and effected deals which exceeded sustainable quotas of timber. As these companies seldom offer their own expertise, management, capital or labour to the enterprise, they can best be described as opportunistic middlemen rather than entrepreneurial associations properly representative of the landowning community, an impression which is further strengthened by the fact that these associations are most often led by a small elite of the more literate westernized tribesmen, rather than organizations with the full participatory involvement of the greater community.[37]

In this case, though limiting the rights of these groups might appear to disempower and undermine the autonomy of these communities, our analysis of phenomena like Bougainville tends to argue that these associations can have a debilitating effect on traditional culture of the community including its possible disintegration, especially where large infusions of cash are present. As we have pointed out, these associations tend to spawn hierarchies and elites which are variance with the traditions and culture of the indigenous community. In this instance limiting, rather than ascribing rights to these associations and landowner groups, may work to preserve the order and cohesion of the traditional community.

With respect to Fiji, I would hold that the idea that the N.L.T.B. is a colonial impediment to higher standards of living because it prohibits direct dealings between lessor and lessee and imposes a 25% service charge, is in part the product of the uncomplicated vision which sees any arrangement which limits the highest possible rate of return as intolerable and patently unjust. On the other hand, Fijian Nationalists might solicit support from Western liberals, especially those tending toward libertarian views, who would agree that such regulatory agencies undermine some essential characteristics of modern liberal society in that these regulatory intrusions deny freedom of contract, economic autonomy and principles of entitlement which apply as the usual outcome of freely assumed contractual relations. However, regulatory agencies which would be normally intolerable within a modern Western economy may play a necessary and beneficial role within the wholly different context of a developing economy. One must remind oneself that the developing world is not the first world in which it is usually assumed that the economic actors are equal and equally knowledgeable and cognizant of their best interests. In short, it is an economic reality in which inequality of bargaining power is often the rule rather than the exception, and where unrealistic expectations and unfamiliarity with market forces and procedures often cloud and prevent sound judgement, often to the detriment of both contractual partners. In this circumstance it is important not merely that there exist some legal apparatus to which one can apply to seek redress through litigation, but rather that there is some bureaucratic agency to monitor all contractual stages from negotiation to performance, through to distribution. Certainly in P.N.G. the socio-economic climate would improve if there existed a third party institution with a mandate both to apply objective principles in all dealings of customary owners to ensure that the terms of agreement are fair to both parties, and that all members of the community receive significant benefit from the use of communal holdings. Eventually when there is sufficient economic sophistication the present system will have to be scrapped in Fiji, however, at present it would be premature to call for its abolition in so far as indigenous Fijians, unlike the Indians, have yet to become active participants in the businesses and economic affairs of the Island; and until they do, any objective assessment must reckon that the present system works to their benefit.

Also this leads us back to our central issue, the continuity of the cultural community and the ascription of special rights to ethnic groupings. One can conclude from the foregoing that though empowering and granting rights to particular groups may appear to work in favour of preserving traditional communities and their way of life, the over generalization of this proposition should be resisted. Events in

P.N.G., especially those surrounding the Bougainville crisis, indicate that somewhat ersatz organizations, often hastily constituted to represent some alleged group interest, may actually hasten the breakdown of the traditional culture and its particular form of life. On the other hand, it is certainly arguable that the land rights accorded to the Fijian *mataqalis*, though they did not nor could not preserve the traditional Fijian land tenure, did preserve the Fijian communities from white encroachment and assimilation, with the result that Fijian communities continue to exist to this day as distinct cultural enclaves. Furthermore, the limited rights accorded to the *mataqali* - usufructuary rather than the right to deal directly with property by alienation, rental or conveyance without the intervention of the N.L.T.B. - gave little scope for the emergence of entrepreneurial subgroupings or middleman brokers who might challenge the traditional feudal structure of society. Also provisions requiring that the nobility receive a proportionately greater share of the rental revenues could only reinforce and maintain the traditional cultural hierarchies, whatever we may think about the desirability of this cultural heritage.

From the foregoing one might reach the conclusion that the principle of ascribing special rights to ethnic communities so that they will have the resources to survive as distinct cultural enclaves bears careful examination. From what we have seen one could qualify the principle and assert that such a policy can only preserve the character of the culture when an exogenous disbursement of resources is consistent with, and reinforces the customary devolutionary direction of social goods. In Fiji, the legally instituted system of land tenure worked to preserve the customary lines of devolution, within P.N.G. the legally recognized system has apparently worked to undermine and disconnect tradition from its political-economic base. However, circumstances in Fiji differ from those in P.N.G. the culture is not universally Melanesian, 50% of the population is Indian, and thus there is a further issue which must be addressed, that of the principles of liberal democracy which demand equal citizenship for all citizens.

The Issue of Justice with Respect to the Fijian Indian

Can we defend a system of land tenure in which the Fijian Indian is constitutionally precluded from owning any part of the 83% of the total land area which falls under customary ownership? Certainly these terms constitutionally entrench an inequality of rights which specifically undermine individual autonomy and equality of opportunity so far as the

Indian is concerned. According to liberal ideology the state is meant to secure the "liberties of equal citizenship" and not special rights and privileges of cultural membership. By according rights of customary ownership to *mataqalis* and their membership, the Fijian state, while precluding other cultural groups access to the same rights, appears to be violating the canons of equal citizenship.

In practical terms the 50% Indian population remains virtually landless and is denied ownership of resources which are available to their fellow Fijian citizens. According to the traditional understandings of Western liberal democracies, the notion of equal citizenship cannot sustain unequal treatment of different groups in cases where the government guarantees certain fundamental rights to one group of individuals while denying the same rights to another group of individuals.

However, recently communitarian critics have argued that this notion of universal rights through equal citizenship is flawed in that it ignores the individual differences which emerge through differences in community and cultural identity.[38] A more thorough understanding of social justice must also encompass ethnic difference through recognition of particular cultural communities and their special needs, claim the communitarians. Accordingly, recent communitarian critiques of liberal theory have questioned the liberal tendency to articulate principles of justice premised on the "bi-polarity" of the individual on the one hand and the state on the other.[39] The traditional liberal perceives the justice of socio-political arrangements in terms of an appropriate ascription of rights and agency to each of these two actors, with the understanding that rights ascribed to individuals will be equally shared. However, this model has been advanced by social scientists with the assumption of a culturally homogeneous society and the facts of ethnic diversity have are now been recognized to pose a strong challenge to this model. Specifically, ethnic groups and communities have sometimes violently rejected this model and have begun to claim autonomy, agency and legal personality which have been previously vested in either the individual or the state.

Within the global spectrum of ideological locations, the idea of enhanced community rights has been seized upon by two very distant groups, the left, represented by Will Kymlicka and others, who believe that these views license the protection of minority ethnic groupings, like Canadian Indians and French Canadians; and the Right specifically the New French Right led by thinkers like Alain de Benoist and Guillaume Faye who believe these ideas support the protection of a majority French culture against the inroads of minority cultures and a dominant transnational American universal culture.[40]

Beginning with the left side of the spectrum we find Will Kymlicka, for example, arguing that cultural communities "indigenous peoples" ought to be accorded special protections of the law so that their culture is not undermined in so far as an attenuated cultural structure damages the individuals who live within it.[41] Kymlicka centres his defence on the notion of the fragility of the cultural community and the dependence of the individual on a "cultural context of choice". Selecting autonomy as the central concern of liberal discourse Kymlicka asserts that the range of choice which allows us to be autonomous is undermined when one's cultural community is in peril. Kymlicka's two examples are Canadian Indians and French Canadians, groups who now face these sorts of threats. These groups are not well established dominant cultural enclaves like Francophone culture in the territory of France but rather minority cultures in the North American context whose survival is threatened by the dominant and majority American/Anglophone culture. Given these realities these groups need to be given special rights so that their cultures will continue to survive and their membership spared the anomie and the other debilitating shocks to self identity and responsible agency which result in conditions of cultural disintegration. It may well be argued that the Fijian state has in fact done just that by ascribing special rights of ownership to the *mataqali*, the Fijian kinship group and so has recognized that Fijian cultural communities possess special rights of ownership which do not devolve to other communities or individuals.

However, it has been argued that Kymlicka's account of the cultural context and relation to autonomous decision making is overstated if not overblown. One critic argues that the concept of being a Quebecois or an Indian from the Northwest Territories is too "thin" to offer much in the way of guidance in modern society. As he states, "In Quebec, as in most other places, people turn for guidance not to in group ideals of their ethnic group but to the beliefs of their religious community, to the consumerist standards of a market society, to the meritocratic standards of the corporations they belong to, to the media and so on."[42]

He concludes that Ethnic solidarity does not provide meaningful contexts of choice except in relatively rare circumstances. The question one needs to ponder is whether Fijian culture provides one of these rare circumstances and so justifies the ascription of special rights to the indigenous Fijian groupings.

In Peter France's definitive work on the history and origins of the current Fijian system of land tenure, *The Charter of the Land*, he states

"To have preserved the actual institution of native society might have stemmed the rapid decrease of the Fijian population, to have encouraged the adoption of European institutions might have enabled the survivors to adjust themselves to the changing world introduced by the white man. The establishment of the communal system throughout Fiji did neither."[43] France's argument is that the communal ownership recognized by the British did not really preserve Fijian culture, nor did it effect the assimilation of the Fijian to the economic and social world of the white man. These remarks point to the possibility that the Fijian cultural community had already been undermined by the very landholding rights ascribed to the mateqali by the colonial power and this is the important point to be considered when we attempt to justify these rights. On the other hand, it is certainly arguable that current life in Fijian villages is more culturally attuned to indigenous traditions than the life of a French Canadian or a North American Indian living on a reserve in Northern Manitoba or North Dakota. Certainly modern Fijian communities are different from pre-colonial Fijian communities, there has been an evolution conditioned by European influences, but life in these communities is distinct and different from that of the North American experience.

But for Kymlika's arguments to work in Fiji's favour, it must be established that for a given group, assimilation is not a viable option which means that future generations will suffer malaise and anomie if they attempt to assimilate completely to the economic market orientated culture of the white man. But again this all seems to be a matter of degree and furthermore an empirical matter which is not easily susceptible to proof. Certainly this century their are countless examples of successful ethnic assimilation in America, Australia and Canada etc. In any event Fijians, more than Papua New Guineans, whose contact with the dominant economic culture has been far more tenuous and recent, are much better prepared to assimilate to the economic culture of a market society.

Let us now turn to the particular communitarian or culturist position of the New French Right. Unlike the communitarianism of Kymlicka, the focus of the New French Right is not the fragile identity of the human individual dependent on cultural affiliation but rather a thoroughgoing return to community through an emphasis on the rights of peoples over the rights of individuals, and the creation of a genuine global pluralism to counter American liberal market universalism. Unlike the American Right, the New French Right is anti-Christian in outlook and also opposed to the principles of an American lead global market economy. With respect to the latter, The New French Right sees the principles of market liberalism, together with the growth and spread of new technologies, as a deracinating process which is destroying distinct cultural communities and transforming man into an atomized homo-economicus - a profit maximizing consumer of American culture and its products. Certainly the substance of these ideas is not without respectable intellectual support. Jurgen Habermas, for example, has warned of the dangers of market intrusiveness which threatens to invade other areas of social and institutional meaning in a de-diffentiation process which subverts all meaningful systems to one overriding economic meaning.⁴⁴ Similarly in the North American context, Michael Walzer in the 1980s warned of the need to maintain distinct spheres of justice to ensure that the distributive procedures of the market did not envelope other spheres of social life and corrupt the varied forms of social existence to a single economic interpretation.⁴⁵ In this respect, some of the ideas of the new Right have already received respectable intellectual articulation on both sides of the Atlantic, but what is characteristic of the New French Right is a diagnosis which identifies the threat to diverse distinct cultural identities with American life and the exportation of its culture through the global market. In order to counter this threat they recommend that the dominant culture within a given territory have a privileged relation to the land and that they control the rights of exit and entry controlling a territorial base of cultural difference.⁴⁶ Their recommendations, also require that resources be diverted to those projects which extend and promote the dominant distinct culture and in this case they are speaking of French culture.

However, this view stands to be accused of simply relabelling positions so that the policies resulting from this form of culturalism are extensionally equivalent to those which would result from racist ideology stripped of the communitarian baggage. For example Pierre Andre Taguieff and others argue that culturalism especially as it is employed by the European New Right, GRECE (Groupement de Recherche et D'Etude de La Civilization Europeone), fosters a racist regime, one that is racist because the lines where mixing is discouraged correspond more or less exactly to the lines which would have been drawn within the racist discourse which it replaces.⁴⁷ This means that culturalist policies aimed at excluding and denying the rights of non-francophone groups like the Arabs and the Berbers would be indistinguishable from those relying on more simplistic racist attitudes. It is difficult to question the appropriateness of this observation as applied to the French Right, the question is whether the land policy in

Fiji and perhaps other measures passed in Fiji since the two coups, are simply racist policies which one might attempt to dress up as communitarian or culturalist discourse.

Ultimately, I believe that one can better defend the rights of the Fijian communities by abandoning question begging arguments based on the liberal value of individual autonomy and indeed fall back on the on some but not all ideas of the French thinkers in the New Right who elevate the value of cultural diversity per se to combat American market liberalism which in many ways does appear to flatten differences and push people into the market as atomized consumers - a humanity transformed into "homo economicus". One can argue that in order to maintain cultural diversity, one need not embrace the fascist or covertly racist positions of the New French Right which argue that we must maintain the exclusive privileged status of one group to the exclusion of other groups. Certainly one may recognize that successful pluralism requires accommodation and the recognition of the validity of other cultural groups and so avoid the imputation of racism. This means we have to look closely at possibilities of accommodating different groups and trading off advantages. In this respect we might argue that the state not only represents a social contract between the government and the individual citizens but also one between the different groups which make up the citizenry, which means that different parties to the contract have different rights and responsibilities. Indeed a form of social contractarian justification has sometimes been advanced to explain the 1987 Fijian coup which firmly entrenched the political hegemony of indigenous Fijians. Thus, despite the coups and the regrettable upheaval and undermining of Fiji's democratic institutions, some claim that these events are part of a process of accommodation between the two dominant ethnic groups which has realized a form of social contract which understands that the Indians hold the weight of the economic power while the indigenous Melanesians hold the preponderate political power. Josefa Kamikamica one of the leaders of the Fijian *Soqosoqo ni Vakavulewa ni Taukei* party (S.V.T.) has stressed the need of Fijian-Indian cooperation through a constitutional review which should seek a trade off between Fijian political superiority and Indian economic strength.[48] Thus the special rights of ownership vested in the Fijian *mataqali* can be seen to be incorporated as contractual terms to guarantee and protect Fijian social, economic and cultural stability in the face of Indian economic dominance and external threats from the global market.

Ultimately one might agree that no society is perfect and no political scientist or political philosopher is going to find his preferred theory of justice mirrored in the political/social reality of any modern state. As I have attempted to demonstrate, the system of land tenure based on *mataqali* ownership which colours and determines the economic realities in Fiji, can be defended from a variety of moral perspectives: utilitarian, communitarian and contractarian, though it will hardly satisfy liberal and libertarian theorists who demand that political arrangements protect a set of preferred universal rights equally ascribable to each individual citizen. Overall when one applies standards of assessment which are contextually appropriate, The Fijian system of land tenure based on the *mataqali* unit of ownership appears to be both generally economically beneficial, and when a number of our moral insights (utilitarian, communitarian, contractarian not to mention libertarian notions of historical entitlement) are balanced or brought into "reflective equilibrium", appears to satisfy important ethical concerns.

---

[1]   Forthcoming, R. Gerard Ward, "Land, Law Custom: Diverging Realities in Fiji," in *Land, Custom and Practice in the South Pacific*, eds. R. Gerard Ward and Elizabeth Kingdon, (Melbourne: Cambridge University Press): 198-149.

[2]   See Will Kymlicka, "Individual and Community Rights," ed. V. Baker in *Group Rights* (Toronto: University of Toronto Press 1994); *Liberalism, Community and Culture* (Oxford: Clarendon Press, 1989); Avishai Margalit and Joseph Raz, "National Self-Determination," in *The Journal of Philosophy* 87, No 9 (Sept. 1990): 439-461; Avishai Margalit and Moshe Halbertal, "Liberalism and the Right to Culture," *Social Research* 61, No 3: 491-510; Vernon van Dyke, "Justice as Fairness; For Groups?" *American Political Science Review* (1975): 607-614.

[3]   Will Kymlicka, *Liberalism, Community and Culture*, 170.

[4]   Ibid., 152.

[5]   My impression is that philosophers tend to call these writers "communitarians" whereas social scientists label them "culturists".

[6]   B.H. Farrell and P.E. Murphy, *Ethnic Attitudes Towards Land in Fiji* (Santa Cruz: University of California Press, 1978), 1.

[7]   Peter France, *The Charter of the Land* (Melbourne: Oxford University Press, 1969), 107.

[8]   B.H. Farrel, "Fijian Land: A Basis for Intercultural Variance," in *Themes of Pacific Lands*, eds. M.C.R. Edgell and B.H. Farrell (Victoria: University of Victoria Press, 1974), 113; see, however, A. Ravuvu, *The Facade of Democracy* (Suva: Reader Publishing House, 1991), 14, who argues that the Fijian chiefs were pressured into an unconditional surrender.

[9]   B.H. Farrell and P.E. Murphy, *Ethnic Attitudes Towards Land in Fiji*, 1.

[10]   A.H.B. Walter, "The Conflict of the Traditional and the Traditionalized: An Analysis of Fijian Land Tenure," *The Journal of the Polynesian Society* 87, No.2 (1978): 89-108, 90).

[11]   Ward, "Land, Law Custom: Diverging Realities in Fiji," 209.

[12]   Ibid.

[13]   B.H. Farrel, "Fijian Land: A Basis for Intercultural Variance," 119.

[14]   C.K. Omari, "Traditional African Land Ethics," in *Ethics of Environment and Development*, eds. J.R. and J.B. Engel (London: Belhaven Press, 1991): 167-175, 173.

[15]   See Glenn Banks, "Compensation for Mining: Benefit or Time Bomb? - The Porgera Case," *Resources, Nations and Indigenous Peoples*, eds. R. Howatt, J. Connell, and Phillip Hirsh (Melbourne: Oxford University Press, 1995) especially page 3, to appreciate the difficulties of an informal system of customary relations has effected on the communities surrounding, Porgera, P.N.G.'s largest gold mine. He states, "Landownership in Porgera consists of a series of rights which an individual may claim through either parent (a system of cognatic descent). This has allowed a large number of kin who were born and living outside Porgera to move in and occupy land to which they do not have full ownership rights, although they can only do so with the permission of the landowners themselves. This group are referred to by the Ipili (the local tribe) as *epo atene*, or "those who have come" or "invited guests". Banks mentions that this trend has continued, and even intensified since the start of mine construction with consequent social disorders.

[16]   R. Gerard Ward, "Pacific Island land Tenure: An Overview of Practices and Issues," *Land Culture and Development in the Aquatic Continent*, eds. D.G. Malcolm Jr & Jeanne Skog, (Kihei, Hawaii: Kapalua Pacific Centre, 1992): 29-40, 31.

[17]   Ibid.

[18]   A. Ravuvu, deputy Vice Chancellor of the University of the South Pacific in Suva, Fiji.

[19]   My source of this information is Mr. Steven Retuva, lecturer in sociology, University of the South Pacific.

[20]   Ibid.

[21]   David North, "Why Mauritius is so Successful," *Pacific Island's Monthly* 64, No. 5 (May 1994):27-29,27.

[22]   See Craig Skehan, "Land of Discontent," *Pacific Islands Monthly* 63, No. 4 (April 1993): 20-23.

[23]   R.W. James, *Land law and Policy in Papua New Guinea* (Port Moresby. P.N.G. Land Reform Commission, 1985).

[24]   Ibid., 45.

[25]   Ibid., 46.

[26]   *Land Groups Incorporation Act*, (1974) Ch. 147, s. 1 (e).

[27]   Revised laws of P.N.G., *Land Act of P.N.G.*, Ch. 185, sec. 73. "Subject to Sections 15 and 15A, a native has no power to sell, lease, dispose of customary

land otherwise than to natives in accordance with custom, and a contract or agreement made by him to so is void."

[28]   See Rasa Koian, "Give More Power to Landowners," *Times of P.N.G.* (May 4, 1995), 3. This article states that the landowners should be given greater control in the management of the forest and control of the timber rights.

[29]   Following established federal legislation, the mining company sought to compensate the traditional owners for the use and abuse of traditional lands on which the mine was constructed through leasehold arrangements. In implementing the lease or leases the company subdivided the leased areas into blocks which were said to belong to particular family groups. Each block was then drawn on a map and registered under the name of an individual title holder, usually a male who had convinced the company of his leadership of the clan. These determinations then founded the calculation which fixed the proportion of royalties, occupation fees and compensation payments the family group received as rent from the lease of their land.

[30]   C. Filer, "The Bougainville rebellion, the mining industry and the Process of Social Disintegration," in *The Bougainville Crisis* eds. R.J. May & M. Sprigs, (Bathhurst: Crawford House Press, 1990).

[31]   Ibid., 91.

[32]   See Ibid.; and also Glenn Banks, "Compensation for Mining: Benefit or Time Bomb?", 9. In his survey of the effects of Porgera, P.N.G.'s largest gold mine, on the immediate community, Banks, with some qualifications, agrees with Filer that the larger the compensation, the quicker the social disintegration.

[33]   See for example as evidence of world wide concern Phillip Shenon, "In Isolation, Papua New Guinea Falls Prey to Foreign Bulldozers," *New York Times* (June 5, 1994) and the 1994 Australian Broadcasting Commission's *Four Corner's* Documentary, "Bush Bugarup".

[34]   The Forestry (Private Dealings) Act of the *Revised Statutes of P N G* , Ch. No 217 allows the customary land owners to deal directly with the logging interests and the Forestry Act, 1991, No 30, s. 57 (2) provides that agreements are valid with the assent of 75% of the customary resource owners.

[35]   *Pacific Island Monthly* 64, No. 5 (May, 1994), 36.

[36]   R. Gerard Ward, "Land, Law Custom: Diverging Realities in Fiji," 221.

[37]   Rodney Taylor, "Sustained Yield Forest management in P.N.G.," *Resources, Development, and Politics in the Pacific islands*," eds. Stephen Henningham & R.J. May, (Bathurst: Crawford Home Press, 1992): 129-144, 141; points out that the so called landowner companies which sprung up on Manus Province to deal with the foreign timber interests failed to satisfy the legitimate reasons for their formation which include: 1) bringing customary land and associated rights under corporate title by use of the Land Groups Incorporation Act; 2) forming a business for the carrying out of forestry and spin off enterprises; 3) managing funds accruing from the enterprise for community development projects. In Reality they simply operated as middlemen between logging interest and customary owners.

[38]   In the 1980s Communitarian criticism effectively challenged Western liberal assumptions with very significant works by Michael Sandel, *Liberalism and the Limits of Justice* (Cambridge: Cambridge University Press, 1982); Charles Taylor, *Philosophy and the Human Sciences. Philosophical Papers 2* (Cambridge: Cambridge University Press, 1985); *Sources of Self: The Making of Modern Identity* (Cambridge: Harvard University Press, 1989); Alstair McIntyre, *After Virtue* (Notre Dame: Notre Dame Press, 1981); *Whose Justice? Which Rationality?* (Notre Dame: Notre Dame Press, 1988); Michael Walzer, *Spheres of Justice. A defense of Pluralism and Equality* (New York: Basic Books, 1983); Will Kymlicka, *Liberalism, Community and Culture* (Oxford: Clarendon Press, 1989).

[39]   This observation and a more thorough discussion of these points is offered by Niraja Gopal Jayal in "Ethnic Diversity and the Nation State," *Journal of Applied Philosophy* 10 (1993):147-153.

[40]   See for example Alain de Benoist, *Europe Tiers Monde Meme Combat*, (Paris: Laffont, 1986)

[41]   Will Kymlicka, *Liberalism, Community and Culture*, 170.

[42]   Brian Walker, "Culturist Dilemmas; On some Convergences between Kymlicka and the French New Right," Draft Presentation at the CPSA Annual Meeting 1995, Montreal.

[43]   Peter France, *The Charter of the Land*, 128.

[44]   Jurgen Habermas, *Theorie des Kommunicativen Handeln* (Frankfurt: Suhrkamp, 1981), 503-514.

[45]   Michael Walzer, *Spheres of Justice: A Defence of Pluralism and Equality* (New York: Basic Books, 1983).

[46]   Pierre-Andre Taguieff, "From Race to Culture: The New Right's view of European Identity," *Telos* 98-99 (Winter 1993-Spring 1994): 99-125, 101.

[47]   Pierre-Andre Taguieff, "From Race to Culture: The New Right's view of European Identity," *Telos* 98-99 (Winter 1993-Spring 1994): 99-125, 101.

[48]   See Ralph Premdas, "General Rabuka and the Fiji Elections of 1992," *Asian Survey* 23 (1993): 997-1009, 1005.

Chapter 4

The Legitimacy Of Different Customary "Ownership" Claims

What I would like to do in this chapter is to consider in greater detail different aspects of customary land tenure. We have spoken of communal land as though it assumes the same form throughout the territory claimed by the clan or community. At the same time it is presumed that the term "ownership" can be applied with equal meaning to all the territory claims of a given indigenous community. In order to achieve greater clarity and thoroughness, it is necessary that we investigate and determine the accuracy of these assumptions before proceeding with further comparative analysis.

In Papua New Guinea during 1995 there was a spate of turmoil over land registration. In July the P.N.G. government began to assess the feasibility of a land registration policy following structural readjustment recommendations from the I.M.F. This triggered a short strike by university students, and demonstrations by students and some military personnel. Demonstrators alleged that registration of "customary land" will lead to its loss through alienation. The connection between registration and alienation is certainly not a necessary one, and during this period the debate was little more than one of hysterical assertion and counter assertion rather than reasonable assessment. In order to gain some perspective on this issue, I believe one needs to conduct a more fundamental inquiry as to the meaning and nature of alleged customary ownership itself.

The colonial government of P.N.G. always recognized the customary land titles of the indigenous people, unlike the parent government of Australia which did not extend the same recognition to the aborigines on its own continent. However, the recent Mabo decision in Australia reversed this policy, and held that land occupied by Aborigines, where native title had not been extinguished, remains Aborigine land according to customary law.[1] Previous decisions held that Australia was empty before the arrival of the white man (*"terra nullius"*) and, therefore, there were no legal persons possessing rights to land. In effect, the Mabo case states that such legal persons existed and continue to exist and that they possess rights which legally cannot be ignored. In P.N.G., however, customary title has always been recognized, and it is understood that any disturbance to this title must be agreed to by the customary owners. What I would like to ask, in light of recent developments, i.e., the Mabo decision in Australia, and the registration issue in P.N.G., is the exact nature and status of these alleged customary land rights.

What strikes one in both cases are two legal/philosophical issues which need to be urgently addressed; 1) can we say that recognizable property rights exist outside and independent of civil society; 2) in what sense can we refer to these customary rights as property rights. With respect to the first issue, and in fact both issues, the question here is one of legal philosophy or jurisprudence and cannot be answered by appealing to the authority of judicial decisions (e.g., the Mabo case, or related cases in the North American or New Zealand context) which are themselves events already occurring within the structure of civil society. This issue is important because it is asserted that customary land tenure antedates the formation of the state and therefore must be recognized by the state. In other words, can we assert in some reasonable sense that these rights exist antecedent to their receiving formal definition and recognition by a fully formed civil society? In this case, we will draw upon a relevant body of thought, principally the writing of Thomas Hobbes and John Locke. The importance of Locke cannot be underestimated as his political writings provide the foundation for the modern understanding of property in the English common law tradition. With this in mind we will weigh the issues in light of this body of thought, bearing in mind that the final court of authority can only be the reasonableness and cogency of the conclusions reached.

Before going into the subject in detail, one can say with respect to the second issue, there seems to be a great deal of imprecision in the description of indigenous customary rights. Sometimes they are stated to be usufructuary, usufructuary but less than full ownership, *sui generis*, "recognized by common law though not common law tenure", rights of possession without alienation etc. To address this issue, I think, one needs also to attend to the general reality of customary tenure throughout the South Pacific. Here I draw upon the work of R.G. Ward of the Australian National University, to demonstrate that the term customary ownership, throughout the South Pacific, is often loosely applied to different forms and aspects of customary land tenure within the same communities. Accordingly, I argue that in the interests of sound policy and precision in decision making, the courts should clarify exactly which aspects of customary tenure are being recognized and why. It is ultimately my argument that certain distinct forms of alleged "customary tenure" have a stronger claim to recognition as "property rights" than others, and that it is in the interests of reasonableness and sound development policy to make the distinction.

The Hobbesian Positivist Approach

If we turn to that old master of pessimism Thomas Hobbes we will receive the clear answer that rights of any kind independent of civil society are inconceivable. Hobbes rejects the idea that rights can be given any just definition if there is no central authority with sufficient power to adjudicate, determine and finally settle these issues. Without this authority, a right can only have a relative validity proportional to the personal power of the individual making the assertion. This is not really a right in the proper sense of the term because in these conditions there is no obligation to obey if one can marshall sufficient forces to resist the imposition of the "right". (Here Hobbes speaks ironically of a right of nature which is a right to everything which the other has including his life, it is precisely this right which must be surrendered if we are to achieve justice and peace through entry into civil society.) For Hobbes it is a matter of logic that rights in their proper sense do not exist in the state of nature, i.e., conditions independent of civil society, because rights logically imply obligations which can only be maintained through the existence of the overwhelming power and authority of the state.

Certainly pre-colonial Australian and P.N.G. societies were effectively without a central state and therefore if we are to maintain that rights of property existed, we will have to overcome this Hobbesian argument that rights cannot exist without a central authority. However, one may argue that though there was no central state, there did exist sufficient adjudicating authorities in the indigenous communities and villages which were to be found across all the islands of the South Pacific. Within the villages there would be a group of elders, a chief, a big man, or in the case of Polynesian islands, a feudal hierarchy, capable of determining land rights and enforcing decisions. For example, if one family had begun gardening on the lee of a certain hill, that property would be usually regarded as theirs, though eventually it would revert to the community when it was abandoned and allowed to lie fallow. If another family tried to interfere and impose its own gardens on the same area, their activities, as contrary to custom, would be stopped and no doubt there would be some form of punishment from the village authorities.

An Intrinsic communal authority structure would certainly exist, and be capable of maintaining customary rights, imposing sanctions and forcing individuals and families to recognize their obligations. However, when we begin to speak of inter-community relations, relations between villages or between communities, it becomes less easy to overcome Hobbes' objections to the existence of rights in pre-civil society. Inter-community relations could not be based on the rule of customary law, for as we know from P.N.G., different communities have different languages (more or less eight hundred) and different customs. The Mabo case, for example, speaks of a "connection" to the land established by traditional laws and customs with respect to the land.[2] However, In the "New World", Spanish conquistadors had the custom of claiming all the land which they surveyed in the name of the King of Spain. This custom obviously interfered with the customs of the indigenous peoples. Whose customs are to prevail? Obviously the Spanish custom did through force of arms. Within East New Britain province of P.N.G., the Tolais drove off other early indigenous people from the coastal areas several hundred years ago. One can obviously conclude that Tolais had a custom of regarding conquered land as belonging to themselves, though the dispossessed group may not have agreed with this custom. On mainland Papua New Guinea, the Kukukukus, a nomadic tribe, had a custom of disregarding the property claims of any other community and so felt free to invade and attack any other clan or community to take and gain what they wanted. The point is that custom can settle disputes within a given community among a common membership which subscribes to the custom, but custom will not determine, and settle property claims and property disputes between communities if there is no agreement as to the relevant custom. Independent of a given community, there is no system of meta-customs by which one can determine that one custom is more appropriate than another. But furthermore, if agreements as to custom existed between communities, the Hobbesian point is still operative because there would exist no superior third party, for example, the state, to ensure that these agreements were met. Each community, would still be like an individual in the state of nature with no appeal to a superior adjudicating authority.[3] Hobbes observed that in these situations when there is nothing to hold men to their agreements, men being what they are, will abandon their agreements when they are regarded as disadvantageous. In these situations the reliability of the agreement and one's operative rights are always proportional to one's capability to maintain them by force; a precarious circumstance - which Hobbes calls the "state of war" - in which rights are defined not by law but by force of arms. Consequently indigenous communal land claims cannot logically fall back on local custom but must depend on some Lockean type natural rights argument or similar argument, based on continuous close association with the land through gardening, cultivation, tilling, pasturing etc., as I will subsequently argue.

Therefore, we can say that land rights within the community are relatively unproblematic, but when we begin to talk of the status of the community's ownership rights, which in P.N.G., are legally regarded as the fundamental rights - as land rights in P.N.G. are deemed to be held by the community rather than individual - and as in the Mabo case, where there is much emphasis "on communal native title" - then, following Hobbesian analysis, matters become very problematic. Land which a given community claims by "custom", cannot be regarded as a right in the appropriate legal sense, absent the adoption by other groups of the customary obligations derived from the customs of the original land claiming community. But as no superior authority like the state exists to legitimate and enforce obligations derived from the customs of the original group, no corresponding right can exist, according to the Hobbesian understanding of rights.

Locke and the Natural Rights to the Products of Labour

One might, however, prefer to abandon the Hobbesian positivist approach, whose premises clearly work to preclude the possibility of rights in non civil society, and embrace instead a natural rights orientation. The antidote to Hobbes was, of course, the political philosophy of Locke. Locke believed that rights or natural rights, including rights to land, did exist in the state of nature, i.e., in conditions independent of civil society, and were generally recognized by all reasonable men and women. This meant that individuals and communities could and would observe their obligations to respect these rights even when this might be disadvantageous. Even independent of the authority of the state, rational men and women feel constrained by a moral law which recognizes the natural rights of other human beings. In the absence of the overwhelming authority of the state, Locke gave us the authority of reason, a construct which Hobbes had endowed with far less motivating capacity. Thus, communities and individuals, compelled by reason, would universally recognize the rights of individuals and other communities to land upon which they had worked and laboured. Labour, according to Locke, established one's right to that land and the products of that labour, and all other individuals were compelled by a moral sense, intrinsic to human rationality, to respect that which one had acquired through one's work.[4]

Locke, however, like Hobbes, does see the state of nature as an impermanent condition which leads ultimately and logically to civil society. Locke acknowledges that individuals have need of third parties to adjudicate disputes when they arise and, among other things, this leads to the creation of civil society and the creation of the state; but this does not obviate the belief that natural rights to land do exist in the state of nature.

If we do accept Locke's account as resolving Hobbes' allegations that rights are inconceivable apart from a sufficient adjudicating authority, one must still establish the character of property rights in the state of "Nature". According to Locke one has a right to what one has laboured upon so that the land which one has tilled and cultivated becomes that of the individual, or perhaps the family which he represents. But what sort of rights are we talking about, are these usufructuary rights, which are rights to continue to use that particular holding but rights which terminate when the holding is no longer used, or are these full blown property rights in the modern liberal sense of the term, i.e., rights to alienate, convey, grant, and bequeath the holding which persist in perpetuity? There has been much debate about Locke's views as to the character of property rights in the state of nature, but it is not within the intent or scope of this chapter to offer a thorough exploration of the issue.[5] My own reading of Locke tends to see these rights as usufructuary as we will see later in the text, but for now this issue is peripheral to our focus.[6] For our own purposes let us assume that there is a formal continuity between property rights originally acquired in the state of nature and those which are later legitimated by civil society, and that these rights more or less approximate our modern notion of private ownership.

Given these assumptions, we can now enquire, more to the point, whether all alleged customary rights associated with land within a customary tenure system meet the Lockean conditions for the ascription of a natural right of ownership. In order to answer this question, one can make considerable progress through a more empirical approach which pays close attention to the paradigmatic features of a typical South Pacific tenure system and the various rights which are acquired within such a system.

Forms of Ownership within a Typical South Pacific Community

Prof. R. G. Ward of the Australian National University, formerly professor of geography at the University of Papua New Guinea, believes it is possible to outline the basic features common to most tenure systems in the South Pacific. He states, that, "there are parts of the village territory to which all must have access; for example, the forested area is a source of timber, firewood, birds or animals for meat or decorations and serves as a reservoir of potential agricultural land. This area is held in the name of the community as a whole. It is not the sole property of any clan, sub-clan, extended or nuclear family or individual. In general any individual or household group can gather from it."[7] Beyond that individual rights generally seem to creep into the picture very much in accordance with Lockean analysis, though in sense which falls short of Western private forms of ownership. Garden land, through labour, remains the property of the family which cultivates it, but reverts to the community with disuse. He states, "Ultimate ownership rests with the whole village community, but as long as a household continues to use a plot its right to continued use is acknowledged."[8]   On the other hand, situations involving a great deal of investment of labour in land improvement, e.g., the construction of terraces or associated water reticulation systems, the construction of compost mounds for sweet potato production, the creation of raised beds for taro, or drainage of swamps etc., may result in these areas being held by a household or even the individual in perpetuity. Finally he says that within the village itself house sites may be owned almost in perpetuity by the resident household.[9]

From the foregoing one concludes that communal lands can roughly be said to include three areas, the immediate area on which the village is located, secondly the cultivated garden sites and third the uncultivated and unimproved forest and jungle, and in some cases, areas of the ocean which are casual sources of food, decorations timber etc. If we are to follow Locke, it is only with respect to the first and second of these three areas to which title may be attached, because no labour has been expended to improve land in the third category. The first and second of these areas are, therefore, relatively unproblematic. Following Locke's labour theory of original acquisition, we can give substance to a notion of ownership based on labour and we can ascribe title of these areas to the individuals or group who expended the labour. The third category of ownership, and the areas to which it refers, however, do not meet the Lockean conditions, whether title is claimed by individuals or the group. But in P.N.G., it is principally this third category of land which has become the subject of compensation claims and disputes.

For example, on July 27, 1995 landowners in the Eastern Highland Province of P.N.G. completed a long and difficult climb of Mount Otto, a neighbouring mountain and damaged a repeater station which relayed telephone messages. They claimed that the station had been placed on their traditional lands without sufficient consultation and demanded 400,000 kina (about $300,000 U.S.) in compensation.[10] They eventually settled for about 3,000 kina and allowed the station to be repaired. Furthermore, because of the relatively sparse population in P.N.G. most mining sites which have become the subject of large compensation claims have involved disturbances to this third category of land. Both the mining companies and the government have tended to acknowledge these "ownership" claims and have sought to compensate the original inhabitants and, in some cases, those who have abandoned the original community but have decided to move back to benefit from the possible compensation package.

Ownership of the Wilds

But let us go back to Locke and ask ourselves some difficult questions about the sort of rights which might be gained by continued hunting, fishing or gathering in a given area. Obviously in the Lockean sense these activities do not establish some form of individual ownership because they do not involve sustained individual activity (labour) on a particular thing, whether a material object or plot of land, activity which would effect a significant change in that object. For Locke, an individual may make claim to own the fruit which he has gathered through his industry, because he has altered the original condition of the fruit, or as Locke says, "..labour removes it out of the common state nature left it in".[11] But one cannot be said to own the trees from which one has gathered that fruit because they are virtually in the same state, unless one has also engaged in some form of silviculture with respect to these trees.[12] According to Locke one can make claim to what one has gathered, acquired or captured from the wild but one cannot make claim to the wilds itself in its unimproved natural state.[13]

It may well be the case that continued hunting, fishing and gathering in certain places creates rights which relate to these areas but these are not accurately described when they are referred to by the English term "ownership". First of all these activities may be associated with rights to sustenance and material welfare such that if these rights are denied or interfered with one's material well being suffers. Thus, non traditional usage of these lands may present a disturbance to the activities of the indigenous tribes which adversely affects the ability to achieve a certain level of material welfare. One can, therefore, establish an infringement of rights based on these needs. But indeed it does not follow that every non-customary incursion into wilds which have been a traditional source of food, ornaments or whatever for a given group, affects rights to a certain level of material well being, unless it is demonstrated that the local people have actually suffered in terms of material needs. To take the extreme yet actual case, It demands an impossible leap of the imagination to believe that a repeater station on the top of a remote mountain interferes with the standard of living of a hundred villagers three thousand metres below.

Beyond these rights which we associate with access to primary goods: food, shelter, clothing and perhaps ornament, one can discern other rights which one could link with the notion of liberties. By this we mean liberties to engage in chase, hunt, wander, pasture, explore etc. The existence of an adjacent area of wilds which a given village claims as its own certainly offers the opportunity to exercise these liberties without interference. From these liberties, therefore we can derive corresponding rights of movement and access, though, of course these will fall far short of what one means by a full blown "ownership" right. For example when I am in New York I have access to the streets in mid town Manhattan in order to shop, wander, socialize and explore and as when I am in Port Moresby, I have similar rights to the "town" area . I may have developed a familiarity through continued acquaintance and residence so that I am led to refer to New York, or Port Moresby as my town, but this in no way means that I actually own the streets of mid town Manhattan or the town area of Moresby. Again with respect to areas of wilds which a South Pacific community may refer to as its own, a large development may or may not significantly disturb these rights. If there is no significant disturbance to these rights, there can be no injury. In other words, if it can reasonably be demonstrated that a development substantially impairs these liberties then compensation for this loss will certainly be necessary, otherwise there is no cause of action.

Again, the existence of the loss depends entirely upon the significance of the development, a repeater station on the top of a remote mountain which is very rarely visited by the local villagers cannot reasonably be regarded as a disturbance to these rights, whereas a large Mine like OK. Tedi in the Star mountain range of western P.N.G. may significantly diminish access to traditional hunting gathering areas. It is worthwhile to point out that not every instance of blocked access can be regarded as a significant loss of liberty. Locke claimed that in the state of nature one was free to take what one needed so long as one left "as good and enough for others".[14]   An individual, therefore, could not claim a loss resulting from another's use of land if there still remained sufficient land to satisfy his own activities and needs without discernible diminution. Thus, it may well be that though a given mine site in a remote range of mountains offers an area of blocked access to the local tribe, yet their traditional hunting gathering lands may be so vast as to offer virtually no disturbance to the exercise and enjoyment of their liberties. In this case the compensation should match only a marginal loss of liberty. It should also be kept in mind that though mines and other forms of industrial development create certain disutilities, they also bring certain benefits of civilization, for example, roads, employment, communication links, the acquisition of new skills etc., and these should not be discounted. Robert Nozick, following Fournier, has argued that compensation for loss of these forms of liberty should only be due those for whom the process of civilization had been a net loss.[15]   Certainly when people talk of injuries to indigenous peoples brought by foreign development, in fairness, one also needs balance this account with the advantages which civilization often brings to remote people, e.g., new skills, employment, transportation and communications links etc. These should not be overlooked as local people are often insistent that compensation packages include provisions

which require that members of the local tribe be given first consideration
in terms of job opportunities at the mine or industrial site.

Conclusion

The conclusion which I reach from the foregoing is that certain
aspects of "customary land rights" have been and continue to be
misleadingly treated as equivalent to full blown property rights as found
in the English common law system. In regarding these rights in this way
we have been led to draw erroneous implications with very
unsatisfactory consequences. Specifically, the liberties, welfare rights
and rights of access which one associates with a community's customary
hunting/gathering areas have been unwarrantedly assimilated into a
rather protean concept of ownership. In elevating these to the status of
full blown ownership rights, we are, of course, led to assume that any
use of these lands, no matter how small or insignificant, must be
consensual, and the residing individual or group is at liberty to demand
whatever price is sufficient to buy this consent. On the other hand, if
these rights are regarded for what they really are, a cluster of related
liberties and rights to necessities which fall short of a recognizable
ownership right, then we will see that the members of the traditional
community have no cause of action unless the use by non customary
people exceeds a threshold at which point there are discernible effects on
their liberties or welfare.

In the language of the courts, this all means that there is strong
justification for moving away from the strict liability which attaches to
the notion of ownership (in which any unauthorised use of the described
property is deemed an injury or trespass) and embracing instead some
formula of cost/benefit analysis involving demonstrable harm. Having
said all this, I think one finds oneself returning to the issue of land
registration. The foregoing analysis should, if anything, impress upon
one the importance of land registration. At present the national
government of Papua New Guinea is prepared to recognize these areas
of the wilds which surround indigenous communities as belonging to
these communities and registrable as the property of the clan or
community. Though in actuality these rights, as they apply to
uncultivated areas, would normally be insufficient, as I have argued, to
effect an overwhelming presumption of ownership, they do offer
evidence of a certain group or community's long standing connections
with certain discrete areas of land, which of course, the civil authorities

are at liberty to recognize as sufficient to establish a more complete title of ownership - though circumstances appear to fall short of establishing a natural right to ownership of the holding.   This all means that at present the central authorities are prepared to recognize the loose package of rights, which I have described, as being equivalent to the full blown modern common law notion of ownership, substituting a community of ownership for individual ownership.   At this point in time, it would certainly be advantageous to the local communities to validate, what I believe, are dubious ownership claims, through the judicial machinery of the state. Unfortunately, within P.N.G. individuals are fond of thinking of the country as *sui generis*, a self contained, self determining system free of exogenous influences.   Nothing could be further from the truth. Change is always occurring, and new political and social events are continually being stimulated from both   internal and external sources. Custom is merely what it is, that which people customarily do, but in dynamic periods such as the present, customs do not remain static, they change. In this situation relying upon custom to validate your claims and rights may be a serious mistake. In another ten years customs and habits may dramatically change.   Social and environmental pressures may effect different attitudes propelled by new exigencies. As social realities change, and no doubt population density augments, it may be increasingly disadvantageous to regard extensive communal land claims as having validity, indeed it may become "customary" to disregard such claims. There is nothing to stop current habits and customs changing to meet changes of situation.   In his forthcoming book   R.G. Ward argues that throughout the Pacific we already observe a divergence between real practice, traditional custom and even the legally defined forms of tenure.[16] These remarks should be sufficient to alert those who wish to safeguard traditional "customary rights". Specifically, there is nothing at present to guarantee that future practice will conform to traditional custom, and certainly doing nothing is no protection at all, as Ward demonstrates. But one would think it should be obvious that customary owners would be best able to meet future challenges to their authority through strong legal precedent established through the unambiguous formal registration of their lands - though, as Ward believes, even this may be insufficient to defeat evolving practices.

---

[1]   Mabo v. Queensland, 66 *Australian Law Journal Reports*, 408.

[2]   Ibid; See also *James Cook University Law Review* Vol. 1, 1994, 57.

[3]   Thomas Hobbes (*Leviathan: Or the Matter, Forme and Power of a Commonwealth Ecclesiasticall and Civil* (New York: Macmillan Inc., 1962), 101) would regard these communities in the same light in which he looked upon sovereign states. Within these states there could be observance of rights in accordance with the rule of law but between these independent entities there could be no reliable system of rights and obligations. In these conditions he states that "...in all times, kings and persons of sovereign authority, because of their independency, are in continual jealousies, and in the state and posture of gladiators; having their weapons pointing, their eyes fixed on one another; that is, their forts, garrisons, and guns upon the frontiers of their kingdoms; and continual spies upon their neighbours; which is a posture of war".

[4]   John Locke, *Two Treatises of Government*, ed P. Lazlett (Cambridge: Cambridge University Press, 1967 [1690]) *Treatise* II: 32, 33. Henceforth, the first *Treatise* will be simply referred to as *Treatise* I and the second will be referred to as *Treatise* II.

[5]   For the more recent developments in this debate see for example Den Hartogh, "Tully's Locke," *Political Theory* 18 (1990): 656-72; Thomas Baldwin, "Tully, Locke and Land," *Locke Newsletter* 13 (1982): 21-33; J. Waldron, "Locke, Tully and the Regulation of Property," *Political Studies* 32 (1984): 98-106; J. Waldron, "The Turfs my Servant has Cut," *Locke Newsletter* 13 (1982): 9-20; G. A. Cohen, "Marx and Locke on Land and Labour," *Proceedings of the British Academy* 71 (1985): 357-88.

[6]   See David Lea, Lockean Property Rights, Tully's community Ownership, and Melanesian Customary Ownership," *Journal of Social Philosophy* 25, no. 1, (Spring 1994): 117-33.

[7]   R. G. Ward, "Pacific Island Land Tenure: An Overview of Practices and Issues," in *Land culture and Development in the Aquatic Continent,* eds. D. G. Malcolm Jr. and Jeanne Skog, (Kihei, Hawaii: Kapallua Pacific Center, 1992): 29-40, 30

[8]   Ibid., 31.

[9]   Ibid

[10]   Papua New Guinea Post Courier, July 28, 1995.

[11]   Locke, *Treatise* II, 28.

[12]   See, for example Locke, *Treatise* II, 32, 33, which states that land and its contents can only be appropriated through improvement by subduing, tilling, sowing etc., as well as enclosure.

[13]   In *Treatise* II, 45, Locke describes the wilds as lands which "...lie waste and are more than the people who dwell upon can use, or can make use of, and so still lie in common". By this he means that these lands remain the common property of mankind rather than the property of any individual or group.

[14]   Locke, *Treatise* II, 27, states that there must be "enough and as good left in common for others".

[15]   Nozick, *Anarchy, State, and Utopia*, 178.

---

[16] R. G. Ward & Elizabeth Kingdon,   *Land, Custom and Practice in the South Pacific* (Melbourne: Oxford University Press, 1995).

Chapter 5

Christianity And Western Attitudes Towards "Property"

Having spoken extensively of communal property in the context of the subsistence culture of Papua New Guinea, it is worthwhile to reflect on the historical origins of Western attitudes towards individual property. In this chapter we will be specifically concentrating on the changes in self description and self definition, which occurred during the Renaissance and Reformation which propelled the emergence of the moral and social significance of private ownership. We will see that this entailed a new understanding of nature and alterations to Man's attitude and self-perceived relation to nature.

In most matters in Western civilization one tends to trace antecedents back to the Classical period of Greek culture. However, in all classes, the Greeks thought of property as family property rather than individual property in the modern sense. As one modern commentator on Classical Greek culture remarks:

> The Greeks set out from a different starting point. In their early world of tribes and brotherhoods and families no one thought of his own "rights" or questioned the claims of society, practically everything that he had belonged to his kin. He would not claim his own life for himself, if they asked it of him in time of need. Why should he dream of claiming his house or his field or his cattle?[1]

However, Plato proposed family loyalties should be replaced by responsibility to the wider community, the *polis*. The desire to enhance the family property could come at the expense of the community's good, he feared.[2] For this reason, Plato proposed that the Guardians of the public interest, the philosopher kings, should be essentially propertyless.

From *History of European Ideas*, volume 18, number 4 (1994), Copyright © 1994 Elsevier Science Ltd.

Though sometimes Aristotle advocated private rather than communal ownership his attitude towards the individual remains very different from that of the modern Western liberal age. The *polis* is prior to the individual, says Aristotle; man is born for life in the *polis*. Individuals and families are not self-sufficient; they have to be part of a *polis* which is self -sufficient, that is, which is of a size and kind to allow us to live well, and to live virtuously. The naturalness of the *polis* as an environment for a successful life explains why it is a premise of his view of political virtue that we are born for life in the *polis*, and this teleological perspective equally explains his belief that the good life is a happy life. We should have no incentive to take part in the life of the *polis* unless it made us happy on the whole; but the argument is neither contractual nor individualist - the state is not a contractually established device to promote our individual interests. We are happy as a result of living as we should.[3]

For both Plato and Aristotle responsibility for the community's interest should take preference over individual interests, and there is no elevation of the rights of the individual in terms of property or otherwise, as has become current in modern Western ideology. The community, articulated through the concept of the *Polis*, has an identity and a definition which is not merely reducible to an arrangement to support individual interests and individual rights. The *Polis* exists with both temporal extension and spatial location, and is always greater than its present membership. It has its own spiritual protectors to ensure its health and well being, for example, in the case of Athens, Pallas Athena, who received the prayers of both the ancestors and the present generations. One can say that generally in both Greece and Melanesia, the community embodied the overriding value which was not derived from or legitimated through individual rights or interests, though in Greece the concept of the community was integrated into that of the city state, a unit of social organization with greater demographic extension and complexity.

Neither the notion of individual's inherent value nor that of private property relations played a significant role in the articulation of social relations, either in ancient Greece or in traditional Melanesian culture. In Melanesia it is the community which is regarded as having an overriding value which legitimates particular social arrangements; in ancient Greece the clan and the extended clan have been overridden by a notion of community associated with the "*polis*", the city state, an arena of public performance which takes precedence over private "individual" interests and familial responsibility. But in the Middle Ages, Christian allegiance to one universal omnipresent God significantly attenuated the European notion of community as it swept aside the local deities and spiritual beings which maintained one's important identity with, and greater responsibility to one's community. Unlike the Classical age when the living community conceived in terms of the "*polis*" or the Republic of Rome, was conceived as the ground of ones public responsibilities, the Middle Ages introduced a new ground of obligation located in the primacy of the Godhead itself. God, articulated in three persons, had created both the spiritual and temporal realities, and all duties in both spheres fundamentally derived from His authority. However, in the decidedly lessor important realm of temporal affairs, God was said to have delegated his authority to the King conceived as an authoritarian predominantly male figure like the Father Himself. In this circumstance we find that ownership is neither private nor communal, but feudal, a hierarchical system of land holding in which ultimate title is vested in the King through some form of bequest from the Creator.[4]

Ultimately, in this pyramid of ascending authority it is the King who occupies the highest position and he himself is subject to no superior human authority. The serfs may owe duties to the lords who in turn owe duties to King but the King's obedience is to a Divine rather than temporal authority. This conveys, in part, the ideational model of two realms which are separate and distinct concerns, as encapsulated in the maxim render to Caesar the things which are Caesar's and to God, the things which are God's. This conceptual model bred two attitudes towards the King's authority. On the one hand, religious authorities regarded property relations as an earthly arrangement appropriate to man's fallen state, and therefore something over which the truly spiritually minded individual should not attach strong moral significance, and accordingly, in so far as some form of social regulation and ordering was deemed necessary, given man's fallen state, this was left to the lessor earthly authority of the King. We have, therefore, one attitude springing from the axiology of the religious intelligencia which does not invest great value in what occurs in the temporal realm, and therefore shows little philosophical interest in founding a moral defense of proprietary relations, communal, feudal, individual or otherwise, after all, the fallen world remains the fallen world no matter how it is arranged.

But on the other hand, the two orders, the temporal and the spiritual, are not unconnected as the King's authority on this lessor plane of material and temporal is derivative from the supernatural authority of

God. Accordingly, the necessary nexus between the two systems gave rise to the doctrine of the Divine Right of Kings. When the authority of the King became challenged especially at the time of the Stuarts, it was argued by Royalist thinkers that the King exercised absolute sovereignty analogous to that of the Creator in the Spiritual realm, however, if we look back to the earlier teachings of the Church we find that the rights granted to human beings are perceived to fall far short of absolute sovereignty.

What is significant is that during the Renaissance and the Reformation attitudes altered and the concept of man's sovereign relation to the natural environment emerged with important implications with respect to Western understanding of ownership rights. This intellectual shift cannot be discounted once we compare it with indigenous Melanesian attitudes and the teaching of the Early Church. In traditional Melanesian culture and that of most other indigenous peoples, human beings are not regarded as separate and distinct from the natural environment embodying a particular dominant status. Humans like the vegetation and the other fauna are simply part of the encompassing environment and equally subject to the cycles and powers which they do not expect to dominate or control. In this ideology, there is scant tendency to claim a superior status or value for human creatures. The modern Western attitude which emerged during the Renaissance is therefore entirely alien to the thinking and understanding of indigenous peoples like the Melanesians, and it was also foreign to the Church's early teaching as to Man's relation to the created order.

Early Christianity taught that human proprietary rights over the natural world and its resources, devolves from the bequest of the Creator who originally created this natural order and necessarily claimed original title. What we shall look at in this chapter is the nature of that bequest.

Exploitation and the Domination in the Christian Tradition

Recently there has been considerable controversy over the environmental impact of Christian teaching. During the beginnings of our increased awareness of the ecological crisis several strong papers appeared condemning Christianity for encouraging environmental exploitation. In response, a number of works have sought to defend the Judeo-Christian tradition by emphasizing different aspects of a message which allegedly promotes environmentally friendly behaviour. Over all, however, these interpretations exhibit doubtful ontic significance. This is because too little attention is paid to the fact that Christianity has been in a continuous state of ideological development since its inception, and thereby nothing is to be gained by isolating some aspect of Christian teaching and universalizing the application to a significance independent of any particular historical epoch.

It is the contention of this chapter that Christianity evolved profoundly after the Renaissance and the Reformation and with attendant intellectual changes encouraged an exploitative attitude towards the natural environment. These post Renaissance attitudes suppressed or supplanted the attitudes towards the created order engendered by certain strains of Hellenic philosophy which were prominent during the Middle Ages. In the course of this chapter we demonstrate how post Renaissance Christianity gave moral impetus to the emergence of new attitudes towards "property" and a new understanding of man's proprietary relation with the created order.

The fact that modern European man viewed the "natural environment" in ways which were and are profoundly different form that of other peoples, especially indigenous peoples, is certainly undeniable. The modern European man in his colonizing activities, exhibited a moral and religious posture which was felt profoundly by other cultures who became subject to these activities. The difference in attitudes towards the nature and human "property" was manifestly evident during the expansion of Western European dominance over the territories inhabited by indigenous and less technologically advanced peoples. On the matter of the ideological and territorial struggles between the European white men and the Indians of North America, one writer has offered the following comments:

> ...and so ignoring and desecrating the Indian's reverence for the land, the white settler spread across the plains with his more exploitative ideology. His attitudes were shaped by an anthropocentric religion which demanded that man exercise dominion over the earth and all the lesser creatures, for the indian, however, the land was incapable of human domination. The Indians did not consider that the land belonged to them. On the other hand, the white man believed that god created the earth and gave it specifically to man for his domination.[5]

The origins of this exploitative ideology have been laid, not surprisingly, at the very origins of the Judeo-Christian tradition. In Genesis Man is told to multiply, fill the earth, subdue it and have dominion over the fish of the sea, birds of the air and every living thing that moves upon the earth. In this period of worsening ecological crisis commentators have been quick to notice the potentially negative consequences of religious imperatives. Most prominent perhaps have been Lynn White and Ian L. Mc Hague who see environmental deterioration attributable to the "Christian axiom that nature has no reason for existence save to serve man".[6]

The Judeo-Christian culture has not been entirely happy with these accusations and there have been efforts to rebut the criticism that their teachings are environmentally insensitive. For example, very recently Jeremy Cohen published a work, *Be Fertile and Increase, Fill the Earth and Master It: The Ancient and Medieval Career of a Biblical Text*, in which he seeks to dispel the notion that the Genesis story must bear responsibility for Western insensitivity to the natural environment.[7] On the other hand, Christian apologists have attempted to demonstrate, among other things, that the Christian ideal of agape rather than the Greek notion of love as eros, prescribes a non-exploitative relation with the world.[8] Also in this vein, a recent paper by L.H. Steffen "In Defense of Dominion" stresses that it is a gross misinterpretation to equate the command to effect dominion with the notion of domination because the latter has its origins in Greek rather than Hebrew thought.[9]

In the course of this chapter I intend to demonstrate, *inter alia*, that in fact, Greek notions of love and rational action were promotional of respect for the environment and in so far as Christianity remained under these influences its teachings were essentially non-exploitative.

However, I would first like to look more closely at Steffen's paper because it raises some interesting points which will form the focus of this chapter. As I said, Steffen labours to establish that the command found in Genesis does not license exploitation of the earth and its resources.[10] The author states that environmental exploitation in the West has been guided by models of rational action which have their origins in from Greek rather than Hebrew or Christian ideals.[11] He argues the biblical notion of dominion points to actions and to the distinctively human capacity for action of a certain sort - obedient action.[12] This is opposed to the Greek model of human agency which is a manipulative model. The author associates this Hellenic model with the rise of Greek philosophy and science which did not occur in Palestine. In contrast, the Hebrew model of human agency is seen in accordance with the command obedience model of action found throughout Genesis.[13]

In his explanation Lloyd H. Steffen argues that both critics and advocates of Genesis dominion have associated the concept of dominion with an instrumental view of nature according to which it is a tool to be used and possesses no integrity of its own. Such a view, he claims, distorts "*radah*" (the hebrew word for dominion) by turning it into a domination concept.[14] Domination specifies opposition, power relations and power imbalances resolved by force. Dominion, in contrast, is an intimacy concept, a concept of interrelatedness. In Genesis 1:28, man is given the job of "subduing" nature, but Steffen claims that subdue ("*kabash*") means preservation and maintenance.[15] Adam's activity is restricted to keeping the garden and not destroying the earth. He states that "...the Yahwist account shows how the human quest for power, which brings disrelationship to God, distorts dominion with negative consequence for the natural world."[16]

There are elements of distorted historiography in these accounts which demand to be corrected. Steffen's analysis is interesting enough but does not accurately reflect the reality, that Christianity is an amalgam of Hebrew and Hellenic influences which evolved together and continue to evolve in the present day. This means that one cannot go back to particularly Hebrew concepts and thinking and argue that these represent the essence of Christianity, without offering an exceedingly truncated version of Christianity. Furthermore, when Christianity and its various embodiments are considered objectively, it has to be admitted that, in part, they supplied the ideology which contributed to the current environmental crisis. This is particularly the case with respect to certain modifications to Christian religious thought which occurred with Renaissance humanism and the subsequent Reformation. If these developments are taken into account, it is clear that Christianity offered a moral and religious rationale for the intense subjugation of the natural environment.

Having made these general remarks we should proceed to look more closely at his specific argument. Much of the argument turns upon the interpretation one gives to the genesis command to populate and effect dominion over the Earth and its creatures, which in turn depends upon an alleged distinction between the Greek and the Hebrew understandings of action, let us say rational action.

If I may be permitted to address the second claim first, I would point out that there is a basic error of analysis in the association of classical rationality with instrumentality, which is supposedly distinguishable from the Hebrew understanding of action as obedience to God's commands. Indeed once this misrepresentation is properly corrected one begins to appreciate how Christianity contributed to the moral and intellectual climate which endorsed the exploitation of the natural environment.

Steffen's characterization of classical attitudes towards action and specifically rational action, which he says is grounded in the manipulative model of instrumental reason, is allegedly based on the fact that modern technologies and modern science had their roots in Greek philosophy and early forms of Greek science. Though it is certainly true that without the initial Greek endeavour to discover rationality and rational order in the cosmos and humanity itself, modern European culture and science would have been improbable, it is not the case that the Greeks idealized the manipulative form of instrumental reason. The model of rationality which the Greeks promoted was contemplative rather than instrumental. The manipulative model, of which Steffen speaks, is more properly the paradigm of rationality which has been promoted since the beginnings of the period of European modernity. It is a celebration of an aspect of reason which finds its early articulation in the writings of seventeenth century philosophers like Hobbes and Descartes, rather than the Greeks.[17]

In contrast, the Classical understanding of reason (especially in Plato and Aristotle) finds its highest form of employment in the exercise of contemplation. This was conceived to be an activity in which the subject comes to know the immanent rational order of the cosmos and in so doing finds his place in this order through a close union, if not identity with the very reality which is known or contemplated.[18] In this activity the subject/object distinction is effectively obviated since knowing one's place within the cosmic order is inseparable from self identification with the higher orders of reality. This understanding of reason differs profoundly from the instrumentalist conception in so far as the exercise of instrumental reason demands that one continuously maintain the distinction between subject and object, because manipulation of the object in advancing the interests of the subject depends upon maintaining this separation. In other words, if one is to preserve the asymmetrical relation of domination which is always implicit in manipulation of the object, one must continuously distinguish between the subject and the object. By way of contrast, the contemplative relationship is more properly a symmetrical one as the knower, in fact, comes to identify and know itself in the object known.

Albeit what has been said exhibits a high level of abstraction, it is undeniable that this Greek notion of rational action and rational order strongly influenced attitudes towards nature and the theological

Cosmology of the early Church. In the Middle Ages the contemplative ideal of Greek thought and Christianity's notion of spiritual perfection were closely associated. Initially this occurred during early Christianity when Platonic and Aristotelian elements found their expression in Neoplatonic philosophy, which flourished in Alexandria and Rome, and which in turn strongly influenced the teachings of the most important Patristic writers, Augustine, Ambrose and Jerome.

Anders Nygren points out that the religious cosmology of the Middle Ages *exhibits* a domination by the simple pictorial scheme of the Alexandrian world scheme.[19] According to this scheme the cosmos exhibits motion in two directions - the procession of everything from God to levels of lesser perfection toward the material world and then a returning ascent from the material and lesser realities towards the higher spiritual levels and ultimately God himself. The latter movement was seen to originate in eros, a love of the greater spiritual reality which engenders a desire to possess this higher reality. The Alexandrian world scheme was a creation of the Neoplatonists derived in turn from the Hellenic tradition, specifically the Platonic doctrine of the Two Worlds, the world of ideas and the material world, and the Aristotelian notion of the ladder.[20] At his highest level of activity, at the apogee of intellectual development, Aristotle saw man abandoning his material concerns, and the deliberations of practical reason, and achieving a contemplative relation with the ultimate spiritual reality of the unmoved mover. The Neoplatonists underlined that the contemplative relation with this ultimate spiritual/intellectual reality was more than a mere epistemic state, and represented the highest ontological reality the subject could attain in a form of union with the ultimate source of value. Far from being a passive condition, this relationship demanded spiritual and intellectual striving because sensual, material and mundane concerns were always present to importune and drag one downwards both ontologically and morally. Medieval Christianity adopted these ideas *mutatis mutandis* and saw man attaining his *summum bonum* through an ascent to the level of the Godhead where he attains a beautific vision of God Himself.

Under the aspect of Classical influence, Christian teaching required rejection of the material world and the concerns of the mundane existence and a concomitant striving to ascend and live on a spiritual, non-material dimension. The message is clear and undeniable, the concerns of this life have little worth and there is a loss of reality and attendant evil when one invests value in this mundane reality. On the other hand, though one may cavil over the exact connotation of the original Hebrew, the Old Testament clearly commands us to involve ourselves in the world, populate it and exercise some form of control over its existents. Accordingly, there has been throughout the history of Christianity this tension between the teaching of the Greeks and the commands of the Old Testament. The commands of Genesis certainly imply that reason is to used instrumentally in some form of even modest manipulation of this earthy reality. In contrast, the classical model of reason as wisdom or sophia demands an attitude of detachment with respect to the affairs of earthly existence and in this attitude one can find little moral support for the intense subjugation of the natural environment.

However, until the Renaissance and the Reformation the Greek ideal of detachment was clearly ascendent, in part this is evidenced by the popularity of the monastic life and other forms of withdrawal practiced by the anchorites. However, the hegemony of the classical attitude was assailed and overthrown through the intellectual developments occurring during the Renaissance and the Reformation.

Renaissance Humanism

Renaissance humanism presented the initial challenge to the ideal of detachment promoted in Classical thought. Curiously enough the most striking philosophical articulation of humanism is to be found in the Florentine revival of Neoplatonism which occurred in the middle of the fifteenth century. At that time Marsilio Ficino, a cleric, was the central figure of the Platonic Academy in Florence under the patronage of the Medici. While Ficino promoted a Neoplatonic revival under the aegis of the Medici, he also effected the transmogrification of Christian Neoplatonism into an anthropomorphic philosophy, an event which is viewed as the genesis of a distinct humanist philosophy.[21] With respect to our subject, this development is significant in that it added substance to the idea that man had proprietary relation to the created world which was to be expressive of his position of dominance.

This new found emphasis on the importance and dignity of man, typical of the humanist flowering, led Ficino to underline man's pre-eminent role within the created order in language which often shades to terms of dominance. Ficino talks of man's creative capacities, his ability to understand the forces of the universe and indeed produce with genius likened to that of the Creator. Ficino spoke of man's divine like intelligence which elevates him to a position of dominance with respect to the other members of creation, and Ficino mentions that the animals are to be subject to his command as that of a head of a family or the state. Furthermore, he spoke of the activity of the Soul (the human soul) as one which attempts to master the universe, as says to produce all, dominate all and penetrate all.[22] The upshot of this, of course, is an explicit notion of Humankind's God-like nature and superiority which equips man to rule the material universe. Nygren, who is himself critical of Neoplatonism, points out that traditional Neoplatonism could be accused of a love or longing based on egoism contrary to the agape which Nygren prefers. However, argues Nygren, Ficino's interpretation of Neoplatonism adds a dimension of anthropocentrism which did not exist in previous Neoplatonic writings.[23]

Ficino's humanism clearly gave supplementary support to the Old Testament command requiring one to exercise dominion over the created order. It is reinterpreted Neoplatonism which now clearly implies rational domination of the natural environment with the important implicit subject object distinction between the knower and the reality to be known and dominated. This important intellectual shift can be seen to be reflected in Christianity's changing view of the social institution of property.

Ficino's Teaching and the Earlier Position of the Church

Among other things, Ficino's anthropocentrism modifies the reasons for man's perceived pre-eminence in the created world and ultimately man's relation to that world. According to many of the commentaries written during the Middle Ages, man's standing in the world is derived from the will of the Creator who conveys or grants the world to man in order that he may fulfill God's will and purposes. This is the interpretation given to Genesis 1-3. In contrast, Ficino's emphasis on man's sovereign standing in the created universe implies a God-like nature and a God-like relation to the rest of the created universe.

This dominant Christian view was reflected in the attitude towards property. In the early years of Christianity and during much of the Middle Ages the preponderant view was that the earth or the created world belonged to God and various forms of human ownership were conventional arrangements necessitated by man's sinful fallen state.[24] In general, Patristic theory held that private property and the resulting differences in Man's possessions were not natural, the earth and its products had been the common possession of mankind before the fall, but because of man's sinful state, social conditions now require this conventional institution of ownership.[25] St. Augustine, whose Christian thinking was a synthesis of much of Christian teaching and Neoplatonic ideas, held that it is only by human right (*iure humano*) that man has possessions not divine right (*iure divino*) because the earth and its fullness belong to God.   He goes on to say that it is the Kings and Emperors who determine human rights including the right to property.[26] At times Augustine says that man's property rights are limited by the use to which one puts his possessions, and he who uses his property badly has no real claim to it and *de jure*, property belongs to the good.[27] According to Augustine, the most admirable course is to renounce all ownership of the earth and it goods and to hold in common the material things that are necessary to support life, and thus he tells us that renunciation of property in God's service is the higher calling rather that ownership of wealth and property.[28]

Similarly that other towering figure of the early Church, Ambrose, whose thinking was also strongly influenced by Hellenic and Neoplatonic thought, emphasized man's non-proprietary relation to the created world and lack of dominant status. Ambrose, taught that only God could have dominion over objects, man could not have exclusive dominion because the criterion of dominion requires bringing something into being.   Dominion was interpreted to mean exclusive control.[29] Aquinas softened this approach arguing that dominion (or *dominium*) was natural to God alone but that man could exercise a form of dominion in terms of the right to use these objects. Aquinas mentions uses for the purposes of preservation and convenience.[30]   If we take Aquinas as the official authority on the Church's teaching, it is clear that man could not be said to have exclusive dominion over the created material world, that belonged to God alone.   However, within the material world, men's rights were rights of use or usufructs. With a use right "a man secures only daily and necessary advantage from another's property without impairing the substance." (Pufendorf 4.8.8.)

Renaissance humanism, reflected in Ficino's formulations, certainly conveyed something quite different, i.e., that man did not merely have the right to use created substances but that man had a God-like dominion over the material world. In other words, Ficino's words implied that man had full property rights, rights of dominion, i.e. to put into execution any purpose that one may have concerning the said thing.

Ficino himself was not a political theorist and accordingly it was left to others to formulate the political and legal implications of this humanist orientation. This was forthcoming in the seventeenth century with the political writings of Hugo Grotius and Samuel Pufendorf. Both offer arguments to support the view that individual forms of property must be guarantee exclusive individual domination of the *res* or object of that right. The influential works of Grotious and Pufendorf sought to demonstrate that man's rights over the earth and it's creatures go beyond rights of usage and extend to the substance of the material thing. These are rights seen as equivalent to modern private rights of ownership, rights to exclude others from one's holding (even when one is not using it) and rights which approximate the modern right of capital which includes, inter alia, the right of alienation and also the powers to waste or even destroy one's holding.[31]

This departure from the traditional Thomistic teaching is obvious in that St. Thomas held that the world belongs to mankind in common, not individually, and for their use but not for absolute dominion. In St. Thomas' eyes, private exclusive domination is not common or natural for human beings. In contrast, Grotious argued that this common right was meaningless as property implies occupation and occupation can only be realized through private or individual property.[32] Pufendorf followed Grotious and denied that common ownership is a form of ownership arguing that the only form of property is private, i.e., property which arises from occupation and which allows one to exclude others and alienate the holding. The writings of Grotious and Pufendorf were extremely influential to the point that the equation of property with individual private property was completely accepted by the mid-eighteenth century. This is evidenced by Blackstone's *Commentaries on the Laws of England* written during that period, in which it is stated that the "right of property" is "that sole and despotic dominion which one man claims and exercises over the external things of the world, in the total exclusion of the right of any other individual in the universe."[33]

Thus, the equation of property with private property and private property with "despotic dominion". Accordingly, the acceptance of private ownership rather than communal ownership (to which the theologians refer) as the paradigm of ownership finds its genesis in the writings of Grotius and Pufendorf, and in the subsequent century, achieves official jural acceptance in England. Macpherson diagnosed this conceptual alteration as resulting from the "new relations of the emergent capitalist society".[34] It may no doubt be true that the economic climate at this time was appropriate for the nurture and fruition of these ideas, however, one should also recognize the profound influence of humanist ideas concerning the relation between the created world and the human individual, which were originally articulated by Ficino.[35]

One can see that the promotion of private exclusive ownership as the paradigm of property rights is the ineluctable corollary of the humanist emphasis on human sovereignty and dominance within the material world. In other words, a God-like sovereignty implies not mere rights of usage but the exclusive despotic dominion as expressed in the words of Blackstone. The ideal of sovereignty cannot be effectively realized through communal ownership, which often requires democratic participation and consensus in decision making. What is demanded by Renaissance humanism can only really be actualized through despotic individual decision making. This is why Ficino's reformulation of man's relation to the material universe, which gave individual man rather than God dominion over this realm, could only imply individual rather than communal ownership of the world's substance.

But though Ficino regarded man as having sovereignty over the material world, he maintains the traditional Neoplatonic prescription with respect to the necessary abjuration of the material world and the ascent to higher levels of spiritual perfection. On this matter Ficino was consistent with the traditional Neoplatonic theme which held that man progresses as he attempts to raise himself to the Divine level and becomes more God-like in his qualities.[36] Thus, man's sovereignty did not seem to relieve one of the obligation to disengage from the material realm and seek a higher spiritual reality. Though Ficino's Neoplatonism gives new meaning to humanity's role in the empirical realm, the continuing attachment to the traditional distinction between the spiritual and material worlds, precludes a reading which implies the moral appropriateness of intense relations with the material world. In order to locate the softening of this attitude towards engagement in the material world, and the further attenuation of this particular aspect of Hellenic influence in Christian thought, we need point to the Reformation.

The Reformation

In this case the significant event is Luther's introduction of the idea of salvation through faith alone and the dismissal of the possibility that man could advance himself spiritually or improve his spiritual nature through his own efforts. Luther taught that man's salvation was ultimately dependent upon faith in Jesus Christ nothing more and nothing less. Almost needless to say, these ideas were decidedly antithetical to certain Hellenic influences, especially those represented most perspicuously in Neoplatonic teaching. Neoplatonism demanded a life of striving for a more perfect spiritual existence, one which denied concern for the lower material existence. Luther, on the other hand, strongly disbelieved that men had this capacity for self improvement, everything that human beings undertook was tinged with self interest and therefore sinful.

The upshot of this theological attitude was a softening of the religious/moral obligations associated with spiritual striving that involved disassociation from the material world. Concomitantly, this generates the corollary denial of the significance of the distinction between the material and spiritual worlds. Medieval Christianity, as we said, had been strongly allied with the Neoplatonic program which taught that salvation was achieved by forsaking the flesh and the material world in favour of the spiritual world. Luther, however, in arguing that it was useless to try and avoid sinfulness by these efforts, would ultimately assert an obverse rejection of the importance of the distinction between the material and spiritual worlds. Indeed, he saw the interior struggles associated with monastic life as not only quite devoid of value as means of justification before God, but even more so, he regarded the renunciation of the duties of this world as the product of selfishness.[37] *De facto*, this abnegated the Neoplatonic demand that the individual disengage himself from material world. It was not, therefore, surprising to find subsequent forms of Protestantism, most especially Calvinism, asserting that salvation is quite consistent with absorption and involvement in the temporal material world, the very corollary of Luther's teaching. It is in this light that one will see the reformation promoting the moral acceptability of relations of private ownership which enshrine a right of exclusive domination.

Property Rights become Moral Rights

However, to say that establishing strong relations with the material world is not morally unacceptable is not equivalent to an assertion that exclusive private property rights are moral rights. To understand how this equation of property rights and moral rights was ultimately realized we need to appreciate the manner in which Protestantism amalgamated the idea that disengagement from the material world was inherently selfish and sinful, and Ficino's notion that man occupied a place of centrality and sovereignty within the material universe. Perhaps it does not require a great deal of prescience to appreciate that Ficino's emphasis on the ultimate importance of the worldly empirical human being laid the ground work for the Protestant view which saw value and even spiritual worth in engagement in the mundane reality of worldly affairs. Once the Reformation had effectively defenestrated notions which tied together spiritual perfection and withdrawal from the world, it was perhaps inevitable that moral value would be seen in an intense engagement in the material sphere, a disciplined almost self-denying engagement which was previously thought to occur only within the other-worldly spiritual arena.

Where previously the moral imperatives applied to a purely inner struggle in pursuit of higher levels of spiritual existence, the moral imperatives under Protestantism, and especially Calvinism now refer to a struggle within the context of the familiar, material, mundane existence. Max Weber has said that Calvinism took the ideals of the monastic life out of the monastery and placed them in the context of the daily struggle within this earthy mundane reality.[38] The form in which this struggle was conceived drew heavily from the humanistic notions introduced by Ficino. The Reformation had clearly taken on board Ficino's notion of the centrality of the human being and concomitantly the idea that the cosmos was designed to be understood, dominated and penetrated by human beings. The logic of this position dictates that this world is arranged to promote the interests and utility of human beings in accordance with Divine design.[39]   Certainly this is the intellectual foundation for the emerging Protestant morality and Protestant ethic, which saw labour in the service of social usefulness to be God's will and productive labour on the earth's resources to be a moral obligation.[40]

Ultimately, with Locke, the great English theorist of property relations, private property can be seen as both a right and a moral duty. Following the humanist tradition, individual human beings could be said to claim a right of private ownership based on human dominion over the material universe. But at the same time, Calvinism, and by extension Puritanism, had developed the idea that we are under an obligation to labour on the material world in order to fulfil functions of social usefulness. Locke saw that in order to effect this goal individuals would have to have exclusive dominion over some part of the world's natural resources on which to apply their labours, and this according to Locke's understanding meant that each individual would have to have exclusive private holdings on some area of the earth's surface in order to work or labour.   Thus, the imperatives of the divine plan required private property, and indeed, each individual was seen to be under a moral duty to acquire private property through labour in order to fulfill God's natural law.

The idea that private property is both a right and a moral obligation can be seen to follow quite naturally from Locke's Puritan background. English puritanism, after all was strongly aligned with Calvinism with its strong emphasis on worldly engagement.[41] Locke simply made these ideas more explicit and thoroughly explored their ramifications, and consequently, the acquisition of private property itself appears as a moral obligation integral to the survival of mankind and the promotion of its interests. In this light the vigorous industrial activity which followed should be quite understandable considering both the original Calvinists and the Puritans saw personal prosperity and the acquisition of extensive possessions as important indicators of God's grace and blessing.

Conclusion

The question of course is whether property rights for which Protestantism laid the moral foundations, gives moral backing to rights to dominate and exploit the environment. In part I think the answer is yes. Once the Reformation had denied the medieval view that spiritual perfection is reflected in other-worldly, non-materialistic life and had taken on board Ficino's inspired humanism which sees man as the central and necessarily dominating figure in the created universe, it becomes unavoidably easy to envision the world as only having instrumental value in relation to human purposes.   Furthermore, Protestantism, and most particularly the Calvinist form, believed that not mere survival but the fact that one flourished and prospered with obvious wealth was indicative of spiritual superiority and ultimate salvation.[42]   With this attitude it is quite easy to see the earth and its resources as a mere means to personal prosperity, which in turn is seen as indicative of God's blessing. Given that human beings can become most vital when self interest has a moral backing, it is not surprising that these attitudes would initially lead to the worst abuses of the environment in the Protestant industrialized countries, though now the problem is world wide and hardly confined to these few.

Very briefly, the conclusion of this chapter is that there were two significant alterations in Christian thinking during the Renaissance and the Reformation which were strongly contributory to the intensive exploitation of the natural environment.   The first, of course, was promotion of man to a position of dominance and centrality within the created universe, as exemplified in the philosophical/theological speculation of Ficino. The second was the tendency of the thinkers of the Reformation to downplay the importance of spiritual and other worldly aspirations and indeed the importance of the distinction between the material and spiritual worlds. These ideas in turn led to the belief that intense engagement in economic affairs and material forms of

productivity (beyond that necessary for mere subsistence) was indicative
God's grace. It would be very unrealistic indeed to discount the role this
type of religious thinking has played in exploitation of the environment
and the present environmental crisis.

[1]   A. Zimmern, *The Greek Commonwealth* (Oxford: Clarendon Press,1935),
287-88.
[2]   Alan Ryan,   *Property* (Stony Stratford: Open University Press,1987), 10-
11.
[3]   Ibid, 21.
[4]   By way of background to our discussion of the intellectual movements
during the Renaissance and Reformation, we should, of course, speak of the
central character of land tenure endemic to the feudalism, which we find in the
late Middle Ages and early Renaissance. Various feudal systems as we know
were and are to be found throughout Europe during the Middle Ages, and at
various times in the Orient and the Middle East. Honore, however, in his classic
work on ownership, (see footnote 31) refused to recognize as property in the
modern liberal sense, holdings associated with feudal tenure. This is to say that
the rights and duties associated with such holdings don't resemble those
enshrined in the modern liberal concept of property. What is essentially lacking
in feudal arrangements is the right to capital. Broadly speaking, the right to
capital encompasses the rights to alienate, modify, waste or destroy the holding.
According to Honore, the system of holdings must support this right (or incident
as Honore calls it) if the system is said to approximate the modern liberal notion,
even if specific modalities within the system deny this right (as in life tenancy).
Of course, it must be kept in mind that we are talking about real property, i.e.,
land.
    The rights which the individual lacks with respect to his holding, are what
Hohfeld calls power rights, i.e., rights which allow us to alter legal relations, in
this case the rights to transfer, sell or will one's holding. Within feudalism,
these rights are always held by one's superior, in the sense that it is one's
immediate lord or the King who may alter the legal relationships. Thus, the
holding which a serf or villein maintained, for example, was neither transferable
nor transmissible, which is to say that it could neither be given away nor
conveyed for money nor could it be freely willed as in the modern form of
devolution.   The power to transfer the holding resided with the holder's
immediate lord. In a system in which duties were primary, unfulfilled
obligations would lead to the lord or King, whichever the case may be, divesting
the holder of his title and determining the rights of a future holder.
[5]   Andrew Reeves, *Property* (London: Macmillan Press, 1986),51-52.
[6]   Lynn White "The Historical Roots of Ecological Crisis," *Science* 155
(1967): 1203-07 esp. 1205; Ian L. Mc Hague, *Design with Nature* (Garden
City, New York: Doubleday and Co., 1969).

---

[7]   Jeremy Cohen, *Be Fertile and Increase, Fill the Earth and Master It. The Ancient and Medieval Career of a Biblical Text* (Ithaca New York: Cornell University Press, 1991).

[8]   See Susan Bratton, "Loving Nature: Eros or Agape?", *Environmental Ethics* 14 (1992): 3-25

[9]   L.H. Steffen, "In Defense of Dominion",   *Environmental Ethics* 14 (1992): 63-80.

[10]   Steffen, "In Defense of Dominion".

[11]   Ibid., 75.

[12]   Ibid., 68.

[13]   Ibid., 69.

[14]   Ibid., 74.

[15]   Ibid., 73.

[16]   Ibid., 74.

[17]   See Charles Taylor, *Philosophy and the Human Sciences: Philosophical Papers 2* (Cambridge; Cambridge University Press, 1985); Jurgen Habermas, *The Philosophical Discourse of Modernity* (Cambridge: M.I.T. Press, 1991).

[18]   Taylor, *Philosophy and the Human Sciences,* 142-44. Here Taylor speaks of platonic understanding involving attunement with the order of things. The Neoplatonists affirmed that attunement meant the achievement of a certain contemplative state.

[19]   Anders Nygren, *Agape and Eros*, trans P.S. Watson (New York and Evanston: Harper & Row, 1969), 613-38.

[20]   According to one aspect of the latter notion, the Divine exercises an attraction while remaining Itself unmoved and unchanged. At the same time the whole material universe bears the mark of eros, the lower reaching out after the higher striving to become like it. In general the ladder signifies the lower realities striving everywhere upward towards the higher spiritual reality.

[21]   P.O. Kristeller, *The Philosophy of Marsilio Ficino* (Gloucester: Peter Smith, 1964), 13.

[22]   Ibid.

[23]   Nygren, *Agape and Eros,* 672.

[24]   See A.J.A. Carlyle, *A History of Medieval Political Theory in the West,* vol. I (London & Edinburgh: William Blackwood and Sons, 1950), 136-137.

[25]   See Herbert A. Deane, *The Political and Social Ideas of St. Augustine* (New York & London: Columbia University Press, 1963), 104.

[26]   Augustine, *In Ioannis Evangelium Tractatus CXXIV* (Turnhoti: Typographi Brepols Editores Pontificii, 1961) VI: 25-26.

[27]   Augustine, *Corpus Scriptorum Ecclesiasticorum Latinorum,* XLIV: 426-427.

[28]   Ibid., XXXIV (2): 514.

[29]   See St. Thomas Aquinas, *Summa Theologica*, ed. T. Gilby (London, O.P., 1964):II. II.66.1., which sets out Ambrose's position and replies to it.

[30]   Aquinas, *Summa Theologica*: II. II. 62.5.

[31]   See A.M. Honore in "Ownership", in   *Oxford Essays in Jurisprudence*, ed. A.G. Guest (London: Oxford University Press, 1964), 107-147, who offers an authoritative and thorough exploration of the essential characteristics or "incidents" of the modern liberal notion of ownership.

[32]   Francis De Pauw, *Grotious and the Law of the Sea* (Brussels, Editions de L'Institut de Sociologie, 1965).

[33]   See James Tully, *A Discourse on Property: John Locke and his Adversaries* (Cambridge: Cambridge University Press, 1980), 73, in reference to Blackstone II.I.I.

[34]   C.B. Macpherson, *Democratic Theory* (Oxford: Clarendon Press, 1975).

[35]   In this case my argument could be said to resemble and even supplement that offered by Max Weber in *The Protestant Ethic and the Spirit of Capitalism* (London: Allen & Unwin, 1966), in which he argued that the protestant emphasis on the religious nature of worldly duties was an essential component in the rise of modern capitalism.

[36]   Marsilio Ficino in   *The Philebus Commentary*, trans. M.J.B. Allen (Berkeley: University of California Press, 1975), 40, points out that spirituality is realized through inner ascent by separation from the body.

[37]   See Weber, *The Protestant Ethic*, 81.

[38]   Ibid, 121.

[39]   Ibid, 109.

[40]   Ibid, 109.

[41]   Ibid, 109.

[42]   Ibid, 7.

Chapter 6

John Locke And The Issue Of Community Ownership

Locke is reputed to be the champion of individual property rights and subsequent defenders of private ownership have tended to rely on one or both of Locke's central arguments.[1] The first argument says that the individual has a proprietary right to that which he creates through his labour. The second says that the individual has a moral right to private property in order to ensure his own preservation and that of humanity in general.

However, though Locke has been traditionally associated with the so called natural right of private ownership, this view has been strongly challenged in more recent scholarship particularly in the work of James Tully and John Dunn.[2] Tully, in particular, argues that throughout, Locke maintained that the communal approach to ownership remained primary, and that ultimately individual rights are founded upon primary communal rights. In this chapter I argue that though individual rights within Locke's state of nature appear to be usufructuary, communal property is never entertained to be a jural reality, a conclusion which has been forcefully made by several commentators on Tully's work.[3]

However, in developing my argument I intend to accept two salient aspects of Tully's Thesis which Tully's critics tend to deny: 1) that individual property rights acquired in the state of nature are essentially usufructuary; 2) that these originally acquired rights are dissolved and reconstituted following the introduction of money and the ensuing scarcity of land.[4] What I intend to demonstrate is that even if these interpretations are attributed to Locke, this is still insufficient to establish that Locke promoted a strong notion of communal ownership which resembles known models of communal ownership as found, for

Reprinted by permission of the *Journal of Social Philosophy*.

example, in Melanesia. Indeed, notwithstanding acceptance of these two points of interpretation, attention to the Locke's text, indicates that throughout Locke maintained the primacy of individual rather than communitarian values.

My *modus operandi* will be one which compares Locke's views on property with those of Melanesian customary land tenure, and in this way, contrast Locke's understanding of ownership with that of a society which does view holdings as primarily communal. Furthermore, I believe the differences are most perspicuously evident when we look at the effect brought about by the introduction of money into the two systems. Thus, I contrast the unfolding of events which precipitate the dissolution of traditional usage rights as the cash economy is introduced into Melanesia with Locke's understanding as to how the institution of money affects the nature of property rights originally acquired in the state of nature. This study will indicate to the reader that Locke's overriding concern was individual rights and consequently that he was never seriously interested in the communal ownership as a jural reality.

Ownership in the Lockean State of Nature

In the initial state of nature, as Locke describes it, man gains exclusive individual rights over particular areas of the world's resources in order to fulfill the primary command of the Creator: "Every one is *bound to preserve himself* and not to quit his station wilfully; so by the like reason when his own Preservation comes not in competition, ought he, as much as he can, *to preserve the rest of mankind...*" (*Two Treatises*, 2:6).

If we are to fulfill God's command, one needs property, but, according to Tully, the right of property amounts to an initial claim right, the paramount and remarkable feature, of which, is that it refers not to the earth itself, but to the man-made products useful to one's life: food, raiment, conveniences of life, meat and drink.[5] What was originally granted to mankind, claims Tully, was not exclusive dominion over the earth but the right to use the earth in order to create man-made products useful to one's life.

Tully then explains that the exclusive right simply individuates the background claim right, in the same way that a right in the use of a seat on public transportation, particularizes a prior right to use public transportation, and humans, thus, have a right to establish exclusive rights over land, only because one has a prior right to use the products of that land. This is necessarily the case because the complementary natural inclusive and exclusive rights, respectively, refer to, and inhere in, the products of one's labour, Tully tells us.[6] Tully asserts that this "unique construction" serves to establish Locke's main ideological conclusion, that fixed property in land does not have a natural foundation. In this light, the right to land is derivative from the primary right to that which is produced. The conclusion, reached, Tully tells us, is that the common remains common and persons remain tenants in common in accordance with God's original grant of common dominion.

Thus, Tully's analysis promotes the conclusion that the relation of individuals to the resources of the earth is essentially usufructuary. Given Locke's proviso against spoilage (that we are only entitled to that which we can use before it spoils), and the condition that there be *enough and as good* for others, together with the notion of original common dominion by humankind in entirety, property rights do appear to be essentially usufructuary rather than approximations of the full blown liberal concept of private ownership.[7] I would agree that the imposition of the above constraints would seem to commit Locke to an interest which is less than that of modern private ownership, and certainly an interest which shares many of the central characteristics of a legal usufruct. Let us therefore, assume the correctness of Tully's interpretation to this stage.

However, a usufructuary right presupposes the existence of a greater interest as the usufruct allows one to make use of the holdings of another on condition that one does not impair the substance. The question is what is the nature of this greater interest and who holds it. Tully claims that the model which Locke intended for his system was the English commons.[8] Here we see a combination of a conditional use right in land, and an usufruct in the products of one's labours. By usufruct we mean the right to enjoy the things of another without impairing the substance (but in this case we must use and enjoy them for God's purposes and not our own), Tully tells us. The concept of the English common is of course quite well known. Certain property in each town or county was set aside so that the inhabitants could use it for various purposes, e.g., growing vegetables, grazing sheep, and cattle, etc. All inhabitants had access to these lands, but individuals could establish exclusive rights over specific areas, where they were using the land for particular allowable purposes. The exclusive claim expired when one ceased to utilize the property. Furthermore, there were necessarily limits over that to which one could make an exclusive claim. Such a claim could only extend to that which was sufficient for personal need and use. If one were cultivating and growing a great deal of produce, but it became subject to non-use and spoilage, then the exclusive claim might be limited, just as if one failed to utilize a portion of one's enclosed land.

If Tully's interpretation is correct, what Locke appears to be describing is communal land tenure which is realized in the state of nature and which precedes the changes which occur with the institution of money. Within this system it is the community which is the ultimate owner while individual members usually have rights of use. If this model accurately reflects Locke's original intent then Locke was describing a system of land tenure which closely resembles customary communal ownership as it existed and continues to exist in Melanesia.[9] With this in mind we should proceed to investigate the Melanesian embodiment of land rights.

Melanesian Customary Land Tenure

It has been remarked that Melanesian identification with the community is intimately and inextricably connected with the parallel identification with the communal land holding. A.P. Power, with considerable experience with the provincial government of the East Sepic, P.N.G., asserts that the lynch pin of the Melanesian group, which ensured the continuity of its community life and history, was the land holding.[10] The communal land holding provided the locus for the community's cultural activities: political, military and social. Power asserts that as land through generations was held by force of arms through social groupings, the fundamental ownership of land is by groups of some sort or other. As we have pointed out, the important constant, he remarked, was that the group owned, and individuals used the land. "Individual land usage rights did not remove the reality that the group was the basis for ownership and the basis for the defense of these rights."[11] Because of this, Power believes Melanesians cannot fully disassociate themselves from their land, for within this construct are bound up notions of communal identity and individual well being.

If we look at the reality of subsistence farming within these communities, one sees that individuals or a family will acquire exclusive rights to a particular piece of land for appropriate purposes, for example, cropping or grazing, but this right does not continue in perpetuity. After one or two generations of use, the exclusive right ceases and the land reverts to the community. This practice often coordinates with natural cycles and enables the resource to replenish itself during periods of disuse. This was the universal system of traditional production in many parts of Africa and during the Melanesian pre-colonial period.[12] In the case of Melanesia, with which I am most familiar, these practices continued without significant impairment through the period of Australian administration into the present era of independence. Even today Papua New Guinea offers a striking example of the "commons" approach to agriculture as 97% of the land remains communally owned.

To this point Locke's state of nature seems to parallel the description of the customary Melanesian community. However, the essential differences between the character of ownership in Locke's state of nature and customary land tenure in Melanesia are brought out in a study of the effects of the introduction of money as it is seen to occur within these two systems.

Money as it affects Ownership According to Locke

The introduction of money, according to Locke, relieves the individual from necessary conformity to the proviso against spoilage because gold and silver can be hoarded without spoiling. This allows the individual to acquire greater acreage because the surplus produced can be exchanged for money and thereby will not waste. However, not only does the introduction of money relieve one of certain moral constraints it also offers a rationale for building up surpluses. In the state of nature, *simpliciter*, it is not only morally wrong to acquire more than you can use, it is also irrational, because the surpluses would perish indicating wasted and unnecessary labour. However, the possibility of acquiring money gives individuals a rationale for acquiring more land than they can personally use to serve the purposes of cash cropping. (When this occurs it is pretty clear that the central usufructuary nature of acquired rights has been replaced by a different sort of right.) In any case, these events, according to Tully, ultimately lead to scarcity of land and surrender of property to the state (since the *enough and as good* condition cannot be met).

In paragraph 2: 45 of the *Two Treatises* Locke states that after land became valuable through money and ensuing scarcity,

> ...several Communities settled the Bounds of their distinct Territories, and by Laws within themselves regulated the Properties of the private Men of their society, and so by Compact and Agreement settled the Property, which Labour and Industry began; and the Leagues which had been made between the several States and Kingdoms, either expressly or tacitly disowning all Claim and

> Right to the Land in the others Possession, have, by common consent, given up their Pretenses to the natural common Right, which originally they had to those Countries, and so have by positive agreement settled a Property amongst themselves, in distinct Parts and parcels of the Earth...

In abnegating natural rights, and drawing limits to the state's territorial jurisdiction, land is withdrawn from the common ownership of mankind as "...several Communities settled the bounds of their distinct Territories". Agreements are reached by "... either expressly or tacitly disowning all Claim and Right to the Land in the others Possession..." and thus, the individuals within the political jurisdiction "...have, by common consent, given up their Pretenses to the natural common Right, which originally they had to those Countries, and so have by positive agreement settled a Property amongst themselves."

In this passage Locke appears to tell us that it is no longer a question of the state faithfully protecting the original legitimate rights acquired through labour, because the very nature of these original claims has been irrevocably transmogrified with the institution of money. With respect to land, one no longer lays claim to the same "res", which is a portion of a limitless "common" in which there is always *enough and as good* for the rest of humanity. Any portion of land, to which one now attaches a claim, will be a portion of a circumscribed area in which the *enough and as good* condition can not be satisfied because, above all, the portion claimed will be part of a delimited political territory which is under the jurisdiction of the political community. In the state of nature (and in the period preceding the institution of money), one's claim to land was based on the fact that one was a member of humanity and the earth was a grant to humankind in common. In laying claim to a portion of the earth which is no longer viewed as a limitless expanse, but rather a discrete area reserved for a discrete number of individuals (citizens), it follows that one's claims (to land) can no longer proceed without reference to the interests of the other individuals who comprise the political entity. The assertion of exclusive claims to land will constitute robbery, robbery of the other members of one's society, unless there is consent to these claims. Thus, the statement that communities have "... by laws within themselves regulated the Properties of the private men of their society, and so by Compact and Agreement settled the Property, which Labour and Industry began..." can only mean that property which is initially acquired independent of contract and agreement inevitably becomes subject to accords and agreed conventions subsequent to the invention of money.

This must be the proper interpretation. Certainly one of the essential aims of the *Second Treatise* is to respond to Filmer's arguments and demonstrate that individual claims in the state nature can proceed without prejudice to or robbery of the rest of mankind.[13] It would be nothing less than willful blindness on the part of Locke not to notice that exclusive claims within the context of civil society, if uninformed by communal acceptance, would constitute robbery of the other members of one's society. At least one dominating theme of the *Two Treatises*, I would argue, is that socio/political arrangements which affect the interests of other members of humanity cannot proceed without consent of these individuals. For example, Locke decries taxation which occurs without the consent of the taxed.[14] This is all part of a general prohibition against taking another's property without his consent.[15] But notice consent is interpreted as consent by the majority or their representatives chosen by them.[16] Similarly disproportionate holdings require tacit consent through the use of money, whereas arrangements in the context of the state of nature do not require consent because they fundamentally do not affect other individuals.[17]

The introduction of Money in Melanesian Customary Society

Now let us proceed comparatively and consider the introduction of money as it affects customary Melanesian communal ownership. Among the forces working to overturn this traditional system of land tenure in Melanesia, the principal agent is the cash economy initiated with the institution of money. Profound changes have been effected in the Melanesian way of life in those areas of Papua New Guinea which have undergone transformation from a subsistence to a cash economy.

In Melanesia The motor of change has been the demand for cash which, unlike subsistence farming, requires the use of land, not on a cyclical basis, but on a more or less permanent basis for cash cropping. The demands of cash cropping, in turn, exert pressure on the community to alienate communal land into forms of tenure other than communal in order to facilitate permanent use. When this occurs control of the means of production no longer resides with the community. Subsistence farming of commons, as we said, would not have such an effect as these lands, after one or two generations of family use, revert back to commons and the permanent title remains with the human community.

However, the Melanesian example further serves to illustrate how the introduction of cash effects a profound alteration in social structures within the context of the cyclically orientated agrarian economy. Within the context of contemporary Melanesia, alienation of land from communal tenure into permanent individual holdings demands complex negotiations and interactions. As seen by the community, the usufructuary right cannot unilaterally be converted into a permanent individual right of private ownership without committing robbery against immediate community and disrupting the traditional community control and the modalities of custom and ritual which embody this control. Thus, in order to effect any permanent transfer of land from communal tenure to individual forms of tenure, it is first necessary to institute agreements and accords with other members of the community with the purpose of transmogrifying the holding into a permanent form of individual title rather than a mere right of use. Additionally, for these acts to be a performative success, it is necessary that there exist conventions which recognize this concept of private ownership which, according to Honore, would usually include the right to capital, i.e., the right to waste, destroy or alienate the holding.[18]

Within traditional Melanesian society this right was unknown, and thus, the very idea of acquiring such a holding was unthinkable. It is only through the Australian colonial administration that such rights have been recognized through the institution of the Anglo-Australian common law. Thus, within extant Melanesian communities, individuals who wish to acquire communal property as a permanent individual holding for cash cropping must enter into agreements which compensate the community for the loss of land and subsequently register these agreements according to the procedures and rules inherited from Anglo-Australian law. If all this is achieved they will have established for themselves the form of individual freehold recognized in Anglo-Australian law.

Differences between the Two Systems

With respect to Tully's interpretation, which sees the primary form of ownership as communal or community ownership, both den Hartogh and Baldwin, in effect, have argued that an original grant to humanity in common is insufficient to license a presumption of communal ownership.[19]   Den Hartogh underlines that Locke employs the term "common dominion" and not "community of ownership" or "common property", the terms employed by Tully.[20] As both Baldwin and den

Hartogh point out, common dominion by humanity and ownership by a distinct community are not synonymous terms with a univocal meaning, and one needs some argument to demonstrate how one legitimately moves from one articulation to the other. I think the presumption must be that Locke never does make the connection and I think this is borne out by the differences one sees in the system which Locke describes and the characteristics of a system which does exhibit a strong sense of communal ownership, as in Melanesia.

There is first of all profound difference in perspective with respect to the perceived effects of the cash economy. Locke points out that money offers a rationale for greater and disproportionate holdings which lead to scarcity of land, and therefore the subsequent renegotiation of property rights through consensual agreements. The rationale is, of course, that once land becomes scarce, the interests of others are affected and prejudiced whenever land is individually acquired - in the state of nature this was not the case because there was always as good and enough for others. In this type of situation it becomes necessary that the individuals affected give their consent to what is happening. It is unmistakable that the central concern is one of individual interest and nothing in the logic of Locke's statements suggests that there is some distinct communal value to be maintained or acknowledged.

If we contrast this with the developments within a Melanesian community, I think the distinction becomes more clear. When this institution (money) is introduced within this milieu, the effects are perceived not simply in terms of particular interests but also in terms of the community as a whole. What is perceived to be occurring is not simply a possible diminution of individual interests and expectations through the alienation of some portion of communal or clan lands, but rather the permanent removal of holdings from the community and disruption of the customary communal modalities of control. In a sense, this is seen as robbery of the community as the introduction of money effects permanent alienation of holdings disturbing a pattern of cyclical use which renders the holdings available to the community at some future date. A form of robbery occurs, not only because money encourages larger holdings with the attendant diminution of what is available for others - though this factor, of course, cannot be discounted - but *a-fortiori* because it effects permanent abnegation of that which belongs to the community and the ensuing disruption of essential communal relationships.

Here it should be noted that the Melanesian defines the community not imply in terms of current membership but all past and future members. Permanent alienation of communal or clan lands into forms of private tenure not only affects the interests of the present members but is also seen to have effects on the other two groups, the future and even past members.[21] In contrast, there is no indication that Locke sees alienation in terms of permanent denial of this organic entity, which we define as the community. According to Locke, permanent acquisition of private holdings, following scarcity, is important because it does not *leave enough and as good* for others. This is important in terms of the interests of the other individuals and there is no mention of the interests of the community nor its long term well being nor any formulation which would indicate that Locke seriously considers the notion of a definable entity which endures over time and maintains its identity throughout alterations in membership.

It is worth mentioning that in Melanesia a community is thought to consist not simply of a particular aggregate of individuals, but individuals in a number of specified relationships.[22] The Melanesian understands the community in terms of these relationships and, according to this understanding, these connections are seen to carry more importance than the individuals who are so related. As The community is thought to be made up these relationships, the community and thus, life itself, may be disrupted or threatened if these relationships are ruptured. According to the Melanesian understanding, the community can sustain the loss of certain individuals but if the appropriate relationships are not maintained the community itself may be destroyed and with it all the individual members.[23]

By way of comparison one should note that the tradition of individual rights is antithetical to the tradition of communal rights and communal ownership which occur within societies which have been labelled holistic, the most striking examples of which are to found in certain extant Melanesian and African societies. Holistic societies are said to be those which, in contrast to the modern liberal paradigm, invest ultimate value in the society itself rather than the individual.[24] As the community is seen as the central value ethical rules can be seen to respond to this value. Thus, Melanesian cosmology expresses itself in an implicit Melanesian axiology, one which finds its basis in the idea of community and whose ethical implications impose severe restrictions on the ideas of autonomous and self-interested behaviour and what contemporary Western culture has come to understand as the rights of the individual. In other words, ethical ideals are more or less the antithesis of those found in the modern liberal tradition which derives ultimate value from the individual, and legitimates social and moral constraints as they are said to guarantee this central value.

One needs to underline the role of individual consent in the Lockean system to appreciate the difference between his system and one which derives private holdings from original community ownership. In the Lockean system the individual already possesses "holdings" acquired independently of civil society or social arrangement; with the introduction of money and the scarcity of land, he then proceeds to enter into contractual agreements with his fellows to form a political entity consisting of a defined territory with the necessary conventions as they apply to property or "holdings". In contrast, in the Melanesian system, communal property always underlies individual property, such that the former is derivative form the latter. This means that "property" has no primary a-social context or character. There is, thereby, no room for the individual to manoeuver and exercise choice in consenting to the communal conventions which will define "his" property and its modes of distribution and acquisition. Within the paradigms of Melanesian customary ownership, the individual is born into defined communal relations of entitlement; he does not legitimate these relations through his consent. In contrast, the Lockean individual must legitimate societal arrangements through consent. According to Locke, the community and civil society, therefore, is the product of individual decision making as individuals agree to terms to enhance and maintain their individual interests and rights - community relations are not simply something one inherits. Each generation, therefore, forms society anew through consent to the social contract or by seeking to modify the terms of the contract.

In summation, individual rights in the Lockean social context are legitimated through the consent of the affected individuals, within the Melanesian communal context, individual rights are legitimated through communal consent. However, methodological individualists may assert that the community is ultimately reducible to the individuals who comprise it and their particular interests. Acccordingly, we have a legalistic distinction without a real difference. But in fact, emergent qualities do appear when we move from a consideration of a group as a mere collection of individuals to that of individuals related through community relations. There are distinct implications to be drawn depending on whether we consider the interests of the community or simply interests of those who currently comprise the community, political entity or whatever. The former consists of past and future membership where as the latter does not. With respect to the community, therefore, there are the interests of future generation to consider which means that the issue of sustainability arises when land use and development are contemplated - that is to say the ability to meet the needs and aspirations of the present without compromising the ability to meet needs of the future generation. On the other hand, if we simply consider the interests of the set of people who are currently identifiable as members, these issues and concerns will not arise.

Furthermore, these differences in concern certainly determine the nature of the consensual jural constructs and modalities which are constituted to safeguard these interests. Where the community, clan, or relevant social grouping originally owns the land, the subsequent alienation of parts of the communal holding into forms of individual tenure may still imply a form of individual tenure which falls short of the modern liberal notion of ownership. Power, for example, in drafting legislation for the registration of communal land in the East Sepik, has sought to stipulate that any sale involving alienation of the latter into a form of individual tenure must be made to clan members and in turn they are prevented from selling their holdings to non-clan members.[25] This certainly contrasts with the extreme position of libertarians like Nozick who conceive themselves falling within the Lockean tradition and believe the essence of property rights enshrines the inviolable liberty to transfer one's holding without any restrictions.[26] Whether or not Locke would fully subscribe to this view, Nozick is not inconsistent with the validating principles of the Lockean universe. According to Locke, the primary source of individual ownership rights derives from individual responsibilities to God and not the one's particular human community, and therefore individual rights are not controlled by the interests of the latter. In contrast the Melanesian system sees the individual as deriving rights through a more or less fiduciary relationship with respect to the communal holding. He may make use of it, but his use must not impair the substance and moreover its uses must be seen to have some benefit for the community which holds the greater interest, for example he must provide for the wishes of the ancestors and at the same time insure that the children and the subsequent generation will also benefit from the land.

Conclusion

Ultimately the achievement of the *Two Treatises of Government* consists in demonstrating how property which is originally granted to mankind in common becomes conventional and private in response to material conditions and the moral exigencies of the natural law. What is significant is that this account is discordant with the history of development in human communities. With regard to the latter, I have suggested that the natural progression (as demonstrated in Melanesia) would be one which begins with communal property in a period of pre-civil society and ultimately becomes individual or private within monetary economy of civil society. I have maintained that though Locke begins from the premise of common dominion, in which the earth is owned by humanity in common, he never does seriously entertain the notion of communal ownership. In actuality, common dominion is not a jural reality, in which communist conditions occur, rather it is a premise from which Locke derives the inclusive individual usufructuary right to the earth's resources. Subsequently, he demonstrates how this evolves into the modern private ownership, as conditions change with the introduction of money.

One may well wonder as to the function of a notion of common dominion in which humanity exists as tenants in common if the reality of ownership is always individual and exclusive. The function of this concept is to remind us that all human beings have an underlying inclusive right to earth's resources, i.e., to be included in the sharing of these resources, but not to advocate legal reality in which individuals jointly claim communal rights to the identical holding. In a way I would suggest that this concept functions in many respects like Kant's notion of a noumenal community of ownership which is said to underlie empirical possession in that it refers to the moral principles which legitimate any actual distribution of the earth's resources.[27]

Finally, with respect to the more difficult matters of interpretation, one ought to be guided by a hermeneutical approach which takes into account both the historicity of Locke's culture and holistic societies in which communal forms of land tenure occur. Ultimately, to associate Locke with notions of communal or community ownership is to misrepresent Locke's intentions and the social forces he was attempting to reconcile within his cultural temporal context. To be specific, Locke was attempting to lay the moral foundation for the tradition of individual rights in opposition to a tradition of Kingly sovereignty, as it had been expressed in the work of Robert Filmer. The fact that the *Two Treatises of Government* was written in response to Filmer's *Patriarcha* should be ample evidence for this point of view.

On this point one needs to appreciate that during the early years of Christianity and during much of the Middle Ages the preponderant view was that the earth or the created world belonged to God and various forms of human ownership were conventional arrangements necessitated by man's sinful fallen state.[28] In some sense God had conveyed the earth to mankind, but the bequest fell far short of sovereignty. For example Ambrose, as we have seen, taught that only God could have dominion over objects, man could not have exclusive dominion because the criterion of dominion requires bringing something into being. Dominion was interpreted to mean exclusive control.[29]   Aquinas softened this approach arguing that dominion (or *dominium*) was natural to God alone but that man could exercise a form of dominion in terms of the right to use these objects. Aquinas   mentions uses for the purposes of preservation and convenience.[30]   It will be also remembered that St. Augustine, whose Christian   thinking was a synthesis of much of Christian teaching and Neoplatonic ideas, held that it is only by human right (*iure humano*) that man had possessions not divine right (*iure divino*) because the earth and its fullness belong to God. He goes on to say that it is the Kings and Emperors who determine human rights including the right to property.[31] The latter thinking of course supported the idea of Divine Right which taught that the King had exclusive authority to settle determinations of ownership in this sinful earthly state.

However, as we saw in the last chapter, Renaissance humanism increasingly emphasized the notion that man exercised a sovereign dominate status within the created order. If human authority devolved through a grant from God to the King, this sovereignty and the attendant exercise of dominion, would be the sole prerogative of the King. Filmer's work, *mutatis mutandis*, can be seen as concordant with this tradition, one which denies that property rights of individual subjects follow directly from God's laws and which promotes the enhanced sovereignty of the King in human ownership and matters temporal. In opposition, Locke reasserts the theory of the patristic thinkers and Aquinas, which sees the Earth and its resources originally granted to mankind in general for their use, and not particularly as the exclusive freehold of the King (as Filmer believed). Locke then carefully demonstrates how exclusive private property rights are derived from these original inclusive rights through the consent of each individual through the social contract which creates civil society. In this endeavor Locke's intentions are roughly threefold: 1) demonstrate that individual property does follow from God's law and command and not from the determinations of the King; 2) thereby introduce a theory of the social organization and civil society which is derived from the legitimating activities of individuals in the exercise of their natural rights, rather than the authority of the King; 3) affirm that the individual's primary duties, both temporal and spiritual, are directly owned to God and not mediated through hierarchy of King and established Church.

Throughout Locke's concerns were individual and not communal. To suggest that Locke promoted the right of the community in answer to the exclusive sovereignty of the King is to interpolate a cultural tradition which would have been alien to Locke's experiences and concerns. Locke himself can be seen as occupying a transitional period between decline of feudalism and the emergence of full blown capitalist society, and historically, both feudalism and capitalism are inimical to the values of a holistic society, and in particular communal property rights.[32] On matters of historicity, anthropologists and other Scholars have pointed out that during the Middle Ages and the subsequent period of the Renaissance there was a steady decline of the value and importance attributed to the community in contrast to holistic customary societies (like those in Melanesia) who throughout maintained the ultimate value of the community. This European trend has been seen as a historical process involving the progressive negation of the community as a whole and a growing emphasis on individualism.[33]

We have mentioned Daniel de Coppet, for example, who contrasts Melanesian society with that of Europe and contends that during the European Middle Ages there was a growing difficulty to assign a place to society in the context of (in and beside) God, Christ and the King.[34] He believes that with the inability to effect an appropriate definition of society there began a very slow and gradual drift of ultimate value from society to the indivisible individual.[35] Locke needs to be appreciated within his socio-cultural context which followed these medieval developments, and understood as a powerful force in the English Enlightenment who had no small role in articulating individual human rights.

It would be therefore be very strange indeed to find a person in Locke's historical context advocating values of holistic communities and their particular form of land tenure. In reality, Locke belonged to that post reformation protestant culture of the early enlightenment which sought to carry on the struggle against the traditional authorities of the King and the established Church who had embodied the hierarchy of the declining feudal world. As against these authoritarian traditions, Locke proposed the rights of individual property and freedom from religious intolerance, and in so doing, he should be seen as laying much of the intellectual groundwork for the modern liberal culture.

¹   The enduring reliance on these arguments by those who seek to establish a natural right to private property is perspicuously evinced in recent work by Ellen Frankel Paul, *Property Rights and Eminent Domain* (New Brunswick N.J.: Transaction Books, 1987), in which she offers two arguments for property rights: 1)every human being as a natural right to acquire from the commons such commodities which are necessary to his or her survival and;2) everyone has a fundamental right to anything useful that person creates through his or her labour and ingenuity.

²   James Tully, *A Discourse on Property: John Locke and his Adversaries* (Cambridge: Cambridge University Press, 1980); John Dunn, *The Political Thought of John Locke* (Cambridge: Cambridge University Press, 1969).

³   G.A. Den Hartogh, "Tully's Locke," *Political Theory* 18 (1990):656-72; Thomas Baldwin, "Tully, Locke, and Land," *Locke Newsletter* 13 (1982): 21-33; see also J. Waldron, "The Turfs my Servant has Cut," *Locke Newsletter* 13 (1982): 9-20; J. Waldron, "Locke, Tully and the Regulation of Property," *Political Studies* 32 (1984):98-106; G.A. Cohen, "Marx and Locke on Land and Labour," *Proceedings of the British Academy* 71 (1985):357-88.

⁴   Waldron, ("Locke, Tully and the Regulation of Property," 105) for example, argues that on entering civil society natural property rights are not abrogated, but rather merely subjected to the conditions necessary for their effective and positive protection. This position is iterated by both Baldwin ("Tully, Locke, and Land") and den Hartogh ("Tully's Locke"). Den Hartogh, in particular, argues that property rights in the state of nature go beyond mere usufructs and resemble modern ownership rights with a power of alienation. G.A. Cohen, "Marx and Locke on Land and Labour", also gives strong support to the view that originally acquired property rights in the state of nature compare with the modern right of private ownership.

⁵   Locke, *Two Treatises of Government*, ed. P. Lazlett (Cambridge, Cambridge University Press, 1967 [1690]) 1: 41, 2: 25.

⁶   Tully, *A Discourse on Property*, 122. Tully, using MacPherson's terminology, refers to the form of property right, which people like Charles Filmer and Robert Nozick promote, as an "exclusive right", because this right gives the proprietor the prerogative to exclude others from that to which the right refers (the "res"), in addition to the other moral and legal powers over the "res" - rights of abuse and alienation. In contrast, the rights assigned to mankind, according to Locke, are inclusive rights, because they invest a right not to be excluded from the use of that to which the right refers. While others have a duty to stay off the property to which Filmer's rights of private dominion or ownership refer, Locke envisions individuals as having a duty to move over and include other right-holders in the use of common property, claims Tully. Thus, the idea of common dominion implies the inclusive right, which ultimately founds the exclusive right, and taken together, these juridical constructs are logical deductions from God's command that, "Every one is *bound to preserve himself* and not to quit his station wilfully; so by the like

reason when his own Preservation comes not in competition, ought he, as much as he can, *to preserve the rest of mankind...*"(*Two Treatises*, 2:6).

[7] See A.M. Honore in "Ownership," *in Oxford Essays in Jurisprudence*, ed. A.G. Guest (London: Oxford University Press,1964):107-47; who offers an authoritative and thorough exploration of the essential characteristics or "incidents" of the modern liberal notion of ownership.

[8] Tully, *A discourse on Property*, 124.

[9] Tully claims that the model which Locke employs for the state of nature was the English commons. However, the English community in which one finds a community commons, does not, of course, universally subscribe to communal land tenure. That is to say, that such a community may have held a designated communal commons area, but individuals would also have private land holdings as well. Thus, this historic situation would not mirror the state of nature where it is supposed that all individual rights are usufructuary and the community itself is the primary owner. This situation is better reflected in the holistic communities of Melanesia.

[10] A.P. Power, "Resources Development in East Sepic Province", in *Ethics of Development:Choices in Development Planning*, eds. C. Thirwell and P. Hughes (Port Moresby: U.P.N.G. Press, 1988), 269-81.

[11] Ibid., 272.

[12] Ibid.; see also R.W. James, *Land law and Policy in Papua New Guinea, Monograph 85* (Port Moresby: Papua New Guinea Law Reform Commission, 1985); C. K. Omari, "Traditional African Land Ethics", in *Ethics of Environment and Development*, eds. J.R. Engel and J.G. Engel (London: Belhoven Press, 1990), 167-76.

[13] Ibid; Locke, *Two Treatises*, 2: 28; see Tully, *A Discourse on Property*, 95-104.

[14] Locke, *Two Treatises*, 2: 140, 142.

[15] Ibid., 2: 138.

[16] Ibid., 2: 140; Furthermore Locke states clearly that "...Men...in society having Property, they have a right to the goods, which *by the Law of the Community* are theirs, that no Body hath a right to take their substance or any part of it from them without their consent..." (2: 138). Thus, Locke does not believe, as den Hartogh claims, that the state merely protects property, it also defines it within the context of civil society. If this were not the case surely Locke would refer to the goods which men have a right to by the laws of nature.

[17] Contrary to den Hartogh, the central motif which animates the *Two Treatises* is not the idea of unalterable rights which predate civil society, but rather the notion that social/political arrangements which fundamentally affect the interests of individuals cannot be instituted without their consent. Ultimately Locke is open to the idea that material and social conditions can alter the content of our rights, but what is constantly maintained is the idea that sovereignty belongs not to the individual or individuals who constitute the government but to the individuals who comprise the entirety of the political body.

[18]   Honore, "Ownership," 112-14.

[19]   Den Hartogh, "Tully's Locke"; Baldwin, "Tully, Locke, and Land".

[20]   Den Hartogh, "Tully's Locke," 659.

[21]   See Ernesto Mantovani, "Traditional Values and Ethics" *in Ethics of Development: The Pacific in the Twentieth Century*, eds. S. Stratigos and P. Hughes (Port Moresby, U.P.N.G. Press, 1987), 188-202. An important aspect of the Melanesian notion of community is associated with the fact that ancestors are thought to be members of the community, thus requiring that land and resources must be used in ways which will not displease the ancestors.

[22]   Ibid.

[23]   Ibid.

[24]   Ibid; Daniel de Coppet, "The Society as an Ultimate Value and the Socio-Cosmic Configuration," *Ethnos* 55 (1990):140-51; Louis Dumont, *Homo Hierarchicus:the Caste System and its Implications* (Chicago: University of Chicago Press, 1980); Karl Polanyi, *the Great Transformation* (New York, Rinehart, 1944).

[25]   Power, "The Future of the Clans in Papua New Guinea in the twenty first Century," in *"Ethics of Development: Choices in Development Planning"*, eds. C Thirwell and P. Hughes (Port Moresby, U.P.N.G. Press,1987), 173.

[26]   Robert Nozick, *Anarchy, State and Utopia* (New York: Basic Books, 1974), 30-33, 171-73.

[27]   Immanuel Kant, *The Metaphysical Elements of Justice*, trans. J. Ladd (New York: Bobbs-Merrill, 1965 [1785]);See also H. Williams, *Kant's Political Philosophy* (Oxford: Blackwell, 1983), 273, who addresses this specific issue.

[28]   See A.J.A. Carlyle, *A History of Medieval Political Theory in the West*, Vol. I (London & Edinburgh: William Blackwood and Sons Ltd., 1950), 136-37.

[29]   See St. Thomas Aquinas, *Summa Theologica*, ed. T. Gilby (London, O.P., 1964):II. II.66.1., which sets out Ambrose's position and replies to it.

[30]   Aquinas, *Summa Theologica*: II. II. 62.5.

[31]   Augustine, *In Ioannis Evangelium Tractatus CXXIV* (Turnhoti: Typographi Biopols Edifores Pontificii) VI, 25-26.

[32]   See C.K. Omari, "Traditional African Land Ethics," 167-76.

[33]   See Daniel de Coppet, "the Society"; Louis Dumont, *Essays on Individualism: Modern Ideology in Anthropological Perspective* (Chicago: University of Chicago Press, 1983); Ernst Kantorowicz, *The King's Two Bodies: A Study of Political Theology* (Princeton: Princeton University Press,1957).

[34]   See Daniel de Coppet, "the Society as the Ultimate Value," 144.

[35]   Ibid.

Chapter 7

The German Enlightenment, Individual Freedom And The Issue Of Community

With Locke we observe a social analysis which posits the very real estrangement of the individual from his social environment and cultural tradition. In the last chapter we emphasized the fact that Locke resists any attempt to derive property rights or the social relations of civil society from the primacy of traditional communal structures or the determinations of Kingly authority. The social order derives its legitimacy from the individual's consent and decision to implement God's natural law. In the state of nature individual man exists either chronologically or logically but in any case ontologically distinct and independent from society; in the ensuing developments he consents to the limitations on his natural rights through acceptance of the social contract which realizes civil society. Civil society and socio-political structure only enter the individual's life through a consent to their intrusion. Locke thereby presents us with the notion of a human identity which is distinct and separable from any social tradition or cultural modality etc.

Here we see the aforementioned rejection of the earlier Classical ideals which see human rationality or simply appropriate behaviour realized through attunement with cosmic and social orders and discovery of one's appropriate place within that order. In concord with Ficino's enhanced vision of man as the dominating presence in the universe, Locke sees the individual as one who stands apart from the created world and the social organism, whose decisions are not guided by custom or tradition or the implicit rational discernment of one's preordained place in the created order. In the spirit of Ficino's humanism, the individual man confronts a world which in some sense he

Reprinted by permission of the *Journal of Social Philosophy*.

must dominate, guided alone by God's command of preservation with respect to himself and the rest of humanity. In the beginnings he has no need of political arrangements or social conventions to establish these ends, but as conditions change he finds that he must join in covenants with his fellows and create a civil order if God's will is to be satisfied.

Locke's depiction of the individual as estranged and separate from the natural and social orders can be seen to have two closely related sources: Renaissance humanism as incorporated in protestant teaching which sees the necessity for man to establish dominance and control over the natural environment to facilitate human utility in accordance with Divine command; secondly, Locke's articulation of the individual as theoretically separable from the social tradition and cultural order, which finds sources in the struggles between parliament and the King. Locke's ideas represent an important contribution to the ongoing debate on these matters as he attempts to derive the legitimacy of civil society from the individual's efforts to fulfill God's command. This, as we have explained, is by way of opposition to the view that political and social arrangements are legitimated through acts of Kingly sovereignty. To promote successfully this interpretation Locke needed to present convincingly the notion of rational, moral individuality which was independent of the forces of tradition, established custom, and societal sanction, particularly in opposition to Filmer's view that we are born into pre-existing relational webs, including authority structures which are hierarchically ordered to pre-eminent males or fathers. At the same time Locke needed to distinguish his "state of nature" from that of Hobbes, otherwise, Locke could not escape the Hobbesian implication that the authority of Kingly order was preferable to the chaotic and dangerous conditions which constitute the natural context where the unconstrained rapacious behaviour of amoral men is unregulated by authoritarian structures.

The picture which is presented is one of a human being who can intellectually dominate and control the natural order and at the same time stands outside the social order and exercises rationality in the assessment of the suitability of social arrangements in terms of the Divine command. In short it is a human individual who in a very significant sense is detached and estranged from both natural and social conditions. Generally this is the vision of human beings and their relation to the natural and social environment which emerges from Locke's analysis of "property".

With respect to the moral ground of "property rights" and their essential character we observed that private property is required so that each individual may realize the utilitarian ends prescribed by God's command. On this understanding survival and preservation of the species through the production of the necessities and comforts to sustain life could not be attempted unless each individual had certain exclusive rights to property. Without these exclusive rights one cannot properly take on these obligations, and thereby private property is seen as a natural right. But of course this would entail that there must be both inclusive and exclusive aspects to this natural right, since in the consensual creation of civil society, the latter must receive the authority to ensure that individuals have access to the resources which would allow them to fulfill God's command, once it is clear that with respect to land, there is no longer *enough and as good for others* and individuals could not necessarily rely on agricultural labour to sustain themselves. It is evident that Locke did think that commerce and trade would function as effective means of distribution once land became scarce, however, given that the right to property and civil society itself is derivative from God's command that "Everyone is to bound to preserve himself and...as much as he can, to preserve the rest of mankind...", civil society would be bound to offer assistance to those in circumstances which denied them the effective private means.

But aside from the Lockean view which sees private property as necessary to efficient production of human utilities in accordance with the designs of God, there is another view which surfaces during the Enlightenment and sees private property intimately connected with the expression of individual liberty and autonomy. On this view private property is required so that the individual can control his destiny and realize his personal freedom. In its extreme form this view proposes that the private right of property is solely an exclusive right and inclusive rights - or what are referred to as positive "rights" - are not central to our notions of justice based on personal liberty. However, we will see that the critics of this position argue that because the individual is always inextricably connected with society, social circumstances are always a determinate of relative levels of autonomy and freedom. Thus, if personal freedom is the central value which animates our theories of justice, and private property rights are both essential to effecting autonomous existence and a function of social circumstance, then private property rights must also be inclusive, and formal social arrangements must guarantee individual access to the necessary resources.

Kant and the Moral Basis of Property Rights

Locke perhaps embodied the beginnings of the Enlightenment embrace of rational unengaged individuality, Kant, however, was the major figure of the high Enlightenment and he went much further than Locke in drawing the connections between a freedom or liberty which is synonymous with this very independence from created or social order. As is well known, Kant based his moral philosophy on the categorical imperative, a principle or fundamental law of morality which the individual in fact gives to himself. Not only did Kant repudiate the view that morality was a product of societal norms, he went further than Locke and denied that the source of morality could be located in any external source, a prescribed natural law or a supposed Divine source, as in God's commands.   Individual rationality alone was capable of discerning moral principle, however, unlike the Classical Greek view this didn't mean the acceptance of a rational order inherent in the external world whether material or spiritual; on the Kantian view the fundamental moral principle discerned through rational contemplation is a product of ones own self-legislation, a law which one gives to oneself. This so called "deontological" interpretation sees the ideal of morality as identical to this individual ultimate autonomy. Kant moves these ideas further in this direction and pronounces that it is this capacity for autonomy which renders one independent of natural or social determinations and endows the individual with his ultimate value and dignity, his status as an end in himself. Accordingly the utopian society consists of Kingdom of Ends or self-legislating Kingdom of Ends.

Kantian theory represents the most significant elevation of the detached, unengaged, non-determined self transparent individual to a status of ultimate value. The highest form of human life is one of self determined existence and this is a view which continues to exert a strong attraction on modern liberal thinking whether it is that of such diverse fellow travellers as Ronald Dworkin and Robert Nozick.

This Enlightenment notion of autonomy also offered a new defense of private ownership which was clearly distinct from the utilitarian overtones of Locke's imperative to human and self preservation; the moral importance of private property is now shifted from concern with human welfare and personal utility to issues of individual control and self determination. Even more so than Locke, Kant sees the individual as fully formed rational agent, with a will which is profoundly independent of any particular cultural tradition or particular normative system. *A-fortiori*, Kant's state of nature is even further removed from the defective moral chaos envisioned by Hobbes. In the context of pre-civil society, the Kantian individual operates rationally to acquire personal property through original occupation in accordance with the operation of practical reason within the sphere of justice; by which Kant understands that the individual's acquisition of holdings is principled by the intent to legitimate these provisional acquisitions through the future formation of civil society. Like Locke, Kant acknowledges that the earth and its resources were originally given to humanity in common ownership, and subject to practical exigencies, resources become individuated through individual occupation of unowned land. However, the legitimacy of this entitlement does not rest upon the moral command of the Creator or any physical act associated with taking possession, for Kant it can only rest upon principles of freedom and individual rationality or as he claims, the *a-priori* laws of reason. These laws involve the concept of the innate common possession of the earth's surface and a commitment to join with one's fellows in the creation of civil society.[1] As we have remarked, the Kantian individual is free when the principles from which he acts are non-heteronomous, that is, when the motives towards action are not adventitious or received externally. It is thereby accepted that when the individual claims a right of property through *a-priori* laws of reason, he is acting from principles which he gives to himself and he is acting in accordance with the fundamental form of individual moral freedom or in a word, autonomously.

In the formation of civil society men subscribe to universal principles through a social contract, by means of a universalized form of self legislation. A will which can bind everyone, he says, must express itself in a proposal which is capable of universal acceptance whose usual embodiment is a social contract.[2] Justice in civil society is founded on a just constitution, one in which we enjoy freedom under external laws, which is itself simply the contractual expression of universal will, i.e., a covenant which is capable of universal acceptance.[3] In so far as the move towards civil society was engendered by the purpose of transforming provisionally acquired possession to the status of de jure possession, interference with private property would seem to deny the expression of the autonomy of the individual in his practical social affairs, at least in so far it undermines the understanding of the social contract.

Property rights, therefore, find their moral basis in an expression of individual freedom of contract, in this case, a general social contract. In this context, whether one speaks of a general social contract or a specific contract of exchange, one locates moral value in the freedom of the will and it follows that this value is what the social mechanism ought to protect, that is, the freedom to enter into contractual relations. Though Kant does not say it explicitly, Kantian analysis strongly implies that the importance of the property right lies in the protection of the freedom of contract. This, I will argue, is a proto-libertarian position.

Hegel and the Moral Basis of Property Rights

In general the political philosophy of the Kantians closely associates the legitimate origins of our social structures with matters of individual autonomy and self determination. Furthermore, as civil society and its social institutions devolve from a form of individual freedom, which is indeed independent from social existence, it follows that these societal structures must not constrain this asocial form of freedom with implications for a minimal state and minimal state interference. However, this is one interpretation of freedom and it seems to dictate the modern libertarian result. It was not the only interpretation and a rival emerges to challenge it at the closing of the Enlightenment. It was Hegel's understanding that liberty as perfect independence from social arrangements and natural phenomena was an illusion; in the modern existential sense of the term man was thrown into a hostile world confronted by a natural environment and often encountered social structures which were antithetical to a sense of individual sovereignty and freedom. Man could not realize his freedom and sovereignty in this sphere by holding himself distinct from this reality in so far as he must necessarily act to realize himself in this context. In a word, the subject and object distinction was a chimera, that is, human individuals could never be entirely independent of the natural and social world, since men and women had to involve themselves in the social and natural order just to survive and maintain existence. If man is to be really free, Hegel believed, he must first overcome and transform this external environment so that it no longer confronts one as an overpowering alien otherness.

In the *Philosophy of Right* the moral function of ownership rights in the realization of the autonomous moral personality is discussed extensively. Like Kant, Hegel was no less occupied with the Enlightenment concerns of freedom and moral agency. However, for Hegel, freedom of the individual will was not a given, i.e., an immanent enduring quality of our essential or noumenal self. In contrast, Hegel saw individual freedom as an on going project to be realized though engagement with the countervailing forces of the external world.

Though the individual will exists as a particularity, its content consisting of determinate aims, it "...has this content, at the same time as an external world directly confronting it."[4] For Hegel the free will was the self actualized will, which had overcome this alienation and realized and continued to realize itself in the face of the confronting, often hostile external reality. This project essentially embodied the human condition, at once an ontological and epistemic issue, but also finally the basis for Hegel's moral and political thought. With respect to the latter aspect, Allen W. Wood has recently emphasized the enduring interest of the "self actualization" theory which grounds Hegel's normative positions.[5] In this account, actions have ethical value not because they are instrumental to some independent good but because acting through forms of freedom gives reality to the individual's conception of itself as free.[6]

Furthermore, Hegel in his treatment of the higher levels of ethical life, regards concrete cultural and institutional structures as having very significant moral import. In contrast, Kantian ethics, couched as deontological formulations, elide actuality, states of affairs, or cultural contexts and, thus, the specific institutions of societal and cultural experience are not regarded as determinants of moral behaviour.[7] For this reason there is a distinct bifurcation within Kantian moral theory which renders a distinct individual morality and a distinct political morality or morality of the polity. The relation between the two remained for Kant partially inchoate. In contrast, Hegel recognizes that self actualization of the will occurs through specific and determinate cultural institutions, which themselves must be evaluated according to their role in the facilitation of individual self actualization. Hegelian self actualization theory is thereby a more complete axiology. Accordingly, Hegelian ethics moves naturally beyond the central principles of moral behaviour to an evaluatory consideration of specific social institutions like the family, property, contractual arrangements, conveyance, civil society and the state etc.

In founding the ethical in the self realization of the human personality, Hegel states explicitly why property and specifically personal property is a moral requirement of civilized existence. Self realization entails a personality which realizes or puts into effect its ideas and he tells us that "Since my will...becomes objective to me in property, property acquires the character of private property."[8] The connection between personal property and the will is such that personal property is a necessary *relatum*, if the individual self is to establish its objectification and thereby its self realization. Hegel states: "A person has as his substantive end the right of putting his will into any and everything and thereby making it his, because it has no such end in itself and derives its destiny and soul from his will."[9]   In other words, the *modus operandi* of self expression is through the personal holding, the means by which one shapes and molds the external environment.

On the matter of exchange and transfer Hegel's reasoning is somewhat different from that of Kant.   Hegel associates the idea of property with a free act of the will and theorizes that as property is acquired by free acts of the will it follows that property is divested, bequeathed or transferred by free acts of the will. He states: "The reason I can alienate my property is that it is mine only in so far as I put my will into it. Hence I may abandon (*derelinquere*) as a *res nullius* anything that I have, or yield it to the will of another..."[10]   Hegel also makes liberty or freedom central to his derivation of private property, however, it is significant that he derives this right from the prior exercise of the right to acquire property through willful control.[11] He states categorically that the right to possess property naturally entails the right to alienate property by "gift, exchange or trade."   Hegel explains explicitly that human personality and agency, in the fullest sense of these terms, entail the recognition of a property right which is inclusive of the right to enter into contractual relations. He affirms that if one denies another the right of contract, *de facto*, this constitutes a failure to recognize an individual as a person.[12]

Kantian and Hegelian Conceptions of Liberty and Distributive Justice

The two positions actually have quite different social implications. The social prescriptions which one could derive from the Kantian theory are easily shaped to support minimal governing arrangement, if, as I will point out, the individual must, as far as possible, remain unimpaired in his capacity to enter into or effect contractual obligations. On the other hand, Hegelian theory would countenance quite different prescriptions, since the Hegelian concept of freedom focuses upon the necessary relation between the subject and its object. Freedom is realized, not through independence from the external phenomenal reality, but rather through establishing relations with the phenomenal. Consequently, it is through these relations that the other becomes transformed by means of my activities such that the subject object relation is partially overcome in that the external object now becomes my property. Here, of course, differing conceptions of distributive justice begin to intrude. Since in Hegel's view, progression towards individual freedom and self actualization cannot proceed without some form of property in order to realize a relation of domination over the external world, it follows that if freedom and real self actualization are the primary values to promote, one must ensure that social conditions do not deny accessibility to the natural resources which allow one to effect meaningful acquisition of personal property. Consequently, socio-political arrangements should ideally enhance this possibility, i.e., make some resources available for every one so as to maximize self realizing possibilities. Kantian theory, on the contrary, would deny these conclusions since for Kant, and also for the libertarians generally, liberty is an asocial quality of the personality which is independent of the social context. It, therefore, follows that social relations cannot enhance or undermine this liberty so long as they don't directly interfere with its exercise, which will occur if there is direct interference with the capacity for entering social arrangements and assuming contractual obligations. Thus, if property is unevenly distributed so that some lack what is necessary for effective self realization this is of no great concern since the capacity can only be impaired by direct negation or societal interference.

In Kant's moral theory, the ontological distinction between the moral or noumenal self which is independent of the phenomenal world, means an autonomous self which cannot be touched or impaired by the contingencies of the external phenomenal world. The logical distinction between the noumenal and phenomenal selves also applies analogously within the social context where the freedom which is independent of social contingencies or distributive patterns finds an analogue in the capacity to enter freely contractual arrangements. Within both the spheres of individual morality and that of social affairs, individual autonomy is identified with capacity which is a capacity to hold oneself independent of contingent circumstances, in the former it is the capacity to resist heteronomy, or actions based on the qualities of the objects of the will, in the latter it is the capacity to consent or withhold consent to contractual arrangements.

Though it might appear to be willfully wrongheaded to assert that absence of opportunity should not count against the existence of a given liberty or freedom, or to assert in this case that the unavailability of personal resources does not deny a personal right of contractual relations - even though presently unexercisable - Kantian thinking is certainly in agreement with the logical grammar of the language game of capacities or abilities. As my capacity or ability to ice skate is not denied by the fact that we live in a tropical country in which there is no ice or ice rink, lack of opportunity does not contradict the attribution of capacity. With respect to the latter example, what would negate or deny my ability would have to be a serious injury which made it impossible to exercise this capacity *in any circumstance*. Kantian reasoning on matters of ethics and practical reason with respect to justice in property holdings operates in the same way. My capacity to trade and exchange holdings is not impaired by the fact that circumstances dictate that there are currently no resources available to allow exercise of this right. In a very convincing sense we can say that this capacity can only be undermined or denied in the circumstance in which society itself does not recognize this right as in many forms of tenure in the feudal system or where all holdings are merely usufructs, i.e., where the exercise of this right would simply be impossible, unrecognized or a fundamental legal nullity.

This brings us to the connected opposition between a social arrangement which might enhance distributive opportunities and the Kantian ideal of individual autonomy with respect to contractual relations. Here one finds that the logic of the Kantian theory can be used to resist any imposed socialist, welfarist or even Keynesian program. According to what has been said, individual autonomy is guaranteed so long as society fully recognizes the right to transfer, grant or exchange holdings, regardless of other social contingencies, hence any restriction whatever on that right will result in the diminution of individual freedom. This formula, of necessity, has an effect that militates against any plan which proposes the redistribution of holdings, resources or property to effect more equitable social conditions. Any such program will perforce operate against the individual's autonomy in so far as enforced redistribution will have to cancel the free choices previously realized in the exercise of contractual relations, and furthermore, strait jacket future choices so that the right of contract is severely constrained. For this reason, the proposal that the distribution of holdings describe a pattern which affords to each individual enhanced access to certain minimal levels of resources or social goods is an anathema to the logic of Kantian and neo-Kantian (libertarian) thought, essentially because such thinking denies the very foundation on which the property right exists, i.e., moral autonomy, as embodied in freedom of contract and exchange.

However, it is important to keep in mind that I am not relating this as Kant's actual position on taxation, rather I am asserting that it follows from the logic of Kant's premises, for as we know Kant himself supported taxation of the wealthy. However, what Kant and Libertarians resist is coercion and imposition, for the right to tax must flow from reasoned consent through the social contract. Even Nozick will accept taxation if it is agreed to by all members of a given society.

From the Kantian and the Hegelian sources two different systems of distributive justice emerge. The Hegelian promotes a liberal welfarist system in which the individual is guaranteed a minimum access to resources/social goods, usually through redistributive schemes based on taxation of the better off members of society. Freedom of contract is guaranteed but somewhat impaired by the fact that individuals are denied the full capacity to dispose of their holdings because some of it is forcibly transferred from them through taxation.

Putting matters in perspective, Kant and Hegel offer us two versions of what has been called the "romantic" argument for private ownership by which is meant a moral argument based on the liberty of the individual. The Kantian version stresses the liberties of exchange and transfer and requires protection of private ownership in order to sustain and maintain these liberties. On the other hand, the Hegelian notion safeguards a fundamental liberty of control and domination with respect to the natural environment. In other words, the individual personality cannot overcome and realize his freedom vis-a-vis the natural environment unless afforded the dominant forms of control realized in the private property right.

As we have seen, the difference of emphasis, in terms of the distinct aspects of personal freedom, leads to different implications concerning distribution and even the understanding of the property right itself. The Hegelian notion, closely associated with positive freedom, strongly implies a fundamental claim or benefit right to some share of society's social goods, over which the individual should have exclusive sovereignty inclusive of the right to exchange the holding. Within this tradition, for example, one can locate the recent work of Jeremy Waldron who argues that if we do have a general right to liberty, which founds our right to property, then this implies a demand that everyone should actually have an appreciable amount of property. He states, "Freedom requires private property, and freedom for all requires private property for all. Nothing less will do."[13] This type of general right we have previously defined as an inclusive right - a right to be included in the distribution of society's social goods. The Kantian foundation, however, centred on a more abstract and general right to non-interference in one's personal affairs (or negative freedom) means that the fundamental right to be protected is not a general claim right to society's social goods, but rather the liberty right to acquire and exchange holdings through some fundamental freedom of contract, and to do so without interference. In this sense the property right which is guaranteed is an exclusive right because it fundamentally emphasizes a right to exclusive control which means a right to exclude others from dealing with one's holding or gaining access.

This attitude, which sees any scheme to redistribute wealth as interference with personal liberty and the essential nature of property rights, is strongly championed by modern libertarians. Accordingly, the Kantian theory can be used to support free trade and Laissez Faire polices with minimal or no taxation or even support extreme libertarian policy which regards forcible taxation as a form of slavery or at least the fundamental denial of freedom and moral agency.

Libertarian Theory and its Kantian Links

This interpretation of Kant's position accords closely with the contemporary libertarian attitude towards private property. Recently Tibor Machan has emphasized "negative freedom" as an expressly normative notion or a social condition that members of the community ought to maintain out of respect for human dignity - each person's responsibility to choose to live rightly.[14] Likewise, Jan Narveson in *The Libertarian Idea* tells us that "...a pervasive right to liberty is fundamentally negative, not positive," and further emphasizes the exclusive priority of negative liberty stating that"...we are therefore repudiating any such (*positive*) right as a fundamental right."[15]

In the same paper Machan conflates negative freedom and autonomy in his approval of F.A. Hayek's remark that freedom is "..always the possibility of a person acting according to his own decision and plans, in contrast to one who is irrevocably subject to the will of another..."[16] On this understanding, negative freedom is seen to offer a protected space of autonomous operations, which is immune to interference, as opposed to positive freedom which requires that resources necessary to the performance of certain actions be accessible.

For the libertarian, therefore, property rights then enter the picture through freedoms of trade and exchange which are linked with freedom of choice. Choice and moral decision making cannot proceed without the possibilities of trade and exchange which would have no reality without private property, he claims. Machan states that negative liberty finds its essential connection to exchange and free trade which is "...logically dependent on (respect for) the principle of the right to property. One cannot get authoritative forms of trade if one doesn't own anything."[17] Similarly, Narveson has stated, "Defense of the free market is clearly prominent on the libertarian agenda. In a sense it is the only thing on the agenda".[18] The moral ground of the private property right is therefore associated with the fundamental exclusivity of contractual relations, and the private right must be only an exclusive right which precludes interference from third parties.

What libertarians, therefore, conceive as liberty is an area of autonomy in which individuals exercise control without social interference, unless through their own permission. Within this sphere fall rights of trade, exchange and contract which demand private property for their existence. This is an interpretation of freedom which sees liberty as equivalent to negative freedom protected by "negative rights" or as we have said "exclusive rights".

Thus, we can see links between the Kantian theory and the modern libertarian position. Nevertheless, there are two important differences which ought to be mentioned. The first is the Kantian attitude towards taxation and the second is the precise link between Kantian theory and moral source of property rights. With respect to taxation Kant tells us in *The Metaphysical Elements of Justice*, that the state is empowered to tax and raise money to contribute to welfare, or as he explains "...in order to support those members of society who are not able to support themselves."[19] Furthermore, Kant reasons that the wealthy are bound to contribute to the support of their fellow citizens because of the protection they receive from the commonwealth.[20] If, as I have argued, Kant really bases his defense of private property rights on some fundamental right to enter contractual relations, why would he countenance state interference through taxation which in some sense denies individual freedom of contract. I think what one needs to appreciate is that Kant sees property relations established through contract, as when provisional holdings become de jure holdings, which occurs when the social contract is realized with the creation of civil society. In this act he sees the realization of an exchange relationship as the more wealthy members of society agree to offer some form of support for their less wealthy citizens in exchange for protection. This indicates an important but not decisive difference between Kantian thought and modern libertarians like Nozick.

This, however, is not to deny the fundamental affinity between the Kantian and the modern libertarian position. First of all, both positions derive the moral importance of property relations from a fundamental notion of human liberty. Both regard individuals as fundamentally free bargaining personalities who acquire rights including property rights through contract and grant. For both, private property must be upheld in order to maintain the inviolability of these exchanges and covenants which are the expression of human liberty. Though Kant saw civil society created through a social contract, Nozick himself preferred to see civil society evolving through voluntarism, or numerous individual contracts, rather than the emergent product of a general contractual agreement - but this is a minor squabble within the contractarian faith. Despite this difference, one sees that within both the libertarian and the Kantian social orders, rights of property are acquired and divested through contractual relations which are freely entered into, whether it is through a general social contract or a series of individual contracts. Within this system of free exchange and transfer, individual property is fundamentally intrinsic and therefore must be inviolable.

In the last chapter I will argue that both notions of the property right lead to the exploitative attitudes to the natural environment. The Hegelian directly in that natural resources are viewed as having no value in themselves apart from the meaning given to them through the control and domination by a human personality. Hegel says this directly. The Kantian on the other hand, fosters the idea of an unregulated free market in which exchange of services and resources is fundamentally unfettered. However, we will take a final look at the environmental implications of both these moral positions in the last chapter.

Before moving on to this final issue, I will argue in the next chapter that the liberal belief in the reality of individual rather than collective entitlement hinges upon an interpretation of the "self" which implausibly prescinds our empirical identity, the characteristics and qualities which we all inherit as members of a given community. In concert with this topic, I would like to complete this chapter by pointing out a fundamental contradiction which lies at the heart of modern libertarian moral theory. This contradiction is intimately connected with the discussion in the next chapter in so far as I argue that though libertarian positions seem to depend upon a Kantian analysis of the "self", the libertarian description of the "self" and its autonomous needs goes beyond the Kantian "thin" interpretation of the human subject, and thereby implies something quite different with respect to the concerns of distributive justice.

As we have pointed out, the modern libertarian traces his/her origins back to Kant and more or less tells us that a right of free transfer is guaranteed by the third formulation of the categorical imperative, i.e., treat people as an end and never merely as a means. What lies at the heart of this difference between libertarians and Kantians is a different understanding of human autonomy.   Though the rights of property which both libertarians and Kantians believe important are those associated with transfer, contract, and conveyance, derivative from a fundamental form of autonomy supposedly independent of the social context, their understandings of this human autonomy are, in fact, quite different.   For Kant, autonomy meant an ability of the will to self determine itself by universal laws which are independent of individual preference and even reference to my individual existence.   This is why the Kantian understanding of autonomy has nothing to do with appreciating the importance of individual existence or personal preference, and therefore property and freedom of contract have little to do with the separate distinctness of my individual existence.   It is certainly significant that Emile Durkheim writing in defense of Dreyfus in the last century used Kantian ethics as a basis for the argument that proper exercise of autonomy does not lead to selfish individualism but in fact binds one to the larger community - the universal.[21] The libertarian, on the other hand, closely identifies autonomy with the value of an individual existence in which pursuit of personal preference without interference is to be protected through personal property. Nozick tells us, for example in *Anarchy, State, and Utopia* that to violate a person's property right is to use the individual as end rather than a means and to do so is to fail to "sufficiently respect and take account of the fact that he is a separate person."[22]

Libertarian Notions of Autonomy and Hegelian Antecedents

The question then arises, what form of autonomy, if not Kantian, does the Libertarian embrace which allows him to say that denial of property rights must result in denial of individual personality? The notion of autonomy, which the libertarian entertains, is much closer to the Hegelian than the Kantian. The divergence becomes most perspicuous if we enquire into the nature of the "self" which is the subject of this autonomous behaviour.

Here we discover that the libertarian analysis of the "self" begins to shade into something resembling the Hegelian approach. It is well to begin with Robert Nozick's explanation as to why private property is essential to a meaningful (autonomous) life.

I conjecture the answer is connected with the elusive and difficult notion: the meaning of life. A person shaping his life in accordance with some overall plan is his way of giving meaning to life; only a being with a capacity to so shape his life can have or strive for meaningful life. This notion, we should note has the right "feel" as something that might help to bridge an "is ought" gap; it appropriately seems to straddle the two.[23]

From the above it is clear that Nozick is not enshrining what has sometimes been referred to as "moral autonomy" - autonomy as guided by universal moral law, as we have intimated - but rather autonomy as "self realization" which entails the characteristic of a consciously deliberated project containing the continuity of a life history.[24] This is extremely apposite for one sees that the libertarian notion of autonomy is indeed more proximate with the self actualization ethic of Hegel: and thereby libertarian notions of autonomy and personality may imply Hegelian rather than Kantian positions, especially with respect to distributive justice.

To begin, the libertarian notion of autonomy entails relating different events (acts) as the expression of some idea or intellectual planning, and thereby, libertarian and Hegelian notions of autonomy concur in seeing a temporal development entailing an actualized "self" with no ontic significance independent of this temporality. In Nozick's second major work, the *Philosophical Explanations* he explains that the self is not a fixed and enduring "thing", which is separate from its disparate and changing elements, the self is that which creates itself in this multitude of self synthesizing acts.[25] This marks the most significant distancing of the Kantian and libertarian understandings. While Kantian autonomy looks to an essential quality of noumenal self which is ontically independent of the temporal empirical or phenomenal inclusive of the distinct social context - the arena in which our acts become phenomenal and socially meaningful events - the libertarian sees the autonomous self as a construction of and indeed identical with the sequence of phenomenal/social events (acts) which are intelligible as a specific life plan. It follows, therefore, from Nozick's analysis that there is no definable self with an essential attribute of freedom which precedes (chronologically or ontologically) social relations and affairs and which, therefore, stands to be imposed upon by the existence of these relations.

But if there is no ontic meaning independent of a certain sequence of (social) events, to what do we ascribe the attribute of autonomy. Well first of all, for Hegel and Nozick, freedom or personal autonomy is something we connect with a unified sequence of events and not to a particular "thing", which stands outside and independent of the sequence. It follows thereby that the attribution of autonomy is synonymous with realization of autonomy and is distinct from the mere abstracted capacity for autonomy. According to both Nozick and Hegel, it is unlikely that the individual remains an autonomous agent despite the fact that he never exercises this capacity (that is, formulates a life plan and proceeds to shape his behaviour to fulfill that plan) essentially because actions (phenomenal events) define the autonomous self and also the heteronomous self. For example, if the individual never bothered to shape his life through reference to some overall plan we could not accurately say that this person is an autonomous agent despite his/her failure to exercise this capacity. With Kant it is otherwise, for it is possible to say that an individual possesses an enduring quality of autonomy as part of his noumenal self, as distinct from his empirical social self, even if he never bothers to exercise this capacity, that is, where all his/her choices are unredeemably heteronomous.

This brings us to a final point which is that both libertarians and Hegelians have also inherited a notion of individual freedom which shares elements which have a close affinity with the romantic vision of Rousseau. According to this notion, the realization of freedom or autonomy entails the exploration and discovery of ones true identity. According to Nozick, for example, personal identity and selfhood are not givens, one must first formulate a personal plan which is appropriate to oneself and then strive to organize one's life and realize that plan in a worldly, necessarily, temporal context. Hegel similarly believes that existence is a matter of self discovery in which personal autonomy is not realized until one has won through to a true understanding of oneself through application of one's own ideas through engagement with and experience of the world. In contrast, Kant believed that personal autonomy was a given, an ontological aspect of the dualistic self which on reflection was universally apparent to any rational person who acknowledged the moral law. Thus on the modern libertarian analysis there is a strong suggestion that selfhood may be denied non-autonomous agents or those whose exercise of liberty is merely heteronomous.

What I believe becomes apparent, from all of the above points with respect to the distinctness of libertarian and Kantian approaches to autonomy, is that it is much more difficult on the libertarian view to maintain autonomy and personal liberty as a-social capacities of the will which are protected so long as there is no direct interference with its operations: 1) because there is no self which precedes social relations and stands to be imposed upon; 2) because the autonomous or free self actualizing individual is not something distinct from the empirical events (acts) which so define it; 3) selfhood is something we achieve through a process of self creation, it does not exist *ab initio*.

Well one might finally ask, does all this mean that libertarian and Hegelian positions are equivalent?   Well hardly, the fundamental difference between Hegel and a libertarian is to be located at the terminus of this discovery; for Hegel, the point of final discovery in our quest for true identity is to bring us back to the universal or the recognition of Universal Spirit, whereas for the libertarian the final terminus in the exercise is the identification of our unique separate identity.

But the significance of the preceding comparison is apposite with respect to concerns of distributive justice. Ultimately one is led to reconsider the relation between property and autonomy so defined. If personality cannot be achieved without personal property because personal autonomy is not a given a la Kant, but realities which develop and exist over time, then there is a strong implication that resources should be distributed so that everyone has the opportunity to achieve self-actualized selfhood. The Kantian can more easily maintain that negative freedom is sufficient, that is liberty and autonomy are sufficiently intact so long as their is no direct interference with their operation, because by definition, the individual self is complete and free *ab initio*, with a fundamental form of freedom which is independent of social relations. Theoretically then, social relations can only restrict and fetter a "self" which is so defined.

But according to the actual libertarian, non-Kantian understanding of autonomy, there is no "self" independent of the process of the creation of identity over time (inclusive of autonomous identity). Therefore, we cannot even state that there necessarily exists some human "self" separable from social contingencies and social events with the quality of freedom which endures so long as the pre-social self is not interfered with by social restrictions. On reflection it is now apparent that since the "self" is not actual (self actual) prior to the implementation of its life plan, something more than non-interference is required if this autonomous self is to be a reality. Not only do we need negative liberty, freedom from interference, we also need positive freedom, that is the guarantee of resources available to implement our plans.

This is readily demonstratable if we reconsider the actual "thick" rather than "thin" view of the self which follows from the notion of autonomy as "self realization". Where one speaks of this "thick self", the self which is the product of the social acts which gain their meaning from a particular societal context, rather than the self as abstracted from any social context or particular empirical identity, the role of transfer and exchange in the protection and nurturing of autonomous agency alters profoundly. Only so long as one maintains the "thin" view of self, the autonomous "self" independent of empirical social conditions, is it sufficient to say that individual liberty is protected so long as capacity to trade and exchange is protected regardless of whether these social events take place. But once we agree that autonomy is a quality of the empirical social self rather that the ideal pre-social, non-empirical self, then it is necessary to ask ourselves what conditions would be necessary to make this empirical social event a reality, since like any empirical event, it is meaningful to enquire into the conditions (necessary and sufficient) which bring a given state of affairs into existence. This is not the case with Kant's dualistic doctrine of self in which an independent non-empirical noumenal self is assumed in order to solve the antinomy arising between free will and determinism - it is a "self" which is presupposed as an ontological construct to make sense of empirical experience, though not part of that experience. Thus, we can't ask the same questions of Kant's "autonomous noumenal self", but of the empirical self of the libertarians we can certainly enquire into the necessary conditions to bring about an empirical state of affairs.

Following this line of thought we can reasonably say that two things now become necessary to achieve this social reality which we call an autonomous self: first of all, minimal (and not absolute) interference in the trade and exchange undertakings; two, the actual possession of a minimum of resources or holdings to trade and exchange.

From the actual libertarian understanding of "self" it now follows, perforce, that the exercise of conveyance or transfer of holdings through contractual relations (and not merely the capacity for such) is a necessary condition in the temporal creation of personal identity, and thereby denial of access to minimum social goods, whether we call these primary goods or social resources, necessarily implies the wrongful denial of the possibilities of autonomous personality. Furthermore, no freedom is restricted in the implementation of these welfarist social schemes because there is no pre-social, non-empirical self to suffer imposition. In conclusion, we can say that if in fact government is committed to achieving a liberal universe where as Jack Crittenden says, "Each person has his own goals and interests and enters into contractual relationships to pursue and achieve these goals and interests,"[26] then a minimalist government would still have to subscribe to something which Jeremy Waldron has described as a general right to property. As he has stated, "Freedom requires private property, and freedom for all requires private property for all. Nothing less will do."[27]

---

[1] Immanuel Kant, *The Metaphysical Elements of Justice*, trans. J. Ladd (New York: Bobbs-Merrill, 1965 [1797]), 56.

[2] Immanuel Kant, *Kant's Political Writings*, ed. H. Reiss, trans. H.B. Nisbet (Cambridge: Cambridge University Press, 1970), 45-46.

[3] Ibid.

[4] G.W.F. Hegel, *The Philosophy of Right*, trans. T.M. Knox (Chicago: Encyclopaedia Britannica, 1952), 21.

[5] Allen W. Wood, *Hegel's Ethical Thought* (New York: Cambridge University Press, 1990).

[6] Ibid., 21.

[7] Charles Taylor, *Hegel*, (Cambridge: Cambridge University Press, 1975), 370, offers an excellent discussion of the formal nature of Kantian ethics. .

[8] G.W.H. Hegel, *The Philosophy of Right*, 23.

[9] Ibid.

[10] Ibid., 29.

[11] Ibid., 29-31.

[12] Ibid., 31.

[13] Jeremy Waldron, *The Right to Private Property* (Oxford: Clarendon Press, 1988), 412.

[14] Tibor Machan, "The Virtue of Freedom in Capitalism," *Journal of Applied Philosophy* 3 (1988): 49-59, 49.

[15] Jan Narveson, *The Libertarian Idea* (Philadelphia: Temple University Press, 1988), 100.

[16] Ibid., 49.

[17] Ibid., 52.

[18] Ibid., 187.

[19] Kant, *Metaphysical Elements of Justice*, 93.

[20] Ibid.

[21] Emile Durkheim, "Individualism and Intellectuals" in *Emile Durkheim: On Morality and Society*, ed. R. Bellah, (Chicago: Chicago University Press, 1973); Also see M.S. Chadis, *A Communitarian Defense of Liberalism: Emile Durkheim and Contemporary Social Theory* (Stanford: Stanford University Press, 1992)

[22] Nozick, *Anarchy, State, and Utopia*, 33.

[23] Ibid., 50.

[24] Cf., Maeve Cooke, "Habermas, Autonomy and the Identity of Self," *Philosophy and Social Criticism* 18 (1992): 269-291, who utilizes these terms and concepts in a discussion of Habermas and argues that the latter notion is implicit in the writings of Habermas even though he is most commonly associated with the former specifically Kantian notion.

[25] Nozick, *Philosophical Explanations* (Cambridge: Belnap Press of Harvard University Press, 1981), 88-91.

[26] Jack Crittenden, *Beyond Liberalism· Reconstituting the Liberal Self* (Oxford: Oxford University Press, 1992).

[27] Jeremy Waldron, *The Right to Private Property* (Oxford: Clarendon Press, 1988), 412.

Chapter 8

Individual Acquisition And Its Moral Justification

In the last chapter we saw that different views of autonomy imply different understandings of the private property right with different implications for the distribution of holdings. With respect to the Kantian interpretation, which we closely associated with the libertarian, we are talking about negative freedom - rights to be left alone or to be free of interference (though, of course, we indicated certain important inconsistencies within this position). In the other instance, the Hegelian, we come closer to an emphasis on positive freedom and positive rights which can describe a claim to a share of social resources. Both these positions, nevertheless, could be characterized as liberal positions in so far as each recognizes a concern for the liberty of the individual and regards formulated social structure and the institutions of private property as grounded in this central value. In a sense, these two position indicate the limits of the spectrum of debate in which liberal thought argues and deliberates. One position describes the preference for an unregulated market economy in which trade and exchange are essentially unfettered; the other describes a system of private holdings within which government will from time to time intervene so as to ensure that the least advantaged receive some acceptable minimum share of society's resources. During the recent period of political philosophy, the former position has received its most noteworthy endorsement in the work of Robert Nozick, while the latter position is most often associated with the work of John Rawls.[1]

In the last chapter we adumbrated some of the problems and difficulties which one meets when one considers the notion of autonomy and its possible interpretations and implications with respect to the private holding of resources. There is at this point, therefore, no further reason to explore the issue to effect some conclusive statement as to what autonomy really implies or demands. From the last chapter, there should be no doubt as to my views on this matter. However, if we leave aside this issue for the moment we might contemplate what is considered a subsidiary or ancillary issue that of personal or individual "desert".

Individual Desert and the Communal Self

The issue of desert is enlightening because, in fact, it reveals the central problematic in the belief that ownership is primarily private and individual. To this point we have offered a fairly extensive discussion of the liberal attitude which regards the institution of private ownership as necessary to maintain the personal liberty or autonomy of the individual. It must be recognized, however, that this is simply an argument for the institution of private property *per se*, there yet remains the issue of acquisition, its procedures, methods and moral justification. There are, therefore two issues which need to be considered when we seek to establish that property is essentially personal and individual; the first involves the moral justification of the institution itself; the second involves the moral justification of the particular relation which establishes some particular bundle of rights and their objects (*res*) as belonging uniquely to myself. It is with respect to the latter issue that private ownership receives its strongest moral challenge. In other words, it is fine to say that private property must exist in order that trade and exchange may flourish thereby allowing individuals to control their own lives and destinies, but what principles justify the particular bundle of goods and resources which each controls? Usually the argument is made that I am entitled to a particular set of holdings because of a relationship of desert which has been antecedently established through my actions. John Rawls writing in *A Theory of Justice* argued that there is and can be no moral justification for what each has acquired through avenues of fortune, market mechanisms and procedures of exchange.

Earlier this century libertarians and economists aligned with the Austrian school of economics attempted to argue that each of us is entitled to the particular sum of goods and resources we control because this sum is directly proportion to our contribution through our market activities. For example, Frank Knight and F.A. Hayek argued that market mechanisms, if not interfered with, will reward the individual according to his productive contribution, thus generating an actual just distribution.[2]   Rawls, however, disagreed and argued that justice or fairness is not at all captured by an argument based on personal merit or desert, simply because there is no antecedent foundation of desert or merit to justify the capacities, talents and traits which have enabled me to make a certain productive contribution in the market economy.[3] That I am blessed with a sharp mind, a particular business sense, a cultural tradition of hard work and enterprise, have nothing to do with my personal desert or merit but rather are the spoils allotted in the random operations of fate; these traits are all mere contingencies and accidents, and justice by any name must go beyond accident and contingency to establish principles of fairness. For example, It is always possible that one could be born poor and disadvantaged with no particular inclination for work or self-initiative and congenitally unable to make any productive contribution. On the basis of this argument Rawls arrives at his now famous "difference principle", which states that since I do not deserve and thereby rightfully possess the particular share of talents, traits and material resources which have fallen into my hands, any unequal pattern or any pattern of distribution can only be justified in so far as it is seen to provide the maximum benefits for the least advantaged class. In other words, since individual desert is an illusion as far as justice is concerned, a given distribution can only satisfy justice if it benefits society as a whole. To put the matter another way, an unequal distribution can only be supported if it is seen to provide maximum benefit to the least advantaged, that is to say, fulfill the conditions of the "difference" principle, which allows that an upper echelon elite may flourish and claim an unequal distribution but only if this state of affairs brings maximum benefits to an under class, in terms of benefits which they would not receive otherwise if matters were arranged differently.

In this demonstration of the difference principle, Rawls implicitly proposes that individual assets are indeed common assets, and therefore, their given devolution can only be justified if it benefits the common good. Rawls' book, *A Theory of Justice*, which was published in 1971 finds its response in Robert Nozick's *Anarchy, State and Utopia*, which was published in 1974. Nozick aligned himself with the libertarians and riposted that Rawls' argument may demonstrate that individuals do not possess or deserve their assets, but this does not necessarily show that society as a whole does possess or deserve them.[4] On Nozick's view Rawls' undermining of the concept of "desert" merely results in an unhappy state in which holdings appear to be ownerless. Given these difficulties with the concept and calculation of "desert", Nozick proposed that we reject "desert" as a basis for entitlement altogether and utilize the simpler concept of "legitimate entitlement". Unfortunately, from the reader's point of view, this discussion proves to be less than satisfactory because *inter alia*, he fails to articulate unequivocally the conditions which underlie legitimate entitlement through original acquisition (though of course he proves to be more definite as to what satisfies the demands of acquisition through transfer, i.e., the voluntary nature of the transfer), and in any case, the concept of legitimate entitlement itself does not provide an underlying ground of moral justification which could be used to support this rather thin juristic notion, since after all we are not looking for juristic clarity but rather moral foundation.

However, an interesting addendum to this somewhat unsatisfactory debate is to found in Michael Sandel's communitarian critique of Rawlsian liberalism, *Liberalism and the Limits of Justice*, written in the 1980s.[5] In this work Sandel argued that Rawls' difference principle belies a commitment which moves away from the liberal dogma which enshrines the priority of the individual self which legitimates social organization through its choices and individual interests, towards communitarian values which assert the overwhelming importance and priority of the community. Sandel argues that Nozick's argument is quite prescient and indicates the weakness of Rawls' position, but he states, if Rawls wishes to reach his preferred conclusion: that a distribution must benefit society as a whole and, *a fortiori*, the least advantaged group, then he need only drop the liberal embrace of unattached, non-engaged autonomous individuality and admit what is really the case, that individuals are situate within communities from which they acquire their identities. Once we make this move one can more easily make a case for the community as the subject and possessor of the individual assets.

Sandel argues for this somewhat along the following lines: the community, he claims, is not just what fellow citizens have but what they are, not a relationship they choose but an attachment they discover, not as attribute but a constituent of their identity.[6] Thus, it must follow that as our identity depends upon our attached relationships in the community, the assets and traits associated with me personally, and which I cannot claim entitlement to by desert, must become the property of the community since as the distinct separateness of individuals is broken down by their wider attachment to the community, so too, the ownership of traits and possessions must also pass or devolve to the community which now appears to be prior to and constitutive of the individual's identity.

In expanding on this view, Sandel sees three possibilities as to the relation between the individual and his endowments (and by extension the holdings he has gained by means of his endowments):

1. I own them absolutely, i.e., I have certain privileged claims with respect to them - a bundle of rights while not unlimited yet at least more extensive with respect to my assets than any bundle of rights that any one else may possess with respect to them.

2. I am the guardian of these rights (endowments) which denies individual ownership in favour of a more ultimate owner or subject of possession of which the individual owner is the agent. This is the notion of ownership reminiscent of the early Christian notion of property in which man had what he had as guardian of assets belonging truly to God, (which we discussed extensively in the fifth chapter), and it is a notion which fits with the communitarian notion and certainly accords with the Melanesian view of property relations. Here Sandel quotes Vernan Bartlet who says that property rights are relative not only with respect to God but also compared with the derivative rights of society as representing the common weal.[7] There is therefore a stewardship of property on behalf of both God and society which means that assets are owned by someone else (God, Society) on whose behalf I exercise these rights (trusteeship).

3. I am simply a repository of assets and attributes accidently located in my person. This interpretation does not presuppose any subject of possession whose endowment they ultimately are, i.e. nobody owns them.

Nozick claims that Rawls' difference principle only proves the third possibility, that all assets and attributes are fundamentally ownerless. But, argues Sandel, this unhappy state of affairs only persists so long as I see an opposition between the individual subject and the wider community, such that the individual is indeed separable and independent from the latter. What needs to be rejected is this Kantian inheritance which has given us the so called thin view of self, which sees the individual subject as an unattached pre-social self which is independent of social relations. By recognizing the communal nature of self, claims Sandel, Rawls can escape the obvious inconsistencies in his own work in which he maintains: 1) that social political institutions can only be justified in so far as they protect the absolute freedom of choice of this unengaged pre-social self; 2) while implicitly alleging that all endowments and holdings are communal and therefore should be distributed so as to benefit the least advantaged class. Sandel concludes that if one properly appreciates that the self is attached to the community and has its identity which is bound up with the community rather than detached from the community, then one can assert without inconsistency that one is indeed the guardian for the assets located here,[8] and moreover the guardian for the community of which I count as a member,[9] otherwise there is no basis on which to maintain that a pre-social independent self has any prior responsibility or obligation towards any communal organization or societal construct.

This analysis, accords remarkably with our analysis of the inherent inconsistency in libertarian thought which was adumbrated in the last chapter. Indeed in the last chapter we demonstrated how libertarians themselves mistakenly pledge allegiance to this concept of the unattached pre-social self, when in fact, their understanding of autonomy demonstrates quite a different notion of the autonomous subject, that of self actualized social self. As we argued, the autonomous self which the libertarians enshrine is, in fact not the pre-social non-empirical subject of Kantian thought, but rather the empirical ensemble of social events or acts which are seen as belonging together in a unified history. What becomes evident is that this atomized unattached self-determining moral unit of the enlightenment dissolves into something greater when one attempts to make it do any meaningful work in the justification of liberal (and specifically libertarian) order and social arrangement. Each time we seek to establish some definite social political position, one finds oneself driven to formulate a self with greater social thickness, which is to say that we discover a subject which must be imbedded in a definite social matrix which depends on the support of a particular context to guarantee its identity, and which, therefore, is ineluctably implicated in the social order from which it derives its identity.

But I believe what Sandel fails to underline is that the central notion of autonomy which Rawls employs also entails a significant communitarian position. I think it needs to be pointed out that Rawls actually implicitly employs two distinct notions of autonomy. Sandel alleges that Rawls reinstates a Kantian pre-social self while attempting to avoid the Kantian ontology which divides the human subject into an noumenal intelligible self and an empirical sensuous self.[10] I think Sandel is quite correct in seeing Rawls utilize this pre-social self in what I regard as Rawlsian initial understanding of autonomy. This first notion of autonomy which Rawls employs is encountered in the description of the "original position". Regardless of Rawls' denial of Kantian ontology, the conveyed meaning of autonomy depends upon a depiction of the self which has great affinity with Kant's understanding of the "noumenal self". However, the second notion of autonomy which Rawls utilizes later, and which I will subsequently discuss, has much in common with Hegel's "self actualization" theory of human liberty and this understanding entails communitarian rather than individualistic positions.

In his description of the "original position" Rawls states that, "Among the essential features of this situation is that no one knows his place in society, his class position or social status, nor does anyone know his fortune in the distribution of natural assets and abilities, his intelligence, strength and the like."[11] In explaining this construct Rawls explicitly affirms the affinity with non-social noumenal self of Kantian ethics. "The description of the original position interprets the point of view of noumenal selves, of what it means to be free and equal rational beings."[12]

The "original position" offers us a picture of individual identity which corresponds closely with the Kantian noumenal subject, which is that of a distinct "self" independent of the defining aspects of its own empirical nature. This notion of noumenal identity is crucial to an understanding of Kantian moral autonomy, because this form of autonomy can only be achieved by maintaining the noumenal self independent from the empirical self, the latter being the practical agent which is subject to social considerations and the natural desires and inclinations which derive from one's fundamental sensuous nature[13]. According to Kant, this form of independence is preserved when we act from universal moral principles defined by their very distinctness from other principles of practical reason which have reference to these particular contingent realities of social convention or natural constitution.[14] To this stage Rawls and Kant are apparently in full agreement. Rawls states, "The principles chosen in the original position...would agree with those which Kant characterizes as moral principles in so far as the principles chosen in the original position do not depend upon social or natural contingencies, nor do they reflect the bias of the particulars of plan of life or the aspirations that motivate them."[15] Rawls further affirms the correspondence in his assertion that, "...acting autonomously is acting from principles that we would consent to as free and equal rational beings...", that is, as noumenal selves constrained by universal impersonal principles.[16]

Thus, in the articulation of the original position we encounter a notion of autonomy which is fundamentally Kantian, and which, I believe, Sandel rightly views as entailing a Kantian pre-social noumenal subject, even though Rawls denies the Kantian ontological baggage. However, what Sandel does not mention is that the Kantian and Rawlsian positions begin to diverge sharply when we consider Rawls' discussion of the priority of the "right" over the "good". According to Kantian ethics, acting through universal principles which disregard my personal interests is its own end, in the sense that this form of constraint creates the good will which is the "supreme good", ultimately and intrinsically valuable.[17] In Kantian language, this form of behaviour is an end in itself, and not a means to some further good. But in explaining the relation between constraint by impersonal universal rules and the pursuit of my personal good, Rawls states, "Now we can add that the assumption of mutual disinterest is to allow for the freedom of choice of a system of final ends".[18] In practical terms this means that the invocation of universal principles is socially apposite because it creates the interpersonal reality in which individuals have maximum latitude or freedom to self determine their own lives according to their particular conceptions of the "good". The latter becomes more evident if we consider in more detail his remarks with respect to the social reality generated from the "original position". Rawls states: "In a well ordered society then, the plans of life of individuals are different in the sense that plans give prominence to different aims, and persons are left free to determine their good, the views of others being counted as merely advisory".[19]

It occurs, therefore that autonomy, as constraint by universal rules is not for Rawls an end in itself according to usual Kantian interpretations. From the above remarks it is apparent that this form of behaviour is meaningful because it creates a social order which allows individuals the liberty to pursue their own rational plans and ends without official interference. Rawls sees this possibility as a good, and we may interpolate that acting from universal principles has instrumental value in creating the form of society in which this form of "good" can be realized. As he states, "...this variety in conceptions of the good is itself a good thing, that is, it is rational for members of a well ordered society to want their plans to be different."[20] In Rawls' view the priority of the "right" over he "good" is significant not because self imposed constraints are intrinsically worthwhile or because conceptions of the good are subservient to or less important than self imposed moral acts, but because the latter enhance our social liberty or capacity to pursue our own particular vision of the "good".

This shift in emphasis becomes further apparent if we consider the principles of social arrangement which would be chosen from behind the veil of ignorance in the "original position". In outlining the sort of choices which would be made, Rawls stresses certain primary goods: greater liberty, opportunity, wealth etc. In explaining the significance of these choices he states, "Rational individuals, whatever else they want, desire certain things as prerequisites for carrying out their plans of life. Other things being equal, they prefer wider to a narrower liberty and opportunity and a greater rather than smaller share of wealth and income".[21] It is arguable that Rawlsian socio-political conditions are concerned not so much with Kantian "moral autonomy" - a will guided by universal moral law - but rather a notion of autonomy which refers to a capacity of the individual for rationally pursuing one's chosen life style or what has been sometimes described as "a consciously deliberated life project which contains the continuity of its life history".[22]

Rawls like Nozick actually employs two senses of autonomy. One sense, the Kantian, sees moral autonomy as a matter of maintaining the distinct pre-social "self" independent from the structures of community or environment which constitute its own empirical makeup, while on the other hand, autonomy is regarded as an exercise in "self realization" in the Hegelian tradition. It would seem that Rawls like Nozick, believes that his primary commitment is to the liberty of the individual self which must be free to choose without impeding determinations emanating from the natural or social reality, however the form of autonomy, which forms the central aspect of the system, is more accurately associated with self realization ethic of Hegel and not the moral autonomy of Kantians (a life informed by universal moral principle).[23] Hegelian analysis asserts that this autonomous self cannot be entirely detached or disconnected from the embedded social reality, which is to say that self realization depends upon the existence of relevant social institutions, it does not exist a-priori and independent of these social institutions. The self realization ethic of Hegel in fact reverses the Kantian standpoint and views the autonomous self as one which participates closely within certain cultural traditions and discovers its purposes as coinciding with those of certain community institutions; it does not operate in absolute independence from the determinations of community and its society. For example, at the very least, this autonomous self must be committed to protecting and nurturing liberal institutions associated with individual rights and the freedoms of the market which supposedly found and protect autonomous existence.

Having made these remarks we should now be in a position to appreciate the inherent contradiction in Rawls' remarks which tend to assert that social and political institutions can only be justified in so far as they protect the absolute freedom of choice of the unengaged pre-social self. We have underlined that this freely choosing subject can only operate within certain specific institutions which allow it freedom of expression. It therefore cannot exist anterior to the community and social context within which it acts. Consequently, it is illusory to believe that we can evaluate our social institutions in terms of this supposed pre-social self. The autonomous subject of the Enlightenment, like the Medieval Christian believer, the citizen subject of the Greek Polis, Or the Melanesian, is imbedded and situated within the community and traditions from which it is generated. The autonomous subject is, perforce, the product of our modern liberal culture and a familiar social construction within modern paradigms of behaviour. Autonomous existence is a specific form of life within the Western liberal tradition, it does not exist in some pre-social state which can be described independently of our specific liberal institutions, institutions which support and give meaning to this particular form of life.

In properly understanding the relationship between the individual and the greater community one needs to appreciate, as Sandel has emphasized, that the empirical social self does not merely choose its ends it discovers its ends as part of its communal identity; whether it chooses to or not, every human subject finds itself in a historical and cultural tradition subject to obligations which it cannot choose to ignore without violating the moral framework within which it must operate. In the moral reality which everyone encounters in differing contexts, one enters the world not simply with negative duties, obligations not to interfere, but also importantly with positive duties, obligations to perform certain actions as part of cultural inheritance, and ultimately no one escapes these obligations without moral consequences, not even in the supposed liberal societies where individuals supposedly have ultimate freedom to choose the ends and purposes which will shape one's life.

Again the latter point was demonstrated very adequately in the last chapter. We have seen that the central article of faith among libertarians holds that there exists a transcendental moral blue print for social organization which commands that each individual be left alone and thus free to self actualize his own life plan. But we indicated that the reality of this conception where each individual is actually (and not just theoretically) free to implement her/his life plan requires a social reality in which sufficient resources are available to each person to organize and realize a chosen personal destiny. It is axiological that this free society will only be a reality if that society is committed to making a certain minimum of resources available to every one, which, since a given community is co-extensive with its membership, entails more than negative duties, obligations to refrain from certain behavior, it entails that all the members of that society be prepared to undertake certain actions which will ensure that a minimum is available for everyone. Even in the most absolute of liberal societies, the envisioned "minimal state" of the libertarians, it will still be the case that individuals can never have absolute freedom to choose their ends, because these individuals will be born into societies committed to individual freedom through exchange and contract, which means they will be subject to obligations both to support these institutions and to provide minimum resources for the disadvantaged so that they too may be free to participate in the activities of exchange and transfer which create an unique individual existence (otherwise the society in which each individual is free to realize his own life plan remains purely ideational like Kant's noumenal self). Indeed it is this self realization ethic which actually founds the welfarist liberal requirement that we aim for equality in resources. It may be thought that the moral basis of equal resource shares is simply the moral ideal of "equality" itself, however, it is misleading to regard the idea of uniformity in individual human condition as a sufficiently defined moral principle. Indeed if the ideal of equality were such a compelling moral intuition why not demand equality in other matters, e.g., equality in stature (taller people will have to take special hormones to limit their growth), equality in eye colour, equality of offspring etc.? Furthermore, as Nozick has suggested, calls to equality may not be moral at all but simply promptings of human envy. The appropriate answer, I believe is that liberals tend to advocate equality in resources not because they are enamored with the idea that all individuals should operate from roughly comparable circumstances but rather because individuals need access to some social minimum in order to realize the liberty of individual existence, that is to be autonomous. This attitude is certainly made explicit in the writings of liberals like Gewirth and Waldron and I believe it is implicit in the writings of Rawls and Dworkin though they prefer to talk about these matters in the language of "equality".[24]

In any event we should now begin to appreciate that matters of ontology specifically with respect to the nature of the human subject can influence profoundly the manner in which we view institutions and particularly the social institution of ownership. What I have sought to bring out in the preceding analysis of "desert" is that what stands in the way of our appreciation of the underlying communal nature of ownership is our allegiance to the enlightenment ideal of the pre-social radically unsituated self. Once we appreciate that the human subject receives its character and moral characteristics from particular familial and communal contexts, one is far less likely to regard one's traits, characteristics and material holdings as being uniquely and individually "deserved" rather than communally held.

But aside from matters of ontology in relation to the human subject, it should be apparent that the essential concept of a "human resource" implies a communal rather than individual personality. Returning again to the debate between Rawls and Nozick, we might begin by rehearsing Nozick's argument against Rawls. In Rejecting Rawls' contention that a scheme of distribution must be formulated so as to agree with the a-priori principles of justice, Nozick argued that no one has a right to decide this issue independent of the historical circumstances in which holdings or human resources are generated. Nozick argued that material things don't fall like manna from skies they enter the world with a history, a history of production etc.[25] We cannot ignore the history and treat them like manna which call for some scheme of distribution. According to Nozick, we must reject desert and uphold a scheme relevant to the history of productive relations which have actually occurred. But what Nozick's argument actually introduces is the fact of cooperative endeavour in the fashioning of those individual products which we describe as holdings. His words remind us that these holdings could not have existed without the cooperative activities which are social in nature and presuppose a society or community. The history of production does not implicate the fact of individual effort but rather communal effort. The individual therefore cannot deserve them in the strong sense in which, for example, the early Christian theologians claimed that God is entitled to his ownership of the earth because it is the work of His sole creative activity. Obviously human products are seldom the work of a single individual creative act - the closest approximation are works of art but even these are not created *ex-nihlo*, the materials which he/she uses are only available through the productive and cooperative actions of others. One cannot avoid the presumption, when one talks of manmade products, that the community is prior to and conspires in and contrives the production of these things, and therefore, logically their distribution and use should benefit the community which is the basis of the cooperative endeavour.

Even with respect to real property, land, this is the case - the cooperative character of the "holding" is obvious. One often reverts to some Lockean argument of original acquisition in which working the land is said to endow this natural object with the character of private property. One will argue that land unlike most forms of personal property is not fashioned by learned human skill through relations of production which depend upon the plurality of cooperation. Land simply exists and one can certainly find an unowned piece, work on it, and claim it as one's own without the involvement of one's fellows in any sort of cooperative undertaking. However, the whole point is that one cannot simply make something one's own by some private act which does not require the complicity of one's fellows. Intrinsic to the meaning of private or individual property is the notion that others recognize it as such - that they recognize this small piece of property lying proximate to whatever as my property. If they did not so recognize, it could never be referred to as my property. Which is all to say that the rest of the community, clan or whatever must agree to recognize it as *my* property, and furthermore, be actively supportive through appropriate institutions and traditions to secure and maintain this recognition. These remarks lead us to recall the words of A.P. Power with respect to customary ownership in Melanesia. As he says, property has always been communal in nature, as land has always been held by force of arms on the part of community, the community remains the primary owner and the individual uses what is primarily community property.

Individual Rights and the Disempowerment of the Community

At this point I would like to move from the ontology of the human subject and its relation to "human resources" to a treatment with certain wider implication. Having said this, we might ask ourselves at this point whether our analysis has application beyond goals of clarity in our political and social thought. Sandel believes that the notion of radically unengaged individuality is more than a construct of the European enlightenment which has mere theoretical importance in the debates of contemporary political philosophers and political scientists.   Sandel asserts that this construct is itself reflected in the contemporary social and legal reality of Western civilization especially in the United States.[26] What Sandel observes is the erosion of community in the lives of individual Westerners as over the last hundred years economic units have become larger, centralized and centrally controlled. The latter has effected a sense of loss of community as the local community itself has become disempowered with respect to its activities in the important sphere of market relations. The community in its disempowered condition can no longer provide individuals with the purposes and goals which make life satisfying and has not been adequately replaced. We have, however, been offered a spurious replacement of the local community in the form of the nation state. But, claims Sandel, this has not worked because the nation state is too vast and anonymous to provide individuals with a sense of community.[27] The Political community as represented by the nation state is simply not the cultural community and so it cannot claim to exhaust the community as such.

In order to counteract this continuing sense of loss and disempowerment, claims Sandel, legal institutions and bureaucratic organization have fallen back upon theories of individuals rights, which represent trumps which individuals can assert to resist and sometimes defeat the policies and actions of the vast anonymous state and the mechanisms of the huge centralized market. Individual rights now exist to protect individuals against these forces.

The effect of these developments has been to render in individuals both a feeling of powerlessness mingled with a concomitant feeling of dependency.[28] This is because the individual feels himself/herself at the mercy of the economic forces which seem to control individual life and community while at the same time he must cling to a system of individual rights which appears to give him some measure of control against these powerful anonymous forces. Sandel's analysis of these Western social/political events is apposite because it helps to underlie differences between Western and customary Melanesian culture. In P.N.G. matters at present still appear to be quite the reverse. As most of the country, 97% of the land, remains under communal tenure, the majority of Papua New Guineans still maintain customary traditional lifestyles. For most Papua New Guineans engaged in traditional lifestyles, local affairs including economic relations are still controlled at the community, clan and family levels. The individual remains closely attached to the community and the land which is the economic base, and these relationships have been maintained through the central notion of communal ownership. In the present undeveloped state of P.N.G., the individual clansman and woman has yet to feel him/herself to be at the mercy of vast economic forces which s/he cannot control or comprehend. Communal relations and customary institutions in these traditional societies still offer individuals a meaningful standing and an avenue of effective input in which to exert control of local economic activities. It may well be the case that proper development will not be enhanced by instilling in individuals an appropriate sense of individual rights including individual property rights, while at the same time centralizing economic affairs through the government or the mechanism of an internationally controlled market. If as Sandel strongly suggests, emphasis on individual rights only underlines the inherent powerlessness of those who have strong need to assert them, one may be better off by maintaining strong communal relations, especially those involving land rather than hastily embracing Western paradigms especially those which refer to private property relations.

All in all the ordinary Papua New Guinean still feels himself strongly attached to the community from which he continues to derive his source of identity and from which he or she receives the responsibilities and duties which constitute his or her moral existence. He or she is a living contradiction to the liberal model which sees the individual detached from his community and ideally choosing his identity and moral obligations in a protected space which is independent of communal demands. Though liberals claim to see this form of individual liberty or autonomy as enlightened progress, it is not to be forgotten that there is a dark side to this liberal vision as Sandel and other communitarians have pointed out. Emphasis on individuality and individual rights has been nurtured in the circumstance in which the local community has been vitiated and attenuated so that it's individual members feel themselves to be powerless and bereft of an effective access to the decision making processes which profoundly affect their lives. Concomitantly this is the same circumstance in which the vast international economic market has grown, prospered and dominated local and international affairs. In order that events in developing P.N.G. resolve themselves in a more happy manner it is imperative that future development avoid replicating these conditions which advisedly means that one proceed on the local level and maintain local institutions. In this respect we have emphasized throughout this work the importance of communal forms of tenure which we believe should not be undermined through paradigms of individual rights and individual ownership. If we wish to maintain the strength and continuity of Melanesian communities, one must continue to support the "communal land base" which A.P Power has described as the lynch pin which holds the traditional Melanesian community together.

But there are also additional cautionary remarks which need to be made. On Sandel's analysis, individual rights have compensatory functions which appear to offer individuals some modicum of control in the face of powerful depersonalized forces. However, it is also the case that individual rights function in a contributory manner to facilitate the empowering of these centralized economic mechanisms. As is well recognized, the modern market economy works through a system in which assets are readily liquified to facilitate relations of credit and debt which work to harness human resources to "optimum productivity". As it stands communal land tenure does not facilitate these simple legal transfers which easily found relations of credit and debt. However, once we successfully introduce individual tenure with unfettered alienation, then credit and financing can easily proceed on the basis of this form of liquidizable collateral. It does not take a great deal of prescience to recognize the tragic possibilities which might ensue when unsophisticated villagers are allowed to avail themselves of easy credit on the basis of their newly derived individual land titles. In these circumstances one could easily imagine a chain of events occurring which might resemble those which overtook the American Midwest in the 1930s as across many states crops failed and banks foreclosed on thousands of mortgaged family estates. In short, finance and credit, as we know, are instrumental in centralizing economic control in large financial institutions. Whether or not tragic events ultimately transpire, it is undeniable that individual land tenure according to Anglo-Australian model will facilitate financing which promotes this form of delocalized economic control.

Thus, to recapitulate matters to this point, we have presented the communitarian view which sees the unengaged pre-social self of the enlightenment as indeed a myth which has produced much muddle headed thought concerning the necessary structure of social organization and social institutions. In our own study we have emphasized certain fundamental problems with the Western understanding of private property which we have closely associated with this enlightenment tradition. We have argued that the notion of the sovereign individual human subject grew out of the humanist tradition of Renaissance Italy and received further articulation through the theology of the protestant reformation. In the last two chapters we indicated that this understanding of human sovereignty required a particular view of the individual self as one which is unengaged, unattached and independent of the natural and social orders. The enlightenment tradition of Kant understood that liberty and autonomy were implicated in the status of this unengaged pre-social self and that private property was necessary to secure freedom and autonomy so conceived. However, I have argued that once we recognize this unengaged, radically unsituated self as being a myth of the enlightenment and understand that all subjects are situate within some form of communal context from which they acquire their identity, we begin to see that private property cannot be morally justified through the associated fiction of radically unsituated personal autonomy. Furthermore, in recognizing the social character of individual identity we readily ascribe value to the institutions in so far as they protect societal and social organizations which sustain ourselves and our identity, and understand that the particular human institution of property should also maintain a communal rather than individual orientation. This certainly means that in addition to the liberal concern for freedom of individual choice and control, one must be ready to balance this value with an overriding concern that this institution serve the ends of the community, its nurture and continuity. This does not mean to deny individual purposes altogether, but to understand as did Medieval Christianity and the Melanesian tradition among others, that with respect to resources, the individual uses, but society remains the primary owner, an interest which persists through generations of individual users.

Concluding Review

In review, therefore, we have traced the genesis and genealogy of the concept of private ownership from the Renaissance, through the Reformation and the Enlightenment to the contemporary deliberations. We have observed that Ficino's articulation of Man's sovereign status, distinct and apart from the rest of the created order, engendered the reformation attitudes which viewed created nature as designed to be mastered by human intelligence, and thereby amenable to human domination in the service of human needs or human utility. Locke's philosophy is to be understood as a product of this intellectual milieu as Locke understood that humans were subject to a Divine command which required them to master the natural environment in order to effect levels of productivity which ideally would sustain both themselves and the rest of mankind. On this account, private property was described as an explicit natural right necessary to each individual in order to carry out God's supreme imperative. Thus, private property was seen as a moral requirement according to utilitarian principles and sanctioned by theological theory. In subsequent intellectual developments during the enlightenment, we described how the German philosophers moved away from utilitarian orientation and emphasized individual liberty or autonomy in their derivation of the private property right. In the case of Kant, we indicated that he enlarged upon the notion that individual humans are distinct and separable form either the created natural or conventional social orders. This separation is associated with an understanding of autonomy in which our essential intellectual self determines itself without reference to, or influence from, our empirical selves - the self which is the product of nature and social contingencies. In his social philosophy Kant associates the right of private property with an intrinsically self determining nature. The product of contractual agreements accord with *a-priori* principles which are principles that have their source in the rational intellectual self defined by its very independence from social or natural states of affairs.

According to liberal thought, therefore, with its sources in both Lockean and Kantian social theory, social and community relations are the product of consensual agreements between individuals whose essential identity is, chronologically or ontologically, independent of these associations. Lockeans and Kantians thus concur in seeing the human subject as possessing an essential nature which is independent of historical social context. But on matters of private ownership, Kantians eschew Lockean issues of human utility, as both Kantians and libertarians like Nozick tend to see private property as intrinsic to freedom of contract which is the expression of autonomous agency. Finally the Hegelians were seen to offer a different perspective on autonomy and its relation to private ownership, one which reintroduces the role of community and social context in the determinations of autonomous agency and self identity. Hegel associates autonomy with self actualization, the successful implementation of a rationally planned life which relates distinct social events through reference to certain controlling ideas. But though this notion of autonomy does not presuppose a self independent of social or cultural traditions and which thereby disregards the importance of community, it does assume that the human subject fulfills a position of distinctness, domination and sovereignty with respect to the natural environment. On this view private property is necessary so that the individual can control and express himself through modification of the natural environment. In the final chapter I will explore the environmental ramifications of this position.

---

¹ "Associated" is the operative word here, for as Jeremy Waldron has pointed out in "John Rawls and the Social Minimum" (*Journal of Applied Philosophy* 3 (1986): 21-35) Rawls' concept of a social minimum opts for the notion of an "ordinal" minimum, that is, the idea that nobody's share should be much greater than anybody else's. In contrast, Waldron opts for a conception of a minimum which is fixed "cardinally" on an assessment of the resources that

basic human needs require. The Hegelian self-realization ethic most probably implies principles of distribution which are closer to Waldron's, which is to state that individual self realization would demand a fairly fixed minimum of resources which would be independent of considerations relative to the proportional share of the more advantaged groups. Rawls' view is to be found in *A Theory of Justice* (Oxford: Oxford University Press, 1971). Also we might mention the views of Alan Gewirth, *Human Rights* (Chicago, University of Chicago Press, 1982) whose views as to the social minimum probably come closer to Waldron's and the Hegelian position we are articulating. However, neither Waldron nor Gewirth have achieved the notoriety of Rawls who is most commonly associated with the liberal welfarist position. Also noteworthy is Ronald Dworkin's work in this field of liberal scholarship. In "What is Equality: Part 1, Equality of Welfare," *Philosophy and Public Affairs* 10 (Sum 1981): 185-246; and "What is Equality: Part 2, Equality of Resources," *Philosophy and Public Affairs* 10 (Fall 1981): 283-345, Dworkin thoroughly explores how a guaranteed minimum of resources would be made available in a liberal Utopia so as to assure equality of opportunity. In these works Dworkin presents in detail a possible program in which each individual begins life with access to similar bundles of resources which each may utilize through trade and exchange to create the form of life which each desires.

[2]   See for example, F. Hayek. *Law, Legislation and Liberty*, 3 vols. (London: Routledge and Kegan Paul, 1978); F.H. Knight, *The Economic Organization* (New York: Augustus H. Kelley, 1967).

[3]   Rawls, *A Theory of Justice*, 312-313.

[4]   Robert Nozick, *Anarchy, State, and Utopia* (Boston: Basic Books, 1974), 228-231.

[5]   Michael Sandel, *Liberalism and the Limits of Justice* (Cambridge: Cambridge University Press, 1982), 96-97.

[6]   Ibid.,150.

[7]   Ibid., 97-98.

[8]   Ibid., 101.

[9]   Ibid., 144.

[10]   Sandel, *Liberalism and the Limits of Justice*, 13.

[11]   Ibid., 12.

[12]   Ibid, 255-256.

[13]   See Immanuel Kant, *The Fundamental Principles of the Metaphysics of Ethics*, trans. T.K. Abbott, (London: Longmans Green and Co., 1949), 84-87.

[14]   Ibid., 90.

[15]   Ibid., 252.

[16]   Ibid., 516.

[17]   Kant, *The Fundamental Principles*, 10.

[18]   Ibid., 254.

[19]   Ibid., 448.

[20]   Ibid.

---

[21]   Ibid., 396.

[22]   Cf., Maeve Cooke, "Habermas, Autonomy and the Identity of Self," *Philosophy and Social Criticism* 18 (1992): 269-291, who utilizes this definition in distinguishing this second form of autonomy from Kantian Moral autonomy. In a discussion of Habermas she argues that the latter notion is implicit in the writings of Habermas even though he is most commonly associated with the former specifically Kantian notion.

[23]   But then how do we reconcile this analysis with Rawls' statements which deny that the theory of justice requires the centrality of the liberal doctrine of autonomy (See John Rawls, "Justice as Fairness: Political not Metaphysical," *Philosophy and Public Affairs* 14, No. 3 (1985):233-251, 247). He states that his conception of justice "...provides an account of the cooperative virtues suitable for a political doctrine in view of the conditions and requirements of a constitutional regime".   Rawls claims that his principles refer to the basic structures of any "well ordered" society and not solely a "well ordered" liberal society based on individuality and autonomy.   However, despite this disavowal, the function of the "original position" which issues in constraint by universal principles, only gains practical significance in so far as this behaviour, when universalized, enables each individual to plan rationally in terms of his/her particular concept of the good which is nothing less nor more than what is meant by the liberal notion of autonomy.   Furthermore, only by ascribing some primary value to this form of autonomy can we begin to appreciate why cultivation of the "cooperative virtues" is morally valuable, since after all, cooperation can not remain a good thing if the results themselves are not seen as valuable.   Diversity may well be claimed as a valuable result, but this is hardly convincing without the additional assumption that a diverse society is worthwhile because this indicates a society composed of intrinsically valuable autonomous agents.

[24]   See note 1.

[25]   Nozick, *Anarchy, State, and Utopia*, 198, 219.

[26]   Michael Sandel, "The Procedural Republic," in *Communitarianism and Individualism*, eds. Shlomo Avineri & Avner De-Sholit, (Oxford: Oxford University Press, 1992):12-28.

[27]   Ibid., 26.

[28]   Ibid., 26-28.

Chapter 9

Environmental Ethics And The Issue Of Individual Versus Community Control Of Holdings

In the final chapter I would like to explain further why the issue of individual autonomy, however interpreted, cannot be allowed to dominate our thinking about the moral character of ownership. This discussion specifically focuses upon certain central issues within the sphere of environmental ethics, and what I wish to demonstrate is that emphasis on the value of individual autonomy will also prove antithetical to growing environmental concerns.

Environmentalism and the Hegelian Basis of Private Property

To this point we have argued strongly against the Kantian notion of an autonomous, socially independent, non-empirical self and have indicated the confusions which result when we attempt to understand ownership through the prism of this Kantian construct. The danger is that we will fail to appreciate the necessary communal framework which sustains autonomy and social institutions like property. However, autonomy as properly conceived according to self realization ethic of Hegel does not suffer from these liabilities in so far as Hegel understood that self realization was only possible in so far as society is committed to maintain the appropriate culture and inherited institutions in which self actualization would flourish. Which is all to say that Hegel rejected the Kantian notion of a pre-social noumenal self whose autonomy was in some sense fully formed, complete and detached from the social order.

With Hegel, therefore, there is no danger that we will emphasize some a-social form of negative freedom at the expense of social concerns.

But emphasis upon the value of autonomy conceived as self actualizing control of the natural environment promotes narrow anthropocentric attitudes, which when acted upon, seriously threaten efforts to instill appropriately environmentally sensitive behaviour. To recall Hegel's position, it will be remembered that private property is said to be justified because our own freedom depends upon subjugating and controlling nature and by this action achieving self actualization by imparting value to nature. On this point Hegel explicitly stated that nature has no distinct intrinsic value except as a vehicle for execution of individual plans and human ideas. Though the Hegelian analysis avoids the representation of an unencumbered self which is radically detached from its social context, it still fails to appreciate that the self is located within the context of nature and cosmos, in which as Charles Taylor points out, the self must find its place in the natural and cosmic orders and not simply hold itself outside these orders. Though Hegel does not deprecate the importance of our social reality in the realization of personal freedom and autonomy, he does embrace the anthropocentric position which sees the human subject as not merely a part of the inherently valuable natural order, but rather apart from and superior to other natural instantiations as the embodiment of Absolute Spirit.

Nevertheless we must distinguish between the positions embraced by the environmentalists. With respect to the conflict between the Hegelians and the so called "shallow ecologists" - those who stress concerns associated with human interests across time, such that our management of resources must also provide for the needs and aspiration of the future generations as well as the present - the conflict between Hegelian ethics is not as great as that to found between the latter and the so called "deep ecologists". Obviously, as originally stated, the Hegelian self-actualization ethic is presented according to a formula which does not seem to account for the interests of future generations. But it is not inconceivable that those who now stress the objectives of sustainable development would accept a modification in the application of this Hegelian ethic so as to extend opportunities beyond the present to future communities, thereby entailing that exercise of autonomous life styles be managed so as not to preclude opportunities for both the satisfaction of future needs and the exercise of similar lifestyles in the future. The practical implication would at minimum require a careful monitoring of the resources available for the exercise of a particular life style. Thus, there is scope for reconciling both the aims of the "shallow ecologist" with those who wish to maintain the values associated with notions of Hegelian "self actualization".

On the other hand Hegelian ethics finds itself in the most profound contradiction with the proponents of "deep ecology" - those who claim that non-human individuals merit the same concern and respect which we extend to human individuals. Among the former phenomena are often included other sentient creatures, species, natural processes, ecosystems and even the biosphere itself. At present the literature on "deep ecology"has been extensive and quite diverse which means that though there exists a common theme, it has been articulated from different perspectives and preoccupations. Nevertheless it is worthwhile to contrast the Hegelian self actualization ethic with that of one prominent representative, Holmes Rolston, who affirms a land ethic which accords with the earlier work of Leopold. He states: "The land ethic rests upon the discovery of certain values - integrity, projective creativity, life support, community - already present in ecosystems and it imposes an obligation to act so as to maintain these."[1] Accordingly, behavioural constraints will be dictated by consideration of the good of the biotic community as a whole, including that of its individual constituents. Following this reasoning it would be morally wrong to undermine the principles and relations which tend to maintain the biological community, which includes the fundamental cyclical principles founded on biospheric interaction (for instance, photosynthesis, sunshine, nitrogen fixing etc).

Most "deep ecologists" would agree with Rolston in the conviction that nature is not some paradigm of featureless *materia prima* awaiting to be imprinted with worth through human activity, in so far as it already possesses systemic order with its own intrinsic value. Hence the proper course is not to subjugate and mold nature into some valuable form, but to respect the purposefullness and immanent value which already exist. From these sentiments follow a contemplative if not quietest attitude towards nature which is at variance with Hegelian ethic of "self expression" through actively engaging the natural environment. As Holmes Rolston states, "We take ourselves to nature and listen for its forms of expression, drawn by a realm of values not of our construction. We ought not to destroy this integrity but rather preserve and contemplate it."[2] Rolston asserts that the valuing experience is not identical with the intellectual representation of facts or the calculations involved in discursive thinking. Valuing, he says, involves an internal excitation in which "...the marriage of the subject to its object gives birth to value."[3]

This interpretation of the axiological process differs profoundly from the Hegelian which understands the human subject, as vehicle for the Absolute Spirit, superior to the natural reality which it must transform and endow with its own value. Deep ecologists would hold that the Hegelian self-actualization ethic promotes anthropocentric blindness to the inherent values of "nature".

The theory of immanent value found in the land ethic, espoused by environmentalists like Leopold and Rolston, and the ethic of self-expression promoted by Hegel are, therefore, in an irreconcilable conflict. According to the former, we must respect the value found in nature and, therefore, we must constrain actions which might alter or change nature, while Hegelian ethics prescribes actions which would transform nature endowing it with human value or value for human beings. Given that in the last two hundred years the earth has suffered the effects of intense industrialization and development, it would seem reasonable to move away from the anthropocentric view of Hegel towards what is sometimes called the biocentric or ecocentric view expressed in the land ethic. Aside from the issue of questionable anthropocentric blindness, this policy also makes definite sense from a purely anthropocentric perspective as some claim that the survival not only of ourselves but of the earth itself may depend upon respecting nature and its systems rather than continuing to tamper with their workings in order to extract advantages for human beings.

Accordingly, the Hegelian moral basis for private ownership appears to be seriously inappropriate if we are concerned that our ethics be responsive to the intrinsic value intuited in the natural environment. Emphasis upon private ownership, as morally required to protect an individual sphere of sovereignty and control vis-a-vis the natural environment, stands in opposition to the environmentalist demand that we forego active engagement and assume a more contemplative attitude towards nature. Beyond the direct philosophical conflict with deep ecologists, the demands of the autonomous life style may certainly have to be deprioritized on grounds of anthropocentric prudence, if the survival and future well being of our species depends upon constraint with respect to the consumption and profligate resource use. This may well imply that we may have to seriously limit rights of control and management with respect to private holdings and subject these rights to the greater social and environmental concerns.

Environmental Protection and Libertarian Ideals

Let us now consider the libertarian attitude towards environmental issues. The libertarian sees the private property right as essentially a right to transfer and exchange holdings and maintains that unless these rights are protected, the individual cannot achieve his autonomy. For the modern libertarian, autonomy is seen as capacity to pursue individual projects without suffering frustration through some form of external interference; and accordingly, contractual relations are seen as the *modus operandi* in the fulfillment of individual plans.

The question is whether maintaining an interpretation of the private property right, in which the central right is the right to transfer or convey, is similarly injurious of the natural environment. Unlike the Hegelian attitude, the modern libertarian does not stress the aspect of control and sovereign management in the use of the holding. In fact, the Libertarian can live with quite strict controls upon the ways one can use one's possession and certainly s/he is prepared to accept a concept of ownership which in a number of respects falls far short of sovereign domination.   Tibor Machan, for example, has recently argued that libertarianism promises the most effective approach to environmental damage in that its principles require that pollution be punishable as a legal offense which violates individual rights to life, liberty and property.[4] Machan claims that because libertarians are adamant that individual rights should not be violated, their position towards environmental damage is less compromising than positions reached through normal forms of cost/benefit analysis, a utilitarian yardstick employed by most Western regulatory agencies. Calculations based on cost/benefit analysis factor in environmental damage as negative value which must be weighted against the general benefits of a given industrial project.   These calculations, Machan says, suffer from the same disability as all forms of utilitarian calculation. Precisely, how do we justify the violation of individual rights through environmental deterioration even if that injury is the unavoidable consequent of enhancing the position of other individuals no matter how numerous they may be? Environmental damage violates the rights of human individuals, claims Machan, and cost benefit analysis cannot undue the fact that individual rights are being violated.

On this reading, therefore, libertarians are unwilling to countenance any use of one's property which results in environmental damage which injures other individuals. Certainly it is evident that they are prepared to implement restrictions upon one's absolute sovereignty vis-a vis the use and management of the holding, which often will go further than most government legislation which is prepared to accept a certain level of environmental damage and personal injury as the unavoidable consequent of modern development. And though Machan seems to be talking about the rights of the extant human population, the demands of the shallow ecologists could be met by libertarian theory through the ascription of inviolable rights to the future members of the human race and thus the demands of the sustainable development could be brought under the aegis of libertarian ethics. But once more this libertarian policy would not satisfy the goals of the deep ecologists who would wish that the Kantian concern envelope not only autonomous human creatures but also non-human individuals.

However, though it appears libertarian theory can be given an interpretation which would agree with the ends of shallow ecology, I believe the accord is more apparent than real. This is because, at its core, libertarian theory proscribes any actions which interfere with free transfer such that these freedoms must remain absolutely inviolable. What the libertarian overlooks is that these rights of transfer, which for the libertarian define the central character of ownership, have been instrumental in facilitating the profligate resource use and over consumption which precipitated the current environmental crisis. Conversely, the intense subjugation and development of nature could not have effectively happened without these rights of alienation which Honore describes as falling within the general right to capital (rights to waste, modify or transfer the holding). It is demonstratable that the industrial revolution whose effects significantly impoverished and degraded the natural environment, could not have occurred without suppression of a specific form of communal ownership and concomitant emphasis on the unfettered rights of transfer and exchange. On this point it is illustrative to refer to the history of industrial capitalism and the period of enclosure which occurred during the beginnings of the English industrial revolution.

The period of enclosure occurred in the early eighteenth century and, as seen from a jural perspective, it marked a time of transition in which communal rights to inalienable land gave way to individual ownership with rights of alienation. T.S. Ashton tells us that during the process of enclosure scattered holdings were consolidated, common rights to arable lands and meadows were extinguished, and each man's portion was fenced or hedged. These events were concomitant with a move from small self sufficient farms to bigger units of production which introduced division of labour, larger capital and more efficient supply to markets.[5]

Seen in the context of the emerging industrial revolution, enclosure was instrumental in creating a social environment in which industrial development could flourish. As Europe moved from feudal systems to full blooded capitalism, there was a necessity to render the population pliant and amenable to long concentrated hours of work without great financial remuneration. By enclosing commonage, the peasant was denied free access to land on a casual basis, and thereby he lost the inclusive rights which are gained through simple membership in a specific community. These are precisely the rights which exist in a commonage situation.[6] The inclusive right, one can say, gives rise to claim on society's resources or more properly a claim right. Once commonage is enclosed, these rights are extinguished, and thus the peasant in the emerging capitalist society is left with a mere general right to trade and exchange. This meant that the peasant with little land and no right of access to the former common land, could do little else but exchange his labour in order to survive, according to the terms set by the employer.

On reflection it is apparent how the this new circumstance created for an emerging capitalist class opportunities for exploitation of both resources and labour which were not present in an early feudal era or during a subsequent transitional period when yeomen and other freemen had access to commonage. In the changing social context, the owner of resources, or the owner of the means of production in the Marxist sense, became free to extract as much labour from the individual as the market would bear so to speak. In the feudal context this form of intense labour would not have been so easily procured, as the bonds which bound the serf to the lord and lord to serf where greater than those of contract, they were life long relations based on custom, tradition, ancestry and these could not be disregarded. In a word, the lord could not simply cast out his less productive tenants and replace them with another group as, for example, the capitalist farmer can more easily cancel his contracts with unproductive help and hire new workers. Likewise so long as communities had access to commonage and individuals enjoyed inclusive rights to work this land on a casual basis, individuals could not be so easily forced into demanding contracts for labour, nor were the circumstances particularly threatening if they failed to perform to expectations. Capitalism swept away the remnants of Feudalism and the residual communal rights enjoyed in the commonage situation, ostensibly this rendered individuals more free by abnegating traditions and customs which bound individuals to a particular lord or a specific place, but, at the same time, rendered the situation more precarious as the worker became more susceptible to the domination by employers intent on forcing him to levels of maximum productivity and with better means to compel compliance.

The notion that the alienation of land has a central function in the subjugation of both nature and the labouring population can be demonstrated further by reference to social and economic developments in Fiji during the last century. It is indeed worthwhile to contrast and compare the episode of enclosure in England with comparative events which occurred in colonial Fiji later the same century. By way of historical context it should be pointed out that before England accepted the annexation of Fiji to its colonial empire, the European community on Fiji had been relentlessly purchasing native land from the Fijian chiefs. As documented by Peter France in *The Charter of the Land*, this activity had a twofold purpose: 1) to secure sufficient holdings on which to build plantations; 2) to deny the local population access to land for subsistence farming so that they would be forced into contracts of employment with the European owners - in other words to compel the native Fijians into intensive labour on plantations principally devoted to sugar.[7] Sir Arthur Gordon, the first Governor General of Figi adopted a policy to protect the Fijians from this form of servitude and protect the traditional Fijian way of life and this involved, *inter alia*, registering all native land as communally owned (as *Metaqali* land) and rendering it inalienable - (a system of tenure which has been religiously maintained by the sovereign state of Fiji through the Native Land Trust Board up to the present day). Indeed this policy worked and the Fijians avoided general servitude, the over utilization of the land resource was arrested, and the Fijians held on to their traditional lands, some of which they now lease principally for the sugar plantations and some of which remains in a protected undeveloped state. In all respects it is clear that the abjuration of alienable real property, played an important role in subverting a massive capital intensive form of agriculture.

Finally, there is the necessary connection between the supposed inviolable right of transfer and exchange, and the free movement of capital. The idea that the individual (and here we include in the notion of individuality, corporate personality) must be morally free to transfer his holdings, offers a moral basis for arguing that capital must enjoy free movement, otherwise individual rights of contract and property stand to be violated. The free movement of capital is intrinsic to the modern industrial capitalist system as we mentioned earlier in the chapter and it has had a distinct role in the intense exploitation of the environment. Within the modern market system it is important that the movement of capital be minimally regulated in order to take advantage of immediate economic opportunities and profitably coordinate large industrial undertakings. However, with the growing complexity and vastness of the dealings, it has come about that decisions are made and policies formulated in centres which are remote from the local areas in which these policies will be carried out. As well as disempowering the community, the environmental consequences can often be devastating and inappropriate.

Many environmentalists argue that one very important way of combatting environmental destruction is to reinstate bioregionalism or local control of economic affairs especially those directly dealing with local resources and land. It is argued that the sustainability of our economic activities cannot be determined unless there is careful and local monitoring of the effects of these activities, and such complex and intensive information gathering cannot be effected at a distance.[8] To maintain that the right to convey and transfer holdings and resources must continue unrestricted will sustain conditions which are contrary to the aims of bioregionalism. When, for example, indigenous and non-indigenous people sell off land rights to large consortiums and multinational corporations, it follows that the control of economic activities, which will occur on the conveyed land, no longer remains local. As these rights have been instrumental in removing local control of the supervision and determination of economic activities, environmental concerns dictate that we restrict rights of exchange and transfer. Accordingly protesting groups have often addressed both the social and environmental aspects. The Chipko environmentalist group of India, for example, stresses its aims as those of instituting bioregionalism and restoring local community control. Also the German Greens have advocated "no growth" economies with alternative economic and political structures - smaller in scale and more amenable to social participation.[9] With respect to control by indigenous peoples, there are additional environmental benefits, because, claim some, these are groups which have far more basic needs, their demands on the environment are far less intense, and they can draw upon a reservoir of cooperative social institutions and local ecological knowledge in managing the "commons"...on a sustainable basis."[10]

Indigenous communities, however, are not the only ones who risk loss of control, through unregulated transfers. Unregulated transfers can affect communities in other ways as, for example with the phenomenon of development by sub-division. The latter is a familiar devise of land developers in Western societies. Unless a specific municipality has passed regulations either to proscribe or control this practice, an owner or developer will always have this option at common law. Nozick's libertarian principles offer strong support for maintaining this general common law right and rendering it immune to supervening legislation. Again, however, if we were to regard this sort of right as inviolable as Nozick maintains, the community's control of its own growth and development would be lost. Furthermore, giving individuals a carte blanche in such dealings can greatly hamper the community's efforts to formulate a rational plan for the disposal of sewage and detritus, which in many places pose equal threats to the integrity of the environment.

Summary

Liberal theory which has enshrined the notion of autonomy understands that personal destiny is self created through relations of trade and exchange which imply the protection of private property. Conversely it is held that without the possibility of freely chosen contractual relations, the autonomous implementation of personal plans which define a life history could not be a reality. These include essential contracts of employment, and contracts of purchase or hire which relate to choice of home, transportation, leisure, avocations and neighbourhood. These choices, as it were, determine the particular content of one's individual life history, and for the liberal it is important that they be freely entered into, if the content of our existence is to be something self determined rather than externally imposed. However, as I have sought to indicate in the foregoing pages, the liberal attitude, which sees autonomy as an intrinsic value which should not suffer limitation, can be strongly questioned from the environmentalist's view point. It may well be the case that environmental protection may force us to view property as primarily communal rather than individual, as the communal notion may be more consonant with a planned employment of the environment on a sustainable basis which ensures its preservation for future generations. Furthermore, if we are to go further and embrace the views of the "deep ecologist" and those who propose a related ethic of the land, then the conflict between autonomy as an intrinsic value and nature as possessing intrinsic value is even less avoidable. In either case, the demands of sustainability and the stronger demands of the land ethic require that human individuals begin to question our subscription to the ideals of autonomous agency, which have required that various aspects of private ownership which relate to a self determined existence remain unfettered. These considerations may demand the reassessment of issues which include, *inter alia*, the extent to which resources are to be made available for autonomous life styles, limitations on alienation and the free movement of capital through covenants restricting sale and land use, and reinstitution of communal rather than individual decision making in the use and disposition of resources.

Property as a Natural Right - A Final Consideration

Before completing this project, I would like to give a final consideration to the issue of the inclusion of the private property right in a list of proposed "natural rights". In this final section our questioning will fall in line with the hermeneutical approach. In this sense we are basically engaged in an investigation of the language of self description employed by liberal societies. This is an exercise in which the language itself is criticized, through inconsistencies and inadequacies measured against institutional realization and appropriateness in the face of certain enduring facts about human existence and survival; and also by means of comparisons made between different languages of description tied to different cultural traditions etc. This investigation will tell us whether there are certain rights which can be labelled "natural" in the sense that they are the most appropriate components in the arrangement of social interaction, given certain basic universal "facts" about social existence.

Usually natural law and natural rights are tied to some natural feature of human beings which we consider to be morally primary. If we look to the theoretical underpinnings of any alleged enumeration of natural rights, we find that traditionally this notion has been generated from a fundamental belief that all human beings are possessed of a common nature and purpose; and in order to fulfil this purpose, the individual must be ascribed certain rights. These are the existence conditions which are said to give birth to the list of so called "natural rights". This isomorphism in terms of telos is to be found throughout the history of the natural law and natural rights theory, for example, Aristotle finds the human natural purpose in the cultivation of the intellect, Aquinas locates natural human telos in the knowledge of the Deity, Locke discovers Man's natural ends in his duties to fulfil God's commands, in a more secular age, Nozick finds man's nature and meaning in his natural freedom and in the unimpeded exercise of that freedom.

At their foundation all natural rights theories concern themselves with the issue of the universal human purpose; what is conspicuous is the absence of unanimity. In this respect, natural rights theories often appear arbitrary and unsubstantiated. This is because philosophers seldom offer reasons to prefer one definition of human nature and human purpose over a competing candidate. I don't believe libertarianism which gives strong support the concept of a "natural right" to private property avoids Mr. Sumner's observation that natural rights theories, in themselves, fail to offer a satisfying derivation of rights in part because adducing natural rights from the nature of man has been consistently inconclusive or circular.[11]

However, H.L.A. Hart has attempted to rescue natural law theory from indeterminateness and has argued that the idea of natural law could serve as a useful concept to indicate those aspects of our legal systems which incorporate morality and justice.[12] In his inquiries Hart proposed that there is a determinant moral content to legal systems in which the ascription of "natural law and natural right" could be given objective application. In doing so Hart describes certain elements of universality and determinateness which, he believes, avoid problems of ethnocentricity, moral subjectivism and relativism.

Natural Rights from a Jurisprudence Perspective

Hart argues that once we prescind contentious elements, the idea of "natural law" can be identified with a certain minimum content derivative from the general goal of all human societies - survival.[13] The aim of survival seems to be a empirical yet contingent truth about the individuals and human communities and, according to Hart, it colours the structures of language, thought, and the rules of conduct which any social organization must contain if it is to be viable. Hart quotes Hume in emphasis of this point, "Human nature cannot by any means subsist without the association of individuals: and that association never could have place were no regard paid to the laws of equity and justice".[14]

A recognizable humanity will always include certain laws of association and if we study those rules or laws we will recognize a certain minimal content which these diverse systems share. There is, he claims, this recognizable core to all moral and legal systems, without which, a system or society could not fulfil the minimal purpose of survival which is arguably the principal purpose men have in associating with one another. Hart links this common content with certain natural facts about human beings - for example, human vulnerability, approximate equality, limited altruism, limited resources etc.[15]

Given the purpose of survival, Hart believes that the content, which is to be found in the viable system, must include rules prescribing mutual forbearance and compromise, the necessity of sanctions, and some minimal form of the institution of property based on the limitedness of natural resources and the necessity to avoid the chaotic conditions contrary to the rule of law.[16] These are the common elements which are found in all legal and moral systems, according to Hart.

The goal of survival, I believe, is the key to the bridge between the natural rights and the hermeneutical approaches, in the sense that the language of "natural rights" will only have sense if we can give these rights consistent application in relation to the invariable facts of human existence and survival. Thus, what is designated as a natural right, or a natural law is not necessarily a matter of commonality or the existence of consensus throughout differing societal contexts, but rather, a matter of appropriateness and consistency with the facticity of human existence and societal survival. Legal and moral structures which are more consonant with the universal facts and goals of all human societies will more completely fulfil this "natural" status. At the same time our enquiry and conclusions will exhibit a hermeneutical character as we utilize a method of cultural comparison to assess and evaluate the language of our normative and legal structures, in efforts to arrive at certain authoritative pronouncements.

Thus, the issue before us is whether the list of rights generated by Hart's approach, based on the end of survival, would extensionally include modern private property rights. In other words, can Hart's system be utilized to yield a list of natural rights which may be extensionally equivalent to the list which is generated intentionally from liberal and libertarian positions based on the priority of individual autonomy. Of course, an affirmative answer demands that one regard private entitlements as necessary for a viable society.

Communal Land Ownership

Regardless of the outstanding success of Western culture it is not the only extant viable system. In the traditional societies of Papua New Guinea identification with the community is intimately and inextricably connected with the parallel identification with the communal land holding. We have seen that the cohesion of the Melanesia group or community life and its shared history was the land holding. The important constant, as we have seen, is that the group owned, and individuals used the land. "Individual land usage rights did not remove the reality that the group was the basis for ownership and the basis for the defense of these rights."[17]

Certainly on evaluative reflection, Melanesian communal ownership is a viable system as traditional Melanesian societies have survived from millennia up to the present age. Therefore, it would appear that the unilateral forms of individual control and transfer, which liberals and especially libertarians advocate, cannot be natural rights because they are clearly unnecessary to a viable system. However, before accepting this statement as conclusive, one needs to consider with greater care the force of libertarian theory. First of all, libertarian theory closely identifies property rights with the individual right to transfer holdings, such that the denial of this individual right entails the denial of "property". This is to say that what we mean by "property" must include these exclusive individual rights otherwise we cannot really speak of the existence of property rights in the proper use of the term. This line of thinking then strongly implies that though certain societies possess social arrangements which approximate or resemble "ownership" or "property", without the existence of these exclusive individual rights, we cannot properly employ the term "property" in describing their social arrangements. More than this, libertarian thinkers also give substance to the view that societies which promote and protect these individual rights generate greater utilities which enhance survival and render them more viable.[18]

The Modern Liberal Institution of Ownership

The most thorough and respected analysis of the modern concept of property has been provided by A.M. Honore. This, by now authoritative account stipulates that the fully formed notion of ownership is best understood by reference to the following list of eleven elements. These are said to be the "legal incidents" or characteristics which comprise the concept. The incidents are: (1) the right to possess; (2) the right to use; (3) the right to manage; (4) the right to income; (5) the right to the capital; (6) the right to security; (7) the power of transmissibility; (8) the absence of term; (9) the prohibition of harmful use; (10) liability to execution; and (11) the residual character.[19]

Interpreting Nozick's position in light of Honore's analysis, we can say that Nozick "natural right to transfer" encompasses incidents 5 and 7, the right to capital and the power of transmissibility. Incident five, the right to the capital, has reference to the power to alienate the holding or to consume, waste, modify or destroy it. Incident seven, the power of transmissibility, endows one with the ability to devise or bequeath the holding. (Honore points out that holdings first became heritable in English law, before they became alienable.)

With this in mind we should for clarity's sake seek answers to the following questions. First, given Hart's analysis which claims the existence of some form of natural right to ownership, must this natural right of ownership include the right to make voluntary transfers? Secondly, must the denial of the right to make voluntary transfers always be regarded as a denial of the natural right to property? Though, the standard theory of material entailment would seem to dictate that a positive answer to the first question will necessarily elicit a positive answer to the second, this should not be assumed without a thorough investigation.

In considering these eleven incidents, Honore makes the point that all existing mature legal systems encompass these eleven, in the sense that without the presence of these eleven we would not recognize the system as being the full or liberal sense of ownership prevalent in the modern world.[20] At the same time, however, he contends that none of the listed incidents is individually necessary, though together they are certainly sufficient for a person to be designated the owner of a given holding.[21] In other words, it is his contention that any system of ownership, in the full modern sense of the term, will exhibit each of these incidents, though in any particular instance of ownership there is no necessity that all incidents or any particular incident be present. What we see is that an individual who is designated an owner, may in certain circumstances, possess certain of the listed rights and liabilities and in other situations different rights and liabilities. For example, ownership of rental property encompasses elements 4, 5, 6, 7, 8, 9, 10, but not 1, 2, and 3. In contrast, life tenancy, which is also a recognized form of ownership, encompasses elements 1, 2, 3, 4, 9, 10, 11, and 6, but not 5, 7, and 8. Other forms of ownership, such as ownership subject to the power of appointment and ownership subject to managerial rights will also render different concatenations or clusters of "incidents".

Thus, the rights which protect voluntary transfers of property are not essential elements with respect to a particular species of property right. In other words, one can possess a private ownership right which is perfectly intelligible and valid without the presence of all the particular "incidents" which are found within the institution. For example, one may have a life estate which determines on the death of the holder (in an important sense this is a forced transfer yet despite the fact that the holder cannot freely transfer the holding, he or she is certainly recognized as the owner of this property). Thus the "power right" to make voluntary transfers is not a necessary or sufficient condition for the attribution of private ownership. But, of course, Honore is saying that the incidents which describe voluntary transfers are essential to the modern institution of ownership - that is to say that unless the institution itself included at least some forms of property holding which recognized these incidents we would be unprepared to accept the institution as a modern form of ownership as we know it. Thus, the modern viable society, according to Honore's analysis, must recognize some forms of ownership which include the right to make voluntary transfers.

Conclusion

In a general way Honore's analysis would seem to support Nozick's position which sees the individual right to transfer as an essential component in the modern system of ownership. However, one can only see this form of holding as a natural right if it is deemed most appropriate to the survival of a viable society. It is clear that it is also part of the libertarian belief that private ownership generates greater utilities and general benefits, and therefore, is more suitable for individual and social survival.

In the foregoing pages we linked the institution of private ownership with some of the important causal relations which have precipitated environmental damage. There is no need to rehearse these arguments which, I believe, demonstrate that overemphasis on the value of the individual self determination and autonomy, through protection of the private property, may well further continued destruction of the natural environment.

Of course recent events within the global arena can be looked upon as the effects of ecological succession, the process by which the structure of the biological community, with respect to both niche structure and species structure, alters as a result of the species modification of its habitat. As happens most often in the case of dominance of one species within an ecosystem, this process ultimately renders the habitat unfit for the dominant species. However, this knowledge in itself should alert us to the necessity for controlling this process and adopting a rational and strategic policy to eschew these developments.[22]

Western development which has proceeded with the idea of exclusive individual ownership and the right to capital at its centre may no longer be suitable for the sustainable development of the natural environment.   Different attitudes towards individual ownership and different modalities of ownership may now be more suitable. I suggest that this may require a return to or at least balancing of individualistic liberal ideals with values embodied in customary communal ownership as found in Melanesia and elsewhere.

According to this thinking, the values embodied in communal ownership entail individual rights which are derivative from communal ownership rights.   This departure from the liberal formula, which regards the community's rights as derivative from the individual's pre-eminent right, implies limitations on the individual's right of capital which includes the right to transfer as well as to waste or destroy the holding.   In the former case, in which the communal right is pre-eminent, this means that the individual will have to obtain communal approval or consent before exercising the right to capital, which, *inter alia*, includes the exclusive power to transfer the holding and control development.

In Melanesia and other indigenous societies, ownership of the means of production - land - has been communal rather than individual. The advantage of regarding ownership as communal based rather than individual based can be measured in the degree to which this will operate to retard the continuing damage to the natural environment. This will be aided by the fact that the community is conceived as consisting not only of the present membership but also future membership (which is somewhat the case in Melanesia). The individual, therefore, whether human or corporate, will possess rights which approximate those of a usufruct, rights to use holdings which properly belong to another so long as one does not impair the substance of the holding.

Though, no doubt, it will be initially difficult to reorganize property relations in such a radical manner, the first steps in protecting the environment may well will require this revolution in our attitudes to ownership rights. Ownership of holdings (which are components of the natural environment) will be understood as primarily communal rather than individual. This can be required on a very strong moral basis which sees such moves as necessary for the survival of human communities.   Thus, on Hart's formula, one will formulate the communal right as being more natural than the individual since it will form an aspect of the legal system which is seen as necessary for the viability of human communities.

[1]   Holmes Rolston, *Environmental Ethics* (Philadelphia: Temple University Press, 1988), 228.

[2]   Ibid., 40.

[3]   Ibid., 28.

[4]   Tibor Machan, "Pollution, Collectivism, and Capitalism," *Journal Des Economists et Des Etudes Humaines* 2 (1991): 82-102.

[5]   T.S. Ashton, *An Economic History of England in the Eighteenth Century* (London: Methuen, 1966), 38.

[6]   Ibid.,47. For example, Ashton points out that cottagers who had picked up a living by casual work on the commons, now had to hire themselves out as labourers to large scale farmers, while some had to fall back on parish relief and some left for the towns.

[7]   Peter France, *The Charter of the Land* (Melbourne: Oxford University Press, 1969):125-126.

[8]   D.B. Botkin, *Discordant Harmonies: A New Ecology for the Twenty-First Century* (New York: Oxford University Press, 1990).

[9]   Ramachandra Guha, "Radical American Environmentalism and Wilderness Preservation: A Third World Critique," in *Social Ethics: Morality and Social Policy*, eds. T. Mappes and J. Zembaty, (New York: McGraw Hill, 1992), 519.

[10]   Ibid.

[11]   L.W. Sumner, *The Moral Foundations of Rights* (Oxford: Clarendon Press, 1987),126.

[12]   H.L.A. Hart, *The Concept of Law* (Oxford: Clarendon Press, 1964),187.

[13]   Ibid., 188.

[14]   Ibid., 187.

[15]   Ibid., 192.

[16]   Ibid., 192-195.

[17]   A.P. Power, "Resource Development in the East Sepik Province," in *Ethics of Development: Choices in Development Planning*, eds. C. Thirwell and P. Hughes (Port Moresby: U.P.N.G. Press, 1988), 172.

[18]   See for example, F.A. Hayek, *Law, Legislation and Liberty*, Vol II, (London: Routledge and Kegan Paul, 1967); Robert Nozick, *Anarchy, State, and Utopia* (Boston: Basic Books. 1974).

[19]   A.M. Honore, "Ownership," in *Oxford Essays in Jurisprudence*, ed. A.G. Guest (London: Oxford University Press, 1961) 112-128.

[20]   Ibid., 112.

[21]   Ibid.

[22]   For an interesting discussion of this concept and its relevance to the capitalist development of the environment see P. Catton, "Marxist Critical Theory, Contradictions, and Ecological Succession," *Dialogue* 28 (1989): 637-655.

Name Index

Subject Index